JANYS HAYES

The Knowing Body

Yat Malmgren's Acting Technique

VDM Verlag Dr. Müller

Impressum/Imprint (nur für Deutschland/ only for Germany)
Bibliografische Information der Deutschen Nationalbibliothek: Die Deutsche Nationalbibliothek verzeichnet diese Publikation in der Deutschen Nationalbibliografie; detaillierte bibliografische Daten sind im Internet über http://dnb.d-nb.de abrufbar.
  Alle in diesem Buch genannten Marken und Produktnamen unterliegen warenzeichen-, marken- oder patentrechtlichem Schutz bzw. sind Warenzeichen oder eingetragene Warenzeichen der jeweiligen Inhaber. Die Wiedergabe von Marken, Produktnamen, Gebrauchsnamen, Handelsnamen, Warenbezeichnungen u.s.w. in diesem Werk berechtigt auch ohne besondere Kennzeichnung nicht zu der Annahme, dass solche Namen im Sinne der Warenzeichen- und Markenschutzgesetzgebung als frei zu betrachten wären und daher von jedermann benutzt werden dürften.

Coverbild: www.ingimage.com

Verlag: VDM Verlag Dr. Müller GmbH & Co. KG
Dudweiler Landstr. 99, 66123 Saarbrücken, Deutschland
Telefon +49 681 9100-698, Telefax +49 681 9100-988
Email: info@vdm-verlag.de
Zugl.: Sydney, University of Western Sydney, Dis., 2008

Herstellung in Deutschland:
Schaltungsdienst Lange o.H.G., Berlin
Books on Demand GmbH, Norderstedt
Reha GmbH, Saarbrücken
Amazon Distribution GmbH, Leipzig
ISBN: 978-3-639-31248-5

Imprint (only for USA, GB)
Bibliographic information published by the Deutsche Nationalbibliothek: The Deutsche Nationalbibliothek lists this publication in the Deutsche Nationalbibliografie; detailed bibliographic data are available in the Internet at http://dnb.d-nb.de.
  Any brand names and product names mentioned in this book are subject to trademark, brand or patent protection and are trademarks or registered trademarks of their respective holders. The use of brand names, product names, common names, trade names, product descriptions etc. even without a particular marking in this works is in no way to be construed to mean that such names may be regarded as unrestricted in respect of trademark and brand protection legislation and could thus be used by anyone.

Cover image: www.ingimage.com

Publisher: VDM Verlag Dr. Müller GmbH & Co. KG
Dudweiler Landstr. 99, 66123 Saarbrücken, Germany
Phone +49 681 9100-698, Fax +49 681 9100-988
Email: info@vdm-publishing.com

Printed in the U.S.A.
Printed in the U.K. by (see last page)
ISBN: 978-3-639-31248-5

Copyright © 2010 by the author and VDM Verlag Dr. Müller GmbH & Co. KG and licensors
All rights reserved. Saarbrücken 2010

The Knowing Body: Yat Malmgren's Acting Technique

TABLE OF CONTENTS

List of Tables   iv
List of Figures   v
List of Researcher's Journal entries   vi
Abstract   vii

CHAPTER 1: Introduction: positioning this thesis and the researcher
1.1 Embodiment in performance   1
1.2 Significance of the thesis   3
1.3 The performative body   5
1.4 Drama Centre, London: the researcher's experience   5
1.5 Character in realism   9
1.6 Contemporary performance in Australian actor training   11
1.7 Physical expression in Malmgren's technique   14
1.8 Ripple metaphor and structure of the thesis   16
1.9 The researcher's position   18
2.0 Outline of chapters   21

CHAPTER 2: Placing Malmgren in history
2.1 Introduction: orality   23
2.2 The first ripple of the foundation of Malmgren's actor training technique:
    heritage from Laban: defining terms   25
    2.2.1 *Inner Attitudes*: further definition of terms   29
    2.2.2 Malmgren's Actor Training Technique in Australia   31
2.3 Rudolf Laban (1879 – 1958): the creation of Movement Psychology   33
    2.3.1 Yat Malmgren (1916 – 2002): founder of Character Analysis   35
    2.3.2 The synthesis of Movment Psychology: Laban's legacy to Malmgren   39
    2.3.3 Malmgren's actor training   43
2.4 *Effort* in Laban's model   46
2.5 The development of Malmgren's technique   50
    2.5.1 *Externalised Drives*   54
    2.5.2 The body/mind   56

CHAPTER 3: Acting Techniques, Malmgren and embodiment
3.1 Introduction: the second ripple of contextualisation of
    Malmgren's technique – actor training for theatrical realism   59
3.2 Bodies of knowledge: acting techniques and differing views of the
    actor's body   62
    3.2.1 The Stanislavski system   63
    3.2.2 Littlewood's improvisational techniques   66
    3.2.3 Copeau and the French classical heritage   69

3.3 The ambiguous site of the performing body: the fragmented 'self' 71
   3.3.1 Malmgren and postmodernism 72
   3.3.2 Embodiment and the limits of the constructed 'self' 74
   3.3.3 Feminism and performance/agency 79
3.4 Conclusion 83

CHAPTER 4: Using a phenomenological methodology
4.1 Introduction 85
4.2 A methodological framework for research on Yat Malmgren's actor training 86
   4.2.1 The body in performance 87
   4.2.2 Assumptions 88
   4.2.3 Qualitative research 90
   4.2.4 Phenomenology and lived experience 92
   4.2.5 Merleau-Ponty and the phenomenal body 97
4.3 A methodology for research on Yat Malmgren's actor training: phenomenological collection of data 100
   4.3.1 Methodological rigour 101
   4.3.2 The settings and participants 102
   4.3.3 Interview design 104
   4.3.4 Step 1. Focus groups 106
   4.3.5 Step 2. Individual interviews 107
   4.3.6 Other sources: field notes, participants' journals 107
   4.3.7 The researcher's journal 108
   4.3.8 Malmgren and trainers 109
4.4 A phenomenological analysis of data 110
4.5 Research participants 113
4.6 Conclusions 126

CHAPTER 5: Experiences in a Malmgren studio
5.1 Introduction 128
5.2 Australian performance training 130
   5.2.1 Teaching Malmgren's technique 133
   5.2.2 Teaching Malmgren's technique at the University of Wollongong 137
5.3 The experiential journey of Malmgren's technique 139
   5.3.1 Step 1: expectations 140
   5.3.2 Step 2: *Motion factors* and their *Elements* 142
   5.3.3 Step 3: considering *Inner Attitudes* 148
   5.3.4 Step 4: the awareness of being viewed 152
   5.3.5 Step 5: the beginnings of transformation through sensation 158
   5.3.6 Step 6: the self-reflexive actor: *Externalised Drives* and *Action Attitudes* 163
5.4 Conclusions 172

CHAPTER 6: A phenomenological analysis of Malmgren's actor training technique
6.1 Introduction 174
6.2 The widening ripples of the transformative process 175

6.3 Gathering the subthemes 178
6.4 The context of the subthemes 182
   6.4.1 Subtheme exemplars 182
6.5 A shared background 190
6.6 A surprising experience 192
6.7 A phenomenological approach 195

CHAPTER 7: Six themes: Merleau-Ponty's *chiasm*
7.1 Introduction 199
7.2 Six emergent themes 200
   7.2.1 General structure of the phenomenon 201
7.3 The actor's *lebenswelt*: the lifeworld of the actor in training 202
7.4 The phenomenal body: new understandings of the actor's body 209
7.5 The *chiasm* : the inextricable link between actor and audience 216
7.6 Experiencing the gap: whose is the body that is viewed? 223
7.7 Refusal and 'it': new possibilities of expressive action 231
7.8 The transformed body: the ongoing process of 'becoming' 238
7.9 Conclusions 243

CHAPTER 8: Pre-linguistic reflective communication
8.1 Introduction 247
8.2 Pre-linguistic reflective communication 248
   8.2.1 Phenomenological insights about and other contemporary approaches to performative action 250
   8.2.2 Transformation through the *Inner Attitudes* and *Externalised Drives* 254
   8.2.3 Malmgren's 'evolution' of action 255
8.3 Malmgren's *Flow* and meeting of the 'other' 258
8.4 Malmgren and sexual difference in performance 263
   8.4.1 Pedagogical considerations 269
8.5 Conclusions 270

CHAPTER 9: Conclusions: four ripples
9.1 Introduction 272
9.2 Malmgren's technique: an actor training in sensation 274
9.3 Malmgren's technique: directional bodies in space 277
9.4 Malmgren's technique: flowing bodies 279
9.5 The narrative description 280
9.6 Many splashes 283

References 284

LIST OF TABLES

2.1	Laban's *Motion Factors* and their *Elements*	29
2.2	Laban's *Basic Actions* and their *Elements*	29
2.3	Malmgren's *Inner Attitudes* and their *Motion Factors* and *Mental Factors*	30
5.1	Six-step transformative actor-training processes in the Malmgren technique	139
5.2	Laban's *Motion Factors* and their *Elements*	143
5.3	Malmgren's *Inner Attitudes* and their *Motion Factors*	147
5.4	Malmgren's *Inner Attitudes* and their *Action Attitudes*	167
5.5	Malmgren's *Externalised Drives* and their *Motion Factors*	168
6.1	Inter-relation between actor training processes and emergent themes	177
6.2	Subthemes pertaining to the process of Malmgren's actor training technique	181
7.1	Emergent themes arising from subthemes	201
7.2	Subthemes constituting the first emergent theme	202
7.3	Subthemes constituting the second emergent theme	209
7.4	Subthemes constituting the third emergent theme	216
7.5	Subthemes constituting the fourth emergent theme	223
7.6	Subthemes constituting the fifth emergent theme	231
7.7	Subthemes constituting the sixth emergent theme	238
9.1	Six-step transformative actor-training processes in the Malmgren technique	276

LIST OF FIGURES

1.1 Diagrammatic image of Malmgren's metaphor of intentional action 16

2.1 The first ripple – Contextualisation of Yat Malmgren's actor training: the heritage of language and meaning from Rudolf Laban's movement theories 25

3.1 The second ripple – Contextualisation of Yat Malmgren's actor training: a system for theatrical realism 60

5.1 The second ripple – Contextualisation of Yat Malmgren's actor training: a system for theatrical realism 130

6.1 The third ripple – Contextualisation of Yat Malmgren's actor training: a study of embodiment 175

8.1 The fourth ripple – Contextualisation of Yat Malmgren's actor training: pre-linguistic reflective communication 250

RESEARCHER'S JOURNAL ENTRIES

1.1 November 1999, Reflections on the embodiment of the researcher.   19

2.1 January 2001, Drama Centre London, Farewelling Yat Malmgren.   24

2.2 February 1998, Visiting Drama Centre, London.   46

2.3 February 1998, Greeting Malmgren and Fettes at Drama Centre.   50

3.1 June 9th, 2000, Presentation at the Postgraduate Colloquium Program, Centre for Contemporary Performance, University of Western Sydney.   75

4.1 January 1988, Drama Centre, London, Movement Class, Group 25   109

5.1 December 2000, Performance of *Enemies* by Maxim Gorky at Drama Centre London. Afternoon Thursday 7th, December.   162

6.1 April 1998, Faculty of Creative Arts, University of Wollongong, *Space* class.   197

7.1 June 18th 2002, Funeral of Yat Malmgren.   223

8.1 November 16th, 2007, 176 Gallery, London.   262

The Knowing Body: Yat Malmgren's Acting Technique

Abstract

Little has been written of Yat Malmgren's acting technique, despite its international influence in mainstream western actor training. Created originally for the construction and performance of characters in theatrical and screen realism, at the Drama Centre, London, in the 1960-1970s, Malmgren's acting technique, known as Character Analysis, forms a body of knowledge, which is transmitted practically and experientially to trainee actors. This thesis outlines the Malmgren technique's traditions, processes of transmission and centres primarily on the modes of understanding that underlie this practical system.

This research sets a series of widening contextualistations of understandings of the modalities of embedded/embodied knowledge disseminated through the technique's process. Interwoven throughout this thesis, the researcher's voice appears as a Researcher's Journal, placing the embodied awareness of the researcher, as one of the principal Malmgren trainers in Australia. The material and engendered locus for this research is my own embodied consciousness.

This research differentiates Malmgren's acting technique both from Laban's movement techniques and from other twentieth century western actor training processes. It begins with the traditions of Rudolf Laban's movement theories, from which the Malmgren technique arose,

Hermeneutic phenomenology is the methodological framework used to investigate the meaning of the Malmgren technique to those studying it, taking into account contemporary performance and communication theories of agency and embodiment. Benner's (1994) hermeneutic phenomenological method of data collection and analysis, used previously in nursing research, is newly applied to the field of acting. Participants from three full-time acting courses, where Yat Malmgren's technique is the principal mode of actor training, provide the interview data to articulate a series of phenomenological themes. This research uses Maurice Merleau-Ponty's image of *the chiasm,* where materiality and consciousness interweave as an underlying metaphorical structure for elucidating processes of embodiment.

This research proposes a six-step progression, through which Malmgren's technique enables trainee actors to develop a growing performative awareness of their bodily-located behaviours. This research also posits the generation of heightened differentiation of sensory inputs and expressions for trainee actors through the Malmgren technique, and how this opens up possibilities for transformation in modes of embodiment for the trainee. Using feminist theories, this research links this development of embodied awareness, in particular the awareness of non-verbal communication and the 'unspoken', with a greater understanding of alterity.

Whilst the Malmgren technique was developed for purposes of theatrical realism, this research indicates that the technique's impact facilitates a range of modes of performance by investigating the less articulated forms of performative communication.

CHAPTER 1

INTRODUCTION: POSITIONING THIS THESIS AND THE RESEARCHER

In free flow the fantasies are always going to happen.
Malmgren January1988.

1.1 Embodiment in performance

The position of the body in performance is by its nature an ambiguous one. It is clear that others are able to witness our bodies from a variety of views whilst our own access to this visibility is limited. Although we can hear our own voice, the voice that we hear sounds differently to ourselves than it does to others. What we sense kinaesthetically, again, is of a different nature than the objective view held by others of our own movements in space. Our sensations springing from our body whilst in performance are ours alone. It would appear that even in these limited sensing parameters, the performer's experience of being a body on stage is at odds with an audience's perception of watching that body on stage.

The journey of the actor in training is one that must come to grips with these perplexing dimensions of embodied performance. The actor in training is required to listen to direction, tuition and criticism and to translate others' perspectives into embodied forms. Rarely can any observations about an actor's body be differentiated in experience from the understandings of the actor herself[1].

Of course this process is not so very different from interacting with others and what they reflect to us about our actions in everyday life. This position of the performing body and its commitment or lack of commitment to performed action has led the postmodern drama theorist, Zarrilli (1995, p. 1) to state, that acting,

> is not an innocent or naive activity separate from or above and beyond everyday reality, history, politics, or

---

[1] Throughout this thesis I choose to use feminine pronouns to emphasise the engendered embodied consciousness of the researcher initiating this research.

economics ... the actors' perception and practice of acting is a complex, ongoing set of intellectual and psychophysiological negotiations

moderni[...] gs are based on the writings of [...]slavski, Michael Chekhov, Jerzy Grotows[...] Adolphe Appia, Bertolt Brecht, Peter Br[...] who are both theatre practitioners and theo[...] tures and times, share a common basis in [...] heatre. They are major influences in acting [...] he traditional canon of thought, expressed by these writers often drew upon scientific positivism in order to legitimise itself. The dominance of the scientific method was paramount at that time and stretched far beyond the confines of the laboratory to influence all aspects of social science and the arts. These canonical writers call on romanticism in an attempt to define the actor's experience. Concepts such as soul, inner illumination and the active powers of the heart, appear in actor training literature from these times. Stanislavski for instance in *Creating a Role* (1963, p. 4), a text compiled from work written before Stanislavski's death in 1938, calls for,

> An actor ... to prepare a mood to incite his artistic feelings to open his soul

Michael Chekhov (1953, p. 100) writes in a similarly transcendent manner,

> The true creative state of the actor-artist is governed by a threefold functioning of his consciousness: the higher self inspires his acting and grants him genuinely creative feelings; the lower self serves as the common-sense restraining force; the illusory "soul" of the character becomes the focal point of the higher self's creative impulses.

Although Chekhov puts the term soul in inverted commas, he still uses it and refers to the notion of a higher self as a source of inspiration. From Stanislavski, to Grotowski to Brook, the actor in training is met with the use of language that interweaves romantic imagery with science. Theatrical trainings relying on such texts often recapitulate this mixture.

In comparison, Performance studies, as a branch of cultural studies, uses epistemologies predicated by philosophies of structuralism and post structuralism. Viewing performance as a cultural text, these philosophical movements have provided strategies for the analysis of an eclectic set of embodied actions as cultural production. Philosophers such as Jacques Derrida, Jacques Lacan, Claude Levi-Strauss, Michel Foucault, and Roland Barthes have formed the discourses through which performance and the body has been investigated since the 1980s. From these perspectives any notion of essentialism, of the body being synonymous with a fixed or core 'self', have been replaced with more discursive concepts of the body as a phenomenon in performance. The modernist understandings of identity or character in relation to the body have been overturned, requiring or instigating new pathways of understandings of the performer's experience.

Informed by these complexities of approaches to actor training, this chapter reveals my own positioning in relation to embodiment in performance and my own experience of being a performing body with particular reference to my own training in, and teaching of, Yat Malmgren's technique of actor training.

1.2 Significance of the thesis

This investigation is the second academic account of the actor training system of Yat Malmgren, which in itself was substantially derived from the work of the modernist movement theorist Rudolf Laban. The first documentation of Malmgren's technique was undertaken by Vladimir Mirodan (1997), the now Director of Drama Centre, London[2], through his doctorate undertaken at the Royal Holloway College, University of London. Whilst Mirodan sets out the full schema of Malmgren's actor training technique of Character Analysis, my investigation not only traces Malmgren's historical influences from Laban, but also carries out a

---

[2] Since its foundation, Drama Centre, London has been referred to without 'The' as a prefix. The current Drama Centre, London website http://courses.csm.arts.ac.uk/drama/ however refers to Drama Centre, London, The Drama Centre and Drama Centre. I prefer to leave 'the' as a prefix out, using Yat Malmgren's and Christopher Fettes' original name for the college.

phenomenological study of Malmgren's techniques. Mirodan situates Character Analysis as a transformational actor training. This research investigates the meaning to the performer of undertaking Malmgren's training. The overarching question that this thesis pursues is: **In what way does Malmgren's actor training contribute to the understanding of the performative body?** My study stands alone as a close reading of the efficacy of this method of actor training. This thesis documents the use of Malmgren's acting technique within the postmodern setting of contemporary performance. The thesis questions what fields of learning and of actor training are authorised by Malmgren's technique in a twenty-first century setting. The emphasis of the thesis is in viewing the technique as a site for exploring and analysing the nature of constructed embodied identities.

Phenomenology predicates my view. It bridges positivist and post-positivist research through the concept of embodied consciousness. In this thesis, although I am aware of Malmgren's use of essentialist/positivist language and quote Malmgren as a means of bringing his theories to light, I aim to highlight the embodied experiences of performing bodies undergoing Malmgren's acting training. In this I theorise a performing body as one experiencing itself as an agency, but which is also subject to a pre-existing set of cultural discourses.

My research offers new understandings of the interrelationship between an actor's conscious perceptions of her actions with an audience. Then through the phenomenological study the thesis investigates the ways in which desires are articulated and enacted through bodies that intuitively recognize identities that are similar or different from their own. This thesis resists a dialogue about representation, and I acknowledge my own representational scriptings in this first chapter. The performer's body as a site of conflicting discourses in theatre, is not the subject matter of this thesis. I deliberately take a phenomenological approach to the body of the actor in training, introducing concepts of alterity based on phenomenological philosophy. The thesis is directed to practitioners and teachers in the field of performance.

1.3 The performative body

This thesis takes the term 'performative body' from the work of gender theorist Judith Butler (1993, 1999, 2004), where Butler uses the term performativity to describe the ways in which bodies enact particular discourses. In *Gender Trouble; Feminism and the Subversion of Identity* (1999, p. 173) Butler writes that

> acts, gestures, and desire produce the effect of an internal core or substance, but produce this on the surface of the body, through the play of signifying absences that suggest, but never reveal, the organizing principle of identity and cause.

The similarities between actors' search for congruence in the embodied creation of any character and Butler's 'performativity' (1999, pp 171-190) struck me. Discourses shaping performed characters are often clearly delineated by actors, leading me to ask whether an acting training technique can throw light on the ways in which bodies in general shape identities. The major research question of this thesis is set in terms of the unrecognised core of any embodied identity; can an acting technique offer new insights into the performative acts that unconsciously embody discourses? In a wider sense, Malmgren's precise detail as to the embodied performance of any character leads to this research questioning what Malmgren's technique can reveal about the ways in which bodies stay unaware of themselves even whilst in conscious action. Consequently I term the notion of any body involved in 'performativity' (Butler 1999) or 'performative acts' (Butler 1999, p. 172) as a performative body.

1.4 Drama Centre, London: the researcher's experience

My tertiary education commenced at the University of Melbourne, where I undertook a Bachelor of Science with Honours degree in Zoology. I then studied for three years at Drama Centre, London with Yat Malmgren from 1979. Prior to this study I had never consciously considered my body on stage, although I had performed extensively. Despite working for a range of theatre companies, Melbourne Theatre Company, Salamanca Theatre Company in Hobart and Freewheels in

Newcastle, my background in science predicated the view I had of my body, that of an anatomical and physiological system. Since I had taken an Honours degree in Ecological Zoology, I was well versed in Darwinian theories and the arising debate of "Nature versus Nurture" in terms of human behaviour. However in 1979 I began to study acting for three years at Drama Centre, London with Yat Malmgren.

Drama Centre, London was established in 1963 by Christopher Fettes and Yat Malmgren (Rubin 1994, p. 932). This independent acting school ran a three-year course for actors and a two-year course for both directors and instructors. It was located in a nineteenth century chapel in Chalk Farm, London. The school was primarily established to house the developing theories of Yat Malmgren on the interconnection between bodily stances and gestures and character intentions. The current Drama Centre, London website (2009) says that,

> Drama Centre was created around the work of the late Yat Malmgren, one of the great solo artists of European modern dance and the creator of the Laban-Malmgren System of Character Analysis. His unique contribution developed the theoretical work on the psychology of movement initiated by Rudolf Laban, the visionary innovator in the field of choreography and movement theory.

In 1979, Drama Centre's Prospectus, which remained remarkably consistent until Malmgren's departure in 2001, described the school's difference from other British acting colleges as the 'methodological bias ... which centres on the institution of the Acting Class' in contrast to the traditional training available in the United Kingdom, 'most of which adopt a pragmatic approach ... taught largely by example'. This training set Drama Centre apart from other London acting institutions of the time. Drama Centre's Prospectus, over the years of 1964 until 2002 described this methodological approach:

> Training is systematic ... In the early days its [ie. Drama Centre's] essentially methodological approach distinguished it from all its rivals. So widespread has been its influence that this is no longer the case, but the Centre retains its distinctive approach. The approach derives from

a fusion of a variety of contributions to the development of European theatre in the twentieth century.

London's *The Guardian* newspaper referred to Drama Centre as 'the first drama school to teach acting from a truly international perspective' (Barter 1995, p. 16). In the BBC2 programme *Theatre School* (1993, Part 1), which profiled Drama Centre, the Acting course is described as 'heavily based upon the Stanislavsky Method[3] ... It's an approach that requires uncompromising introspection'. Whereas other independent acting schools in the United Kingdom from the mid to late twentieth century concentrated on the look or sound that any actor created on stage, Drama Centre's technique required actors to investigate their own behaviour, the motivations that propel action, and the differing individual modes of action.

Improvisation was the means through which the training at Drama Centre proceeded. Text was often set aside in order to explore the individual actor's creative and imaginative responses to exercises designed to assist in the interpretation of any playscript. Systematic improvisational exercises were employed in the teaching of each acting technique.

> At Drama Centre the emphasis is not upon finished production, it's upon improvisation and acting exercises that are designed to provoke and liberate the student both physically and emotionally. Method acting has it that the text of a play must be related to the actor's own experience, so that the students have to abandon inhibition and learn to release emotions that can then be controlled and used on stage (*Theatre School* 1993, Part 1).

The introspection elicited throughout the three-year training was inexorable and from it a new body, that was I, emerged to function in a new way. The combination of introspection, improvisation and the emphasis on the actor's own experience brought about a profound personal transformation in relation to my understandings of my body on stage and the meaning for me of acting itself. Any objectivity that I had previously maintained with regards to the notion of myself on stage, of myself as a character, even as to why I should choose to act, became a swirling subjective journey from which the only way to achieve any consistent view of myself was to commit myself more fully to what I might choose to believe was my purpose in performing in the first place.

Although Drama Centre stressed the methodological approach, this methodology was directed from teacher to pupil as an experiential journey. There was little emphasis on reading Stanislavski, Laban or Saint-Denis, although all three theorists' work was taught and all three have written of their methods (Stanislavski 1963, 1973; Laban 1948, 1971; Saint-Denis 1982). Instead the experience was a person-to-person set of relationships, structured within the systematic methods that were the fundamental offerings of the school. The discourses of these methods of acting were imparted through personal, and often individually performed exercises, where having a visceral connection to the work was uppermost.

Standing in an acting class of Yat Malmgren's was like having a beam of light probing the deepest recesses of my visceral being. Every muscle twitch, every idiosyncratic gesture, every shift in posture suddenly seemed exposed to layer on layer of readable meanings. Muscles, alignment, movements, all were scrutinised by Yat Malmgren and revealed, through his system, as expressing fundamental understandings about me for an audience, aspects of myself which I recognised only too readily and often to my chagrin. It was then that a gulf appeared between the person I *wanted* to express in action on stage and off, and who I seemed *able* to express. Malmgren's ever-present eye seemed to knowingly elicit all this, as if he understood that the task of embodying actions, which truly represented ourselves, was a lifelong quest.

The acquisition of knowledge about performance at Drama Centre was taught via an oral tradition, rather than through discursive analysis. Malmgren, like Laban (Newlove & Dalby 2004), taught his technique expressed as exercises, physical, vocal, and improvisational. Malmgren created a new formulation of acting exercises based on Laban's theories of bodily effort-actions.

1.5 Character in realism

---

[3] The use of the term 'Stanislavsky Method' reoccurs throughout Drama Centre literature, in the prospectus and online.

Theatre as an expression of realism was an unspoken assumption at Drama Centre, London. The aim of all exercises was a commitment to the notion of acting as transformation of oneself into character. Here Reuven Adiv (Drama Centre Prospectus 2002) describes his class,

> The purpose of the class is ... to secure for [the actor] the correct inner state of being, to open the doors of the subconscious, by means of which he can bring to performance the spontaneity of actual life. Improvised exercises, designed to free the student physically and emotionally, provide a basis for complete identification with the character ...

Although students were often asked to consider the purposes of being an actor, and the purposes of theatre itself, Drama Centre, London remained separated from the emerging new directions of the bustling theatre, film and television industry that thrived in London all about it. External influences from the new directions that theatre was taking through the 1970s and 1980s, did not change the modernist directions of Drama Centre, which were firmly based on servicing the well made play, written by one author, with clear authorial intent and characters who belonged in a reality, presumed to be common to us all.

Yat Malmgren speaking about the purposes of his teachings on the BBC2 programme, *Theatre School* (1993, Part 3) states,

> My teaching is to make the people definitely create characters and create different psychological types. Actors will think, "I can walk, so I can walk. I can talk, so I can talk", but how ... can I make my voice expressive, or my gestures expressive?

Here Malmgren, in his idiosyncratic mode of speaking in broken English, emphasises the notion of character, as a psychologically constituted entity. The trainings at Drama Centre, although radical for London in the 1960s in using improvisational exercises assumed character was an innate aspect of any human body. I acquiesced unquestioningly to a performance style, realism, which unwittingly was to prove limited due to the very basis of my being, my sense of sexual identity.

I did however gain a rich and lasting influence that provided understandings of performance and the emphasis on process as the actor's work. The improvisations at Drama Centre, allowed me to see that the actor's work is a constantly, moving, fluid and dynamic procedure rather than a performative artefact, viewed by an audience at an arbitrary time. Moreover I understood, after my Drama Centre training, that these processes of performance involve considerations of embodiment and that body and motivation are inextricably linked.

Whilst at Drama Centre, I had chosen to specialise in Yat Malmgren's doctrines of the body in performative action. In my third year of studying Acting, I also attended extra movement and Character Analysis classes by Malmgren, in order to teach his technique in Australia.

Malmgren's theories, whilst being influenced by Stanislavski's system as taught at Drama Centre by American trained Stanislavskian exponents are the basis of Chapter 2. Malmgren's work is built primarily on the 1954 work of Rudolf Laban[4] (1879-1958). Although Laban's work has become repopularised through recent texts (Newlove & Dalby 2003; Preston-Dunlop 1998), little has been written of Malmgren's theories. In 1954 Laban provided Malmgren with a set of tables and notes linking Jungian psychology with Laban's movement terminology. As a movement theorist whose work spanned the 1930s to the 1970s, Rudolf Laban's underlying presumption was of the essentialist nature of human expression through movement and gesture. Laban's models and scales of human movement in space, and formulae for choreographic notation were expressed as quasi-scientific concepts. Laban's theories of movement assumed that expressive movement formed patterns shared by all human beings. He sought the same legitimacy as has been accorded to scientific physiological models of movement, stating 'Our movement notation is based on the elementary motor principles of the human body' (Laban 1975, p. 11). The influence of this on Malmgren was considerable.

1.6 Contemporary performance in Australian actor training

---

[4] Laban's Glossary of terms and Movement Psychology tables are held at Drama Centre London.

On my return to Australia from the United Kingdom, I taught Malmgren's method throughout the 1980s, emphasising realism and the development of character in relation to text, at the Drama Studio, The Actor's Studio and the National Institute of Dramatic Arts (NIDA)[5] in Sydney and The Victorian College of the Arts (VCA)[6] in Melbourne, a range of institutions encompassing both independent acting colleges and university courses. My first encounter with postmodern attitudes to performance was at The University of Wollongong's Faculty of Creative Arts, where I took up a position as a Lecturer in Theatre Performance in the early 1990s. At that stage I began to recontextualise my own understandings of the Yat Malmgren teachings in terms of performance.

When teaching the university student actors, often those who struck me as being highly creative could find little engagement in the realm of realism. These limitations were sometimes imposed, as the constraints of pre-existent texts often excluded actors whose class, ethnicity or gender were at odds with texts chosen from a traditional literary canon. Sometimes these students discerned that realism would never facilitate their creative drives to perform, either because there would be few parts in which they would be easily cast or because they themselves understood the socially constricting effects of much of this genre and they were opposed to that per se.

Through Malmgren's actor training technique, with its emphasis on improvisation and investigation of the actor's world and actions within it, these acting students extended their own expressive performance qualities and set no cultural boundaries as to the content of their work. In Malmgren's technique, the performer, no matter what gender, race or class is always set at the centre of her own action and creates her own text. These students responded to the technique with enthusiasm despite or as well as their growing discontent with realism, which they often found at best limiting and at worst oppressive. Often these students were contributing substantially to their artistic field when they left the university, working in areas such as physical theatre or contemporary performance.

---

[5] NIDA, the National Institute of Dramatic Arts is Australia's premiere actor training institution, a centre of excellence in training for theatre, film and television.

I formed a growing understanding that realism reflected an historical and culturally constructed reality, whilst at the same time solidifying the very reality it often purported to be questioning. Feminist perspectives enabled me to question the actor training offered to women in a university setting. Despite an ongoing theme in many contemporary western plays being the changing nature of female social roles, the lack of female representation in written texts reinforces the inequality that many texts appear to be probing. The inability of realism to truly challenge the cultural status of women led to a deeper investigation of my own role as a director, actor and Malmgren trainer.

Firstly, in order to counter the problem of the way realism silences women, I began to produce and direct texts written by women or texts with large female casts. My Masters in Creative Arts (MCA), Advanced Techniques in Theatre subject, at the University of Wollongong, took the form of a study entitled, 'Space for women on stage' (Hayes 1999). The concretising effects of realism's reliance on fixed, gendered, identities shattered the boundaries of my conceptual frame-work about performance in general for as Hart (1993, p. 5), a feminist performance theorist has shown,

> Realism like/as ideology, needs subjects and subjects are constituted through divisions and losses that are always already gendered.

Every character in any play is also a subject-position that can be read by an audience as endorsing a social, political and gendered construction of a reality. Every character represents an ideological stance, so that female characters, who may be victimized or oppressed, operate to suggest or even reinforce these terms to an audience. This search for the meaning of female representations through realism led into an understanding of the complexities of the signification of the performing body, itself.

Butler (1988, p. 521) in her philosophical writing on the body, and the performative ontology of gender has stated that the body is not:

---

[6] The Victorian College of the Arts is a faculty of the University of Melbourne. VCA Drama, one of the departments of the VCA, runs the full-time acting course.

> merely factic materiality; it is materiality that bears meaning, if nothing else, and the manner of this bearing is fundamentally dramatic. By dramatic I mean only that the body is not merely matter but a continual and incessant *materializing* of possibilities.

It became clear that the body on stage, the performative body, was a nexus, materializing subject positions, normalising restrictive and/or radical modes of action. The access that bodies have to performance became a concern and what bodies are given the right to speak through performance became a question fuelling new directions.

As the 1990s progressed, forms of theatre and performance other than realism were burgeoning in the community using new stylistic choices to open performance across boundaries of class, gender and ethnicity. Often these performance modes were not based on written text and had deliberately abandoned notions of linear narrative and/or fixed characters. I began immersing myself in Performance Studies, where cross-disciplinary notions of performance posed challenges to traditional canons and dramaturgical readings of texts. I wanted to grapple with the meaning of Malmgren's work in this larger context of performance where pluralism and heterogeneity have shifted the ways in which an audience views and comprehends any performance. I began to understand how Malmgren's technique of actor training had applications across a broader range of performative styles than the style of realism for which it had originally been designed. Viewed as a constructed 'text' the Malmgren technique resonated with insights about the reading of any performative body.

Geertz (1983, p. 31) has discussed the broadening possibilities that occur with the extension of the notion of 'text', allowing semiotic readings to take account of:

> how the inscription of action is brought about, what its vehicles are and how they work, and on what the fixation of meaning from the flow of events – history from what happened, thought from thinking, culture from behaviour – implies sociological interpretation.

Through this broader framework I helped establish a course at the University of Wollongong, where devised performance was given the same weighting as text-based performance and where Malmgren's training methods were offered across all styles of performance. Performance Studies theorist, Reinelt (1995, p. 124) described a shift of postmodern theorists, 'Moving from a content analysis (who is represented?) to a more formal interrogation of the theatrical apparatus (for whom does it function, what are its codes?)'. Not only did my thinking about performance shift for me through these new paradigms of acting, but my student performances, which I directed or facilitated began to shift in terms of where I placed them, moving out of theatres into community settings or site-specific settings. Character no longer formed the underlying basis for every performance and students were able to analyse their performances from cultural as well as dramaturgical positions.

1.7 Physical expression in Malmgren's technique

My investigation as to the usefulness of Yat Malmgren's method of actor training for performers involved in contemporary performance centred on Malmgren's emphasis on physical expression. Malmgren's technique addresses the body first and foremost. Through Malmgren's use of Laban's categories of physical action, actors can identify and describe action through physical rather than psychological means. Malmgren's categories of character types are also identifiable through the physicality of any performer. Improvisational exercises in the technique are based on memory, on the lives of those studying the program. This engagement with actors' sense of themselves positions the actor as performing a kind of 'realism' as the events depicted are reflections of their own history. However the actor is also positioned as constructing this 'reality' by the choice from their lives of events or actions that they present. In this thesis, I propose that the Malmgren technique can present a bridge between modernism's quest for a meta-narrative of truth and postmodernism's understandings of subjectivity and constructed realities; actor's in Malmgren's training hunt for scenes and language that best address their understandings of themselves whilst at the same time construct their presentation of 'self' through these corporeal choices.

These corporeal demands awakened me to the realisation that my body in performative action not only housed my own meaning-making system, but it also carried a set of implicit signifiers that I knew little about. The way I spoke, dressed, moved, my posture, what I chose to be concerned about in the world, plus the inescapable fact of being female, were all being read without me even being aware of it. These two constructs, the creation of my own unconscious reality through my actions and how I was implicitly read through the identifying signals of my engendered socio-political history through my body, became apparent to me through Malmgren's technique. This awareness of the possibility of constructing realities through differing physical actions enabled a reflection on the differing uses of styles of performance and how performance style can alter the meaning of bodies in action.

Through dealing with the body and its sign systems rather than the content of the scenarios presented, and through dealing with identities formulated by performers themselves rather than characters imposed by given texts, the Malmgren technique functions to highlight the physical nature of any performative body; an identity, no matter how fleeting, is created in Malmgren's technique though a set of perfomative acts. Malmgren's technique emphasises the use of the body to bring text to life, rather than actors hunting for 'a truthful' or 'life-like' performance to enact a realistic text.

Over the decade that I have taught and directed performances at the Faculty of Creative Arts at the University of Wollongong, I have witnessed that students, through the Malmgren training become more aware of their own ideological positions with regard to performance, whilst still staying engaged in the Malmgren work. Whilst Malmgren's technique clearly deals with concepts of identity and character, it is apparent to me that it also highlights the nature of the audiences' readership of texts, which are always active, subjective and socially contextualised.

1.8 Ripple metaphor and structure of the thesis

One of Malmgren's metaphors, which illuminated his concept of character action within his actor training technique, serves as the structure for this thesis. The image that Malmgren often repeated was that of a pebble being dropped into a pond and forming a set of concentric circles, ever widening around each other. In his metaphoric story these circles were likened to the actor's grasp of the intentional motivations of a character's behaviour.

An actor's first understandings of a character's actions in Malmgren's technque are like the first ripple, rudimentary, the motivations being perceived, perhaps, as fixed on the acquisition of material objects or outcomes.

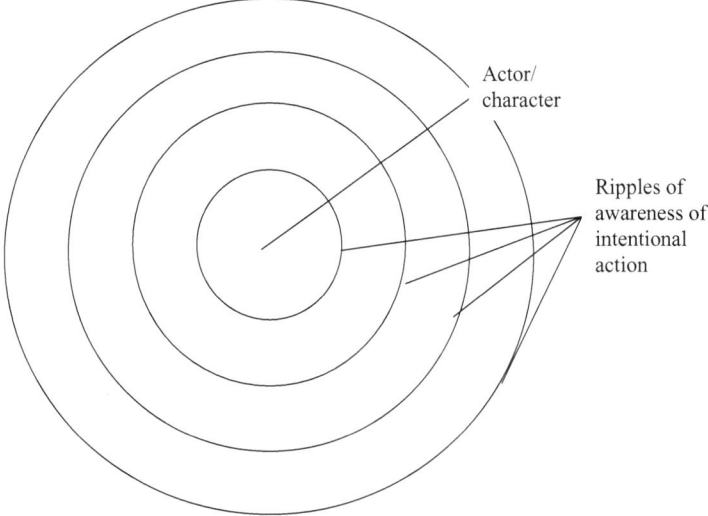

Figure 1.1 Diagrammatic image of Malmgren's metaphor of intentional action.

With empathetic and socio-historic knowledge of any literary, constructed, character, the actor may begin to develop a more expanded view of the motivational intentions of the character under study. The intentions of the character may then be understood as encompassing the first ripple, but expanding to include a second and further ripples of intentional motivation.

In this metaphorical illustration, the actor can become aware of the intentional motivations of any character at many successive ripples of width, until the character's personal motivations extend to the universal. Each ripple is a widening awareness of the motivations for any human action.

In this research Malmgren's image of the ripples created by a pebble dropped into a pond is used to represent a broadening contextualisation of processes and embodied knowledge embedded in Malmgren's method of acting for trainee actors and the researcher. The first ripple in this research encounters Malmgren's work as an interweaving of concepts, about physical action and human bodies, with those of his mentor, Rudolf Laban. Laban's theorizations of movement provide an historical background to the terminology used in Malmgren's technique but also 'astonishing insights into the meaning of the expressive quality of movement that supplied the all important foundation for the training' (Fettes, 1989, p.76). Later, in Chapter 3 and Chapter 5, the second ripple will be added, examining Yat Malmgren's technique of actor training as one of a number of European, complex, embodied techniques of actor training developed for the purpose of performing realism in the theatre. In Chapter 5 the processes that have allowed the Malmgren's actor training technique its international presence are examined in the light of embodied performance practices. Chapter 4 is situated as a Methodology chapter. However, later in Chapters 6 and 7, the ripples will widen, to investigate the Malmgren technique's contribution to the more holistic phenomenon of an actor's consideration of her performative actions, which, in this thesis, I am defining as a subject becoming aware of the organizing discourses that may be structuring her bodily actions. Finally in Chapter 8, I investigate Malmgren's technique as contributing to an understanding of communication with 'otherness', where the term is defined through feminist phenomenology. It is at this level of contextualization that the use of Malmgren's technique as a training for contemporary performance practice is considered.

1.9 The researcher's position

In embarking on this study, my position emerges explicitly in relation to Malmgren's technique. As a female theatre practitioner and academic in the field of performance I am immersed in a masculinist world. Although women are present and active in academia and the theatre, their access to the power structures that govern each of these areas are still restricted. At another level my gender is a real consideration in investigating Malmgren's technique. The technique has been constructed by a man, Malmgren, for application to modernist theatrical texts and in particular to realist theatre, which privilege the social position of the masculine.

In order to integrate the sense of myself as a gendered body, in this investigative journey of Malmgren's training, I weave my own reflective voice into the thesis. This contemplative voice is presented in my doctoral text through the device of an altered style and font as the Researcher's Journal. My dissertation presents primarily an academic investigation of Yat Malmgren's actor training technique, fragmented or interrupted by my reflective voice, that accompanies the academic research and includes my own writings; phenomenological, and from diaries. This reflective voice is presented to the reader as a personal journey of awakening consciousness, a meandering non-linear growing awareness of myself, as a woman, teaching and working within a matrix of systems, set historically for the representation and upholding of masculine advantage. In some ways this voice may be regarded as a performative element within the thesis, for it is the thesis itself as a process of flexible inquiry, that has shaped the growing consciousness of this reflection. I have become something new in action through this investigation.

I appear in this thesis in three positions. Firstly, I am the primary researcher. I document and critique Malmgren's work and drive this research and documentation. Secondly, I appear in this thesis as one of the principal Malmgren trainers in Australia at The University of Wollongong's Faculty of Creative Arts. The Performance course students, as participants in the research study, refer to me in their interviews. Thirdly, I appear as the reflective pilgrim, my consciousness of my sense of self shifting through the experience of this investigation. These three voices interspersed throughout the thesis, via the use of a variety of textual forms are also offered in recognition that each voice is interdependent on the others. The thesis then is offered as a multi-vocal investigation.

In stating my own subjectivities as constructed through my gender as well as through my social and historical context and in particular through the socio-political positioning of being a lecturer in performance at an Australian university, I concede that my context and history have shaped the manner in which I have embarked on this journey. To the extent that I have been able, I have developed my consciousness of my position so that I can be more aware of how that position affects my research. For instance, in interviewing subjects, my own position in relation to the Malmgren technique has influenced the areas of questioning that I have pursued, and postures or gestures of mine may have encouraged interviewees to privilege certain articulated positions or attitudes about the Malmgren technique. These acknowledgements are pursued more fully for the reader through an engagement with my methodology.

However at this point, this thesis is introduced with an acknowledgement of my own subjectivity. I journey from a scientifically based consideration of the body, almost as a machine that is subject to human will and intervention, through my experiences of acting. In acting I journey from a Stanislavskian model of will propelling action, to an unfolding understanding of the body via Yat Malmgren's models of expressive action, where meaning is materialised through engendered bodies. In Malmgren's model of action, imagination and physical action are continually in flux and continually and subjectively being understood by others.

I introduce my reflective voice with an extract from the Researchers's Journal, which establishes the context of my gendered positioning in the theatre.

My ponderings have revolved around my own experiences of gender constrictions – the world for women in the theatre in Australia's 1970's. After all, I had been sacked as an actor by a major theatre company at a young age for being too political. I had been called "Equity Hayes". I had been told in another company by a male director that, "I was too intelligent to be an actor",

for this I read female actor, and at acting school I had been told by many that "I looked more like a director than an actor". It seemed that in my desire to place

19

myself on stage, I was encountering surprisingly restricted expectations of what constituted female behaviour and female attributes. The space on stage for women appeared to have narrower confines than in life!

What has changed? In my first naive attempts to address the invisibility of women on stage and to create new and less confined niches on stage for female representation, I searched earnestly for the work of female playwrights, with female protagonists, even for casts with large numbers of females in them, to direct. I hoped and believed, at that time, that by merely placing female bodies on stage and requiring an audience to give them their undivided and uninterrupted attention, a situation at once at odds with societal norms, I would be creating a difference in the reception of the feminine.

Saturating the space on stage by feminine representation was only one of the directions that I have taken over my years as a director. I also hunted for plays in which constructed images of femininity were less limited and repressive than the norm and I devised performances playing with the construction of gendered identities.

In one of these devised productions, a short scene was shown at a lunchtime performance, in my Faculty. A colleague suggested that I advise several of the women in the play to lose a bit of weight because they were looking 'bulgy'. Had he made the remark in opposition to the material or totally unaware of the intention of the production? It didn't matter. Either way it was and is still indicative of the day-to-day mechanics of the regulatory practices of gender

Researcher's Journal 1.1[7]. November 1999, Reflections on the embodiment of the researcher.

2.0 Outline of chapters

---

[7] I have numbered each Researcher's Journal entry and listed these in the Contents to indicate this differing mode or 'voice' in this thesis.

In Chapter 2, I introduce the major terms in use in Malmgren's actor training technique. I use references to transcriptions from a set of interviews with Malmgren, eighteen months prior to his death. I argue that both Laban and Malmgren developed complex understandings of the human body in action, as a means of creating systematic, performance trainings, with aims of actualising embodied transformations of consciousness through performance. I indicate the various names that Malmgren used for his developing actor training technique, culminating in terming it Character Analysis and I suggest retaining Malmgren's name in association with his technique.

In Chapter 3, I set Malmgren's actor training technique within the framework of a group of European late twentieth century performance theorists, influencing Drama Centre's curriculum. Moving from models of training established within the confines of modernism, to postmodern insights of performativity gained through feminist perspectives, Malmgren's technique is compared with and investigated for its relevance to these particular fields.

In Chapter 4, I establish an hermeneutic phenomenological research framework to investigate the meaning generated when actors in training encounter Yat Malmgren's performance technique as a phenomenon. Phenomenological inquiry models of embodiment and meaning are used to analyse interviews about Malmgren's technique.

In Chapter 5, I paint a set of images of a generic Malmgren studio and its ongoing practices, using participants' descriptions. I establish a six-step transformational process in acting that I present as the present form of the Malmgren actor training technique. This aims to reveal the structures in the Malmgren technique that enable the development of a heightened awareness in the receiving and transmitting of sensory impulses for trainee actors.

In Chapter 6 using an hermeneutic phenomenological analysis of the data, I establish twenty-seven subthemes, categorizing the experiences of the participants' encounters with Yat Malmgren's actor training technique. The subthemes are clearings or horizons where the meaning of certain experiences in the participants' actor training resonate with other participants' experiences. These subthemes illuminate a developing awareness of the modes in which the material and socio-historic aspects of the performers are enmeshed with the performers' subjective sense of themselves.

In Chapter 7, furthering the analysis of the data I draw out six major emergent interview themes relating to the embodied processes of actor training in Yat Malmgren's technique. Each theme is based on Maurice Merleau-Ponty's metaphor of *the chiasm* as an interweaving locus of both materiality and consciousness. I link the six themes with the previously established six-step transformative process developed in Chapter 5. This chapter establishes procedures in Malmgren's technique through which an actor is able to develop a heightened understanding of herself as a set of interlinking embodied processes with her imagined self and others.

In Chapter 8 I establish the Malmgren actor training technique as contributing to an awareness and understanding of pre-linguistic reflective communication. I investigate the processes through which this communication constitutes alterity in relation to agency in performance. I use this to argue the use of the Malmgren technique for actor training in contemporary performance processes

In Chapter 9 I conclude the thesis, integrating the findings of this research and their relevance to Australian actor training in a contemporary setting.

CHAPTER 2

PLACING MALMGREN IN HISTORY

In the world of emotion, the inner state affects the body. Walk a character around. Sit, eat as a character. Text is absolutely outer. You couldn't be more outer than text. You have to go behind to find the inner life.
Malmgren February 1998.

2.1 Introduction: orality

This chapter aims to capture the background and structure of Malmgren's actor training technique. It represents the first ripple of contextualisation of the meaning of Malmgren's actor training technique in this research. This chapter presents Character Analysis as an orally taught tradition of actor training practices, which interweave terms from Rudolf Laban's work with Yat Malmgren's theories about performative action. The descriptions in this chapter are of a documented yet unpublished phenomenon[1]. Malmgren, wrote nothing of his actor training technique. His oral mode of training emphasises the craft-based nature of the technique. Although Malmgren designated certain students to teach his technique, each one knew less about the whole actor training system than Malmgren himself. Malmgren's (1979) tables and diagrams, which formed part of his teaching notes at Drama Centre, London, do not encompass the totality of the concepts with which he worked. Each student grasped only what she could comprehend and add to the limited pages that Malmgren offered as notes to his classes each year[2]. My authority in offering this chapter stems firstly from Malmgren's recommendation that following my training (1979-1982), on my return to Australia, I teach his actor training technique at the Drama Studio in Sydney. This was an independent actor training institution, established by Drama Centre graduates, running from 1981-1990. Secondly, my relationship with Malmgren as a trainer of his practices developed over my visits to Drama Centre in 1988, 1998 and 2000/01 as I continued

---

[1] Vladimir Mirodan's 1997 doctoral thesis outlines Malmgren's technique. It is not available on-line.
[2] Malmgren's lecture notes are referred to within this thesis as primary source material.

to teach his work in Australia. This chapter represents my training notes as well as my documentations of Malmgren's teachings on those visits.

Ong (1982, p. 34) in speaking of orality suggests that communicating organized sequences of thought in a primarily oral culture occurs through intertwining these thoughts in mnemonic patterns. Malmgren often danced in his acting classes to emphasise certain theories of movement. He told repeated stories of his past, his dreams, theatrical productions and texts, characters and stories of the success of certain students who had grasped key elements of his work. In this chapter I begin with the most pertinent oral tradition of Malmgren's work, that of Malmgren's involvement in Rudolf Laban's previously established movement practices. Malmgren developed his actor training theories from Rudolf Laban's work. The chapter outlines Laban's theories of movement that led to Malmgren's development of Character Analysis. Like Laban, Malmgren created tables and geometrical figures to symbolise his understandings and practices and like Laban, Malmgren chose to impart his knowledge through chosen students, to whom he gave the freedom to teach his work in their own manner. This 'master- apprentice' style of teaching is the mode through which Malmgren's technique has been disseminated internationally. This chapter also sets out the professional links between Yat Malmgren and Rudolf Laban, who were colleagues.

> I stand at the entrance to the room, Room 2, Yat's room, or so it has been for the last thirty years. The class files out. I look in. He is seated at his table – a frail old man. His cheeks are flushed. I have heard that he has a cold.
>
> One student is lingering, Branco, a handsome, fair-haired Serbian student. He wants Yat to look at his Xmas photos. He wants to share some secret – a snap of a lover perhaps ... the need to feel cherished in the competitive climate of this relentless institution.
>
> I walk to the table. Yat is pleased to see me and grins waving the boy away. So many things I want and yet in these last few moments I have no will to assert my own needs. I sit as Yat speaks of Laban again. Laban's scales of movement. His voice is soft and rapidly pattering over a myriad of concepts and remembrances that that I can hardly grasp. I struggle to absorb the meaning of

> it all, this space, Yat's physical presence, our shared knowledge and the weight of some task that I feel is my lifetime's work.

Researcher's Journal 2.1 January 2001, Drama Centre London, Farewelling Yat Malmgren.

2.2 The first ripple of the foundation of Malmgren's actor training technique: heritage from Laban: defining terms

Heritage from Laban

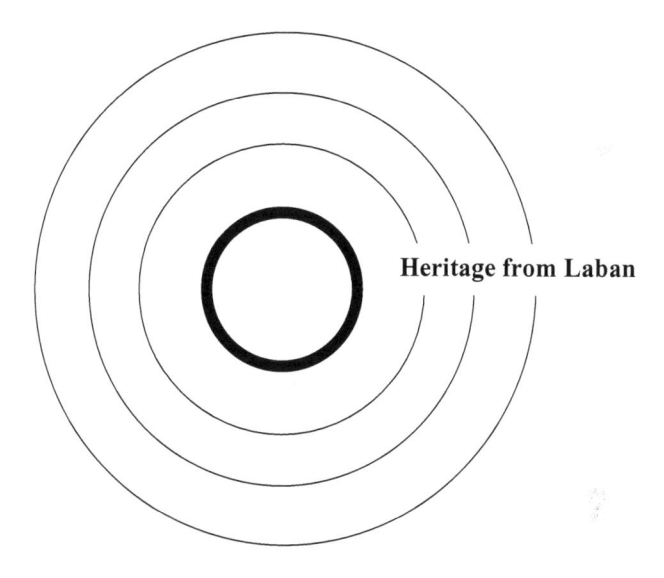

Figure 2.1 The first ripple – Contextualisation of Yat Malmgren's actor training: the heritage of language and meaning from Rudolf Laban's movement theories

Yat Malmgren's actor training technique is one, which despite its presence in mainstream training institutions of Australian theatre, has not yet been formally recognised. The foundation of Malmgren's actor training is directly inherited from Rudolf Laban's (1948, 1950) movement theories and in particular the terms that Laban applied to his systematic analysis of the human body's expressive movement. Christopher Fettes (1989, p. 76), Co-Director of Drama Centre London from its inception in 1963 until 2001, relates Laban's theories underpinning Malmgren's technique in the following manner.

> His [Laban's] theory implies that creative expression is not dependent on gaining control over an essentially alien medium, since the medium of expression is the body itself. Also, everybody is potentially a creative artist provided those qualities that serve an expressive purpose are first raised to consciousness and then systematically developed. This can be accomplished through a wide variety of exercises which, from day one, also involve the use of speech in order to develop an awareness of the relation of gesture to other things, such as the tone of the voice.

In order to comprehend the differing ways in which Malmgren's technique is currently used in Australian actor training and the way in which Malmgren himself developed his technique, often termed Character Analysis, this chapter begins by setting out the basic terms inherited from Laban that are pertinent to Malmgren's actor training technique.

Fundamentally, Laban's analysis of human movement and its meaning have been summarised by Gaumer (1960, p. 32) into five 'discoveries':

> (i) That all human movement has two purposes, functional and expressive.
> (ii) That dancing is symbolic action.
> (iii) That all movement of a part or parts of the body is composed of discernible factors that are common to men everywhere. These factors are contained in two overall terms: *effort* and *shape*.[3]
> (iv) That there are inherent movement patterns of *effort* and *shape* which are indicative of harmonious movement.
> (v) A system of notation that makes it possible to record accurately all movement of the human body.

With these tenets, Laban conceived the human body as expressive in relation to its movements in space. *Effort* and *shape* of the human body's movements in space reflect Laban's Masonic principles of cosmic architectural rules (see p. 34 for Laban's links with the Masons), as in the geometry of crystalline structures. He modelled the human body as standing theoretically in the centre of a many sided

---

[3] I have placed all terms belonging to Malmgren's actor training technique in italics for immediate recognition. Some of these terms belong to a wider general use.

geometric figure, the *icosahedron*. The *icosahedron* is a twenty-sided solid figure, with equilateral triangles for each of its faces. He called this space, the space within personal reach, the *kinesphere*. He used this image of the *icosahedric kinesphere* as a scaffold to illustrate the division of space by the moving body. He then formulated the directions or paths towards which any part of the body could move. In *Choreutics* (1966, quoted in Foster 1977, p. 65) Laban states,

> Movement is, so to speak, living architecture ... and is made of pathways tracing shapes in space, and these we may call trace-forms ... The living building of trace-forms which a moving body creates is bound to certain spatial relationships.

Laban, in *Choreutics* (1966), derives a set of sequences of movement often termed *scales* that he believes to be logical movement sequences of the human body. Thus his model of the three dimensional *icosahedron* represents the human body with linking arrows to represent pathways of movement of the body. Laban, through observation, analysed human movement into four common *motion factors*:

> *weight,* the measurement of the strength and force of an action,
> *space*, the quantitative measurement of the body's angles and pattern when moving,
> *time*, the temporal span of a movement,
> and *flow*, the assessment of the continuity, pauses and restrictions of a movement (McNiff 1981, p. 126).

The common movement factors that Laban codified are placed firmly within his *icosahedral model*, three of them in fact as the struts representing the height (*Weight*), width (*Flow*), and depth (*Time*) of this three dimensional figure, so that a cursory understanding of the model is necessary for the study of Laban's principles (Barker 1983, p. 140). Attitudes towards the movement or *motion factors* expressed through the body result in bodily exertions termed *effort*. In speaking of *effort,* Laban (1948, p. 10) states that:

> ... *actions* in all kinds of human activities, and therefore also in dance, consist of *movement-sequences* in which a definite *effort* of the moving person underlies each movement.

Laban (1971, p. 76) derives *eight basic actions* from investigating the attitude that a moving person takes towards the common movement factors, or *motion factors*.

> These attitudes can be described as:
> a relaxed or forceful attitude towards *weight*,
> a pliant or lineal attitude towards *space*,
> a prolonging or shortening attitude towards *time*,
> a liberating or withholding attitude towards *flow*.
> A specific combination of several of these eight elements of movement is observable in every action, and is most evident in the so-called *basic actions* in which the easily discernible factors of *Space*, *Time* and *Weight* are mainly considered. In a quick reaction to some external stimulus four different actions are mainly used:
> a *direct* and *strong punch*,
> a *flexible* and *strong slash*,
> a *direct* and *light dab*,
> a *flexible* and *light flick*.
> By outer resistance or inner hesitation the action can be delayed and become sustained in the following four actions:
> a *direct* and *strong press*,
> a *flexible* and *strong wring*.
> Or, if the resistance is less strong:
> a *direct* and *light glide*
> a *flexible* and *light float*.

In Malmgren's actor training the relationship between Laban's *motion factors* and *the eight basic actions* is derived through dividing each *motion factor* into two *elements* based on Laban's more descriptive breakdown above. Table 2.1 indicates the readily applicable set of dualisms used in Character Analysis, as each *motion factor* is divided into two *elements*. Table 2.2 indicates how each of *the eight basic actions* is a combination of one of the *elements* of each of the *motion factors* of *Weight*, *Space* and *Time*, whilst *Flow* modulates the expression of *the eight basic actions*. So for any movement or action in performance it can be asked, 'Is it Strong or Light? Is it Direct or Flexible? Is it Quick or Sustained?' and the answer to each of these will construct one of *the eight basic actions*.

MOTION FACTOR	CONTENDING ELEMENT	YIELDING ELEMENT
Weight	Strong	Light
Space	Direct	Flexible
Time	Quick	Sustained
Flow	Bound	Free

Table 2.1 Laban's *Motion Factors* and their *Elements*[4]

Table 2.1 is referred to again in Chapter 5 (Table 5.2, p. 143) in relation to particular students undertaking Malmgren's actor training. Malmgren's technique refers to the *eight basic actions* in the following terms as shown in Table 2.2.

BASIC ACTION	ELEMENT OF WEIGHT	ELEMENT OF SPACE	ELEMENT OF TIME
PUNCH	Strong	Direct	Quick
SLASH	Strong	Flexible	Quick
PRESS	Strong	Direct	Sustained
WRING	Strong	Flexible	Sustained
DAB	Light	Direct	Quick
FLICK	Light	Flexible	Quick
GLIDE	Light	Direct	Sustained
FLOAT	Light	Flexible	Sustained

Table 2.2 Laban's *Basic Actions* and their *Elements*[5]

2.2.1 *Inner Attitudes*: further definition of terms

Including the terms set out above, Malmgren's actor training technique predicates itself on Rudolf Laban's work from the later part of his life. Rudolf Laban turned to this research in 1953, at the age of seventy-four. At that time Laban called it 'the psychology of movement' (Preston-Dunlop 1998, p. 262). Laban entrusted his final documents, regarding this body of research, to Yat Malmgren in 1954. This

---

[4] & [5] The information in these tables is available in Yat Malmgren's Character Analysis lecture notes (1979- 2002) from Drama Centre London.

work connects the psychology of differing personality types with specific *movement sequences*. At first, outlining his concepts in a set of six tables, Laban drew on his understandings of the psychologist Carl Gustav Jung to interconnect his *motion factors* with Jung's psychological functions of *Sensing Thinking Intuiting* and *Feeling* (Hall and Nordby 1973, p. 99). Laban's intention was to describe the movements of character types, dominated by particular *motion factors* as an expression of personality. In *The Mastery of Movement* (Laban 1960, p. 127) which Lisa Ullmann, Rudolf Laban's wife, revised and enlarged from the original of the same name written by Laban in 1950, C. G. Jung's personality functions of *Thinking, Sensing, Intuiting* and *Feeling* are correlated with Laban's *motion factors* of *Space, Weight, Time* and *Flow*. Ullmann (Laban 1960, p. 127) names *Inner Attitudes* as the combination of two *motion factors* and gives them the six distinct names: *awake, dreamlike, remote, near, stable* and *mobile*. The tables handed to Yat Malmgren and never published by Rudolf Laban were outlines of particular *movement sequences* and *shapes* that are formed in *action* by each of these *Inner Attitudes*.

Malmgren spent his years at Drama Centre London refining and extending the concepts of *Inner Attitudes* for the use of actor training. Table 2.3 indicates the pairs of *motion factors*, and corresponding psychological functions, which together form the six *Inner Attitudes* used in his technique for actor training. In Malmgren's actor training technique Jung's psychological functions are termed *Mental Factors*.

INNER ATTITUDE	MOTION FACTOR	MOTION FACTOR	MENTAL FACTOR	MENTAL FACTOR
STABLE	Weight	Space	Sensing	Thinking
MOBILE	Time	Flow	Intuiting	Feeling
NEAR	Weight	Time	Sensing	Intuiting
REMOTE	Space	Flow	Thinking	Feeling
AWAKE	Space	Time	Thinking	Intuiting
ADREAM	Weight	Flow	Sensing	Feeling

Table 2.3 Malmgren's *Inner Attitudes* and their *Motion Factors* and *Mental Factors*[6]

---

[6] The information in this table is available in Yat Malmgren's Character Analysis lecture notes (1979- 2002) from Drama Centre London.

Malmgren's *Inner Attitudes* form a typology that directs actors to the use of particular *movement patterns* and bodily *shapes* in performance. The character types that each of the *Inner Attitudes* reflect are maintained through the constant presence in action of one or other of the two *motion factors* in that *Inner Attitude*. Each *Inner Attitude* suggests through its linkage to the *eight basic actions* ways of translating intentions into action for any constructed performed character.

2.2.2 Malmgren's Actor Training Technique in Australia

At the National Institute of Dramatic Arts (NIDA), Tony Knight, the Head of Acting, introduces Malmgren's technique and its application to text, with knowledge from his own training in the director's course at Drama Centre, London. The technique, as taught at NIDA, requires students to consider Laban's *eight basic actions* (Laban & Lawrence 1974, p. 25) or *basic efforts*, recognizing these *efforts* in text. Students apply Malmgren's *Inner Attitudes* of *Near*, *Adream* and *Stable* to the analysis of text-based characters. The emphasis is on the *Inner Attitudes* that are constructed by *Weight* or *Sensing*.

At Adelaide's Centre for the Arts Acting course, Malmgren's technique was taught via systematic exercises investigating the six *Inner Attitudes*, as set out in Table 2.3 (p. 30). This systematic approach requires students to investigate one *Inner Attitude* at a time, using improvisation to either create characters or to create scenarios based on students' lives, which comply with the character type under investigation. This teaching was initiated and carried out by David Kendall, from 2001 until his retirement in 2006.[7] Kendall had taught Malmgren's technique in Adelaide since 1987, firstly at the Centre for Performing Arts before its amalgamation with the North Adelaide School of Art to become the Adelaide Centre for the Arts. Kendall referred to the technique throughout his teaching as Laban technique for actors, even though he was trained by Yat Malmgren at Drama Centre London.

---

[7] Information about the processes of teaching Yat Malmgren's method of actor training at the Adelaide Centre for the Arts Acting course is taken from personal interviews with David Kendall and Acting students undertaken on the 13th. and 14th May 2003.

At the Performance course in the Faculty of Creative Arts in the University of Wollongong Malmgren's technique, taught by the author, often simply termed 'Yat', is via systematic *Inner Attitude* exercises, covering the six *Inner Attitudes* over three years of training. Malmgren's technique is also applied to both scene and monologue performances.

Two other Malmgren trained teachers run courses associated with actor training in Melbourne. Penelope Chater, a former Director of The Drama Studio in Sydney, describes Character Analysis in her actor training biography as 'a distinctive, rigorous, diagnostic tool for developing Character based on the final thesis of Rudolf Laban in conjunction with Jungian Psychology which was further developed by Yat Malmgren at the Drama Centre, London' (Byron Dance Dynamics 2009). Chater has taught Character Analysis at both the Victorian College of the Arts (VCA) and in Byron Bay at Dance Dynamics. Christopher Snow in Melbourne directs his Malmgren training towards vocal training for actors. Snow who has taught at Monash University's Performing Arts course and at Verve Studios in the Nicholas Building in Swanston St., Melbourne describes his teaching as 'integrating voice and speech work with Laban and Carpenter's Movement Psychology' (Verve Studios 2009).

Whilst it is true that the actor training technique which Yat Malmgren developed through his teaching at Drama Centre London, was prefigured by Rudolf Laban's expressionistic movement techniques and principles in the 1940s (Laban, 1948, 1950), the application of Laban's terms to the interpretation of texts for performances was solely developed by Yat Malmgren and Christopher Fettes, his partner, at Drama Centre, London. Rudolf Laban's teachings have been disseminated throughout the world in the form of educational dance and modern dance teachings. Laban's input to actor training was in movement for actors, which Jean Newlove (1993, 2004), Laban's personal assistant in his latter years, helped to direct. Yat Malmgren's technique, whilst retaining Laban's terminology and principles, concentrates on *Inner Attitudes*. This thesis acknowledges the various names used to term Malmgren's actor training (Laban for actors, Movement Psychology, Character Analysis) and recognises the name Character Analysis as that which Malmgren himself finally chose as the name of his technique. However in this thesis I choose Malmgren's or Yat Malmgren's actor training technique as the definitive term for this actor training as it encompasses all the other terms and highlights the initiator of the technique which utilises *Inner Attitudes* for actor training.

Yat Malmgren was never a student of Rudolf Laban. Their lives and their artistic trajectories in the world of dance and dance training intersected and these intersections became determining moments in the development of Malmgren's technique. Malmgren regarded himself as the inheritor of Rudolf Laban's Movement Psychology. The following section of this chapter is designed not only to chart the interweaving circumstances of the lives of Rudolf Laban and Yat Malmgren, but also to bring to light an almost mythical dimension of Malmgren's oral tradition.

2.3 RUDOLF LABAN (1879 – 1958): the creation of Movement Psychology

Rudolf Laban was a choreographer, dancer and movement theorist. He is probably best known for his comprehensive and precise system of recording human movement, known as labanotation. It is still one of the most efficient means of notating choreography.

Born in 1879 in Poszony, in Hungary, now Bratislava in Slovakia, Laban was influenced by the ideas of the Rosicrucians, when studying art at the Écoles des Beaux Arts in Paris at the turn of the century (Preston-Dunlop 1998). Rosicrucian philosophies of harmony and structure underpin much of Laban's later choreographies and movement theories. In constructing movement exercises, termed *movement scales*, he aimed to reflect in movement the harmonies of music. His scales were based around the geometrical shapes of the cube, the tetrahedron, the octahedron, the dodecahedron and the icosahedron (Newlove & Dalby 2004). These studies of the spatial forms of movement, which he termed 'choreutics', led to his concepts of space harmony, that humans through his movement sequences could achieve balance and stability. His design of the human body as an icosahedron and his other geometrical designs of the body, including that of an *effort cube*, are all linked with the Rosicrucian idealisation of geometry (Foster 1977). Foster recognises that Laban's categorised movement sequences and rhythms owe a heritage to Françoise Delsarte, who like Laban systematised gestures and movements for stage performance in connection with inner emotional experiences. Foster (1977) indicates direct links between Laban's terminology and Delsarte's teachings and that Émile-Jaques Dalcroze's music educational technique of eurhythmics influenced Laban's practices. However in particular Foster considers the mystical and psychological influences on Laban's theories. Laban, active within a number of Masonic lodges, formulated his interest in mysticism and esoteric teachings into movement principles aiming 'for a total harmony of soul and spirit (which) led him from movement observation and analysis into dance theory and performance' (Connolly & Lathrop 1997, p. 32).

Valerie Preston-Dunlop (1998, p. 11) who worked closely with Laban in his teaching, at Weybridge in Surrey in the 1950s writes,

> Laban seems to have developed the conviction that the body holds truths which, through sensitising practices, can be reached and should be sought. Movements of gathering and scattering, which any Laban student will recognise as common in his work, also have a place in the building up of energies and centres in Rosicrucian practice, which in turn lead to psychic energy flowing outwards.

Laban's desire to embody his idealism in an art form led to his involvement firstly with theosophy in Munich and later with the Dadaist movement in Zurich between 1916-1920. During his Zurich period, Laban also developed his use of symbols, rather than words, to express movement and his diagrams often reflected Masonic principles. He stayed connected with the Rosicrucians and may have risen to the rank of Grand-master (Foster 1977). Laban began dancing and teaching dance in new abstract and symbolic forms in Munich in 1913. It was through this work that Laban's name began to quickly spread through Europe. He worked intimately with Mary Wigman, the famous expressionistic dancer who was to carry into her future work many of Laban's notions of dance. Laban's desire to discover an underpinning set of rules for movement, as a major means of communication, led to Wigman's and Laban's collaboration on numerous dance works. These were the beginnings of modern dance as we now know it.

Of Laban, Wigman is quoted by Preston-Dunlop (1998, p. 49) as saying,

> Laban had the extraordinary quality of setting you free artistically, enabling you to find your own roots, and thus stabilised to discover your own potentialities, to develop your own technique and your individual style of dancing.

Laban had established his models of movement related to geometry, in both the *iscosahedral form* and the *octahedral form,* by 1918 (Preston-Dunlop 1998, p. 49). These were *space models* in which personal movements could be mapped. On his return to Germany Laban continued to choreograph wherever possible, as well as to publish his philosophies of movement. By 1930 he rose to the ranks of Choreographer and Director of Movement of the Prussian State Theatres in Berlin.

It is through Laban's numerous European schools of dance, established by Laban as well as his students that Yat Malmgren first came into contact with the movement theories and practices of Rudolf Laban.

2.3.1 YAT MALMGREN (1916 – 2002): founder of Character Analysis

Malmgren was born in Gavle, Sweden in 1916. Named Gert Eriksson Malmgren, he was always called and known as simply Yat. His great desire had been to become an actor. At the age of seventeen he left home for Stockholm, in order to study acting with Julia Hakanson, an actress with the Svenska Teatern, whose repertoire included many of the works of Strindberg and Ibsen.

It was for his dancing however that, at the age of nineteen in 1935, he was recommended to study with Tanya Grant, a Russian dancer who had been working with Kurt Jooss in the Laban School in Esssen, Germany. It was through Grant that Malmgren first heard of Laban's icosahedron. His contact with Laban's ideas however were limited, partly because he preferred to work on individual choreography whilst Laban was primarily creating work for groups, (often termed movement choirs) and partly because Laban's students were all encouraged to develop their own styles and often directly passed on little of Laban's theories.

In a series of interviews with Yat Malmgren, conducted at Drama Centre, London in November 2000[8], I asked Malmgren what of Laban's teachings he was receiving at the time. Yat, whose English always remained an enigmatic but deeply engaging and unique aspect of the man for his students, replied:

---

[8] The bibliographical information about Yat Malmgren is taken from personal interviews with Malmgren at Drama Centre, London on the 28th and 29th Nov. 2000. Some information has been corroborated via personal correspondence with Christopher Fettes, British director, Co-Director of Drama Centre, London 1963-2001 and life partner of Yat Malmgren.

> she [Tanya Grant] came from Kurt Jooss in Essen, and then she had some sort of conception of the *icosahedron*. It was the first time I ever heard about the *icosahedron* – but not about these so called *working actions*, that are so misunderstood. It's dangerously popular, I think. So they misunderstand all these so called *working actions*, ...has just become physical doings (Malmgren 2000).

He continued,

> [It] ... has destroyed Laban, and Laban knew that and later he spoke to me about his situation and found himself in a tragic situation and misunderstanding ... just before he died really (Malmgren 2000).

Here Yat Malmgren first turns to the problem of the dissemination of Rudolf Laban's concepts of movement. The simpler, more functional aspects of Laban's work were spreading rapidly. Malmgren, however, complains that this dissemination was occurring without any of Laban's accompanying understandings of the linkages of the work with concepts of an 'inner', imaginative life. Laban emphasised intentions and often criticised gymnastics as being merely physical movements to promote a healthy body. He differentiated these movements from dance, performed for theatrical or ritual purposes, where intentions of either communication or spiritual expression might play a part.

This European-wide spread of Laban's name and his many dance schools, despite Malmgren's claims, must have been embodying much of Laban's essential philosophies of human development and harmony because, under the growing Nazi regime, Laban's work was heavily scrutinised. His choreographed group dance for the Berlin Olympic Games, held in 1936, met with the disapproval of Goebbels who viewed the work in rehearsal. Laban was subsequently put under house arrest, his notation and books banned and his name forbidden from use in schools. In 1937 he fled to Paris, destitute.

In an unattributed preface in Laban's *Effort* (Laban & Lawrence 1947, Biographical note), the British publishers Macdonald and Evans, who supported Rudolf Laban in Britain during the war years, despite his Germanic heritage, suggest that, the Nazi regime, ... looked upon his teachings of harmony and fulfillment through re-educating the sense of rhythm and movement as a threat to its own discordant philosophy.

During the years from 1935 to 1939 Yat Malmgren's career as a European solo dancer grew. From Stockholm, Malmgren moved to Berlin, in 1936, to train with Eugenia Egorova, for two years (Fettes 1989, p. 76). He called her his 'third Russian teacher'. By this stage Malmgren was already creating the character performances in dance that earned him his reputation as a modern recital dancer. His interest lay in a character's dramatic circumstances and he wanted to explore characters' temperaments. He performed solo recitals of character dances throughout Sweden, firstly in 1938, then in Paris, Berlin, Stockholm and Warsaw. He also trained with Trude Engelhardt who had been an assistant to Mary Wigman in her company. At this stage of his career, although Malmgren had never encountered Laban he was clearly aware of his work.

In 1939 Malmgren performed at the Concours Internationale de la Danse in Brussels and was awarded the gold medal. At that time Malmgren had been studying classical ballet with Olga Preobrajenska, one of Diaghilev's company, in Paris. The fame of Malmgren's success in Brussels, led to Kurt Jooss contacting Malmgren, asking for him to audition for the Ballet Jooss, which by then had relocated to England to avoid the growing vicissitudes of war. The Ballet Jooss was established by Kurt Jooss and Sigurd Leeder. Their choreographies and dance techniques were based on Laban's principles of eukinetics. Malmgren auditioned and was accepted.

> ... so I came. He offered me to come to London ... for an audition. And I was then in Paris, studying for Preobrajenska – classical. And there I did dance and then came a second round and so they invited me for the whole week's stage to show as many compositions of myself as I wanted to show ... and he offered me a contract and I said I didn't know, because I, I have an idea that I wanted to develop my own characters and he was a group and I have never been very good in group work ... I was a sort of individual character dancer (Malmgren 2000).

Extraordinarily, Malmgren's eventual decision in 1939 to join the Ballet Jooss (see Winearis 1968) was the propelling force that brought him into direct contact with Rudolf Laban. Kurt Jooss had invited Laban, in 1938, to also work for the Ballet Jooss, which had its base at Dartington Hall, Devon. This is where the two men were to meet.

Dartington Hall was established in 1931, by Leonard and Dorothy Elmhirst, on their estate, as a trust, overseeing a range of experimental arts activities. John Foster in *The Influences of Rudolf Laban* (1977, pp. 28-29) states that, 'Laban was accepted into this rather intimate symposium as a 'Guru' figure'.

> Into this circle came Laban as 'the master'. He experimented with movement as a unifying element in the arts disciplines, gave advice on the training schemes for reducing the physical strain on estate workers, and generally imbibed the atmosphere of living with this exceptional group of artists.

It was at Dartington that Laban became the close colleague of Lisa Ullmann, an association that lasted until Laban's death in 1958 (Willson 1997, p. 12). Ullmann had visited Laban in Paris and seeing how unsupported he was, after escaping from Nazi Germany, Ullmann requested Kurt Jooss to assist Laban. At Dartington Ullmann engaged Laban in her educational dance work. This translation of Laban's theories into the educational field was in part due to his exile status and hence need of income, but it was also due to Dartington Hall's links with the main English educational innovations of the time. Yat Malmgren paints a very particular image of Rudolf Laban at Dartington in those war years.

> Rudolf Laban was there and he had been saved from Hitler's Germany by Lisa Ullmann ... She fetched him. ... So anyway she, Lisa said, "Oh. You must meet Laban." This Laban – and that was a big name. So she took me in her car from Dartington road down to where he stayed... And then he immediately took some sort of interest and started to speak to me as if he asked me so many questions that I'd never thought about and I answered them fully... And we unfortunately were in accordance that Kurt Jooss started to go the wrong way ... Kurt Jooss had got *The Green Table*. Everything – we worked on the *dynamic* qualities. ... So he became more choreutic – you know asymmetrical. They have this peculiar name – choreutic – simply the abstract and more choreographed and not so much quality in the work. So that was the first time that I looked at all these figures that was hanging on the wall ...

> There was a skeleton there ... It was not just the *icosahedron*. It was all different formations by movement. Then later on he asked me to come have tea with him up at the castle ... He must have been very lonely because nobody definitely really ever spoke about him ... Nobody seemed to care for him at all (Malmgren 2000).

In this colourful description Malmgren points to a first meeting with Laban that laid bare the two men's joint preoccupations with movement, that of the quality or inner life of the performance.

Laban was critical of Kurt Jooss, his brilliant student. Nonetheless Jooss' company would tour the great pacifist choreography of *The Green Table,* throughout the world, using all of Laban's formulations of space harmonies in the work. Laban himself, however, was hunting for greater expression than formulaic movements. Malmgren, despite his misgivings about this direction of Kurt Jooss', joined the Ballet Jooss in its tour of seven ballets, including *The Green Table* throughout the war years. Malmgren danced in many of the Ballet Jooss repetoire, firstly in the United Kingdom and then in the United States, Canada and South America.

It was not until fifteen years later in 1954 that Laban and Malmgren were to meet again.

2.3.2 The synthesis of Movement Psychology: Laban's legacy to Malmgren

Rudolf Laban re-established himself in the United Kingdom, from Europe, through the new context of educational dance. He moved to Manchester and then to Addlestone in Surrey in 1953. It was Lisa Ullmann who introduced the Art of Movement into British schools and who established the Laban Art of Movement Studio in Manchester in 1946. Laban's practices and findings in the realm of movement had become widespread throughout the United Kingdom and later achieved similar acceptance in Japan, Israel, Iceland, South America and Europe, as a result of Art of Movement practitioners (Newlove 1993).

Laban, whilst still involved in the Art of Movement Studio, worked closely with the theatre makers, Joan Littlewood and Ewan McColl at Manchester, who were the founders of the Theatre Workshop Company (Lacey 1995). Jean Newlove was employed by the company as a Laban movement trainer and choreographer and has directed Laban's movement theories towards actors through workshops and writings (Newlove 1993). Laban had a studio attached to the Theatre Workshop studio and often observed and commented on the theatrical and movement studies in progress (Warburton 1993; Willson 1997).

However Valerie Preston-Dunlop records Littlewood as suggesting that it was Ullmann who carefully steered Laban away from his theatrical connections and kept his work, in particular his theoretical writings about movement, aimed at educational dance (Preston-Dunlop 1998). It was however, through a different sphere of influence that Laban's theories were passed, in a newly synthesised form, into the hands of Yat Malmgren, to be used for the training of actors.

In the war years at Dartington Hall, in 1942, Laban had begun collaborations with F.C. Lawrence, an industrial management consultant, in order to create new means of assessing, selecting and training personnel for factory work. The selections were based on Laban's research into the nature of human rhythms (Willson 1997). Laban, in this research, concluded that his *eight working actions* in fact defined a set of movement rhythms that could be correlated to particular movement types or personalities and these could then be matched with particular types of work. From Dartington Hall the Laban-Lawrence Industrial Rhythm was created and taught to factory workers in order to enhance industrial output in war beleaguered times (Newlove 1993). It is vital to note that one of the other refugees from war torn Europe residing at Dartington Hall at the same time as Laban was Michael Chekhov (Fettes 1979). There is a clear influence between Chekhov's application of Stanislavskian concepts to acting and Laban's ideas about human expression. Stanislavski had previously considered both the notion of *tempo-rhythms* (Stanislavski 1988) and character typology (Stanislavski 1989) as means for the use of actors.

The research with Lawrence was the beginning of Laban's investigations into the effect of personality on movement. In *Effort* (1947), the published collaboration of Laban and Lawrence, interpretations of psychological states are listed alongside movement observations. This new direction of Laban's thinking, equating movements with intentions and so with psychological types or personality types was only in its formative stage at this time. It was at Laban's studio in Addlestone, in Surrey, in the years of 1953-4 that Laban attempted to consolidate this work in collaboration with William Carpenter, a manufacturer greatly influenced by the works of Carl Gustav Jung. Laban met William Carpenter through Bill Elmhirst (Preston-Dunlop 1998, p. 262).

Laban and Carpenter's collaboration was intended to address the psychology of movement and an intended book was provisionally entitled, *Movement Psychology*. This book was never published as the collaboration was cut short through the untimely death of Carpenter in June 1954 (Preston-Dunlop 1998, p. 263).

In first naming this research Movement Psychology, Rudolf Laban clearly linked his investigations to psychology and Jung's work on personality theory. This interconnection was deliberate and more than a consequence of finding a collaborator in William Carpenter. As Foster (1977, p. 51) notes, Laban and Jung:

> both expressed the view that the psyche in part was not confined to space and time. Both were mystics who approached their search for the soul from their own interests, Jung using depth analysis and Laban using kinaesthetic experience.

Jung's process of individuation has been compared with the study of Laban's movement techniques by Foster (1977, p. 51). In Jung's process an individual grows into a fully differentiated, balanced and unified personality through psychological consciousness. Through Laban's movement process an individual also develops through bodily awareness.

> By observing and analysing movements (which can be conscious or unconscious), it is possible to recognise the need of the mover and to become aware of his inner attitude which precedes the action (Newlove 1993, p. 11).

> The aim of his work was to assist the harmonization of the individual through the Art of Movement by giving him insights and a heightened perception of consciousness into his physical, intellectual, emotional, and spiritual relationship and inter-dependence (Foster 1977, p. 41).

It was at Addlestone, Surrey, in 1954, during the years of this growing research, that Malmgren once more met and this time worked for Rudolf Laban.

Malmgren had danced internationally since 1939. In Rio de Janeiro in 1940 Malmgren left the Ballet Jooss to recommence performing solo dance works.

Malmgren became the director of choreography at the Casino Copacabana in Rio de Janeiro, performing one solo character per evening there. It was in Rio de Janeiro that Malmgren met and danced with Nina Theilade and Tatiana Leskova, both from the Ballet Russes in Monte Carlo. He also befriended Ruth Draper whose dramatic character monologues made a big impression on him. On his return to Europe in 1947, Malmgren toured Denmark, dancing with Nina Theilade. He then toured Sweden and Finland. He was invited to study classical ballet in Paris and then in London with Anna Northcote in order to perform with the International Ballet. Malmgren was directed by Leonide Massine with the International Ballet Company in the role of the Baron in *Gaité Parisienne*. However whilst working with the International Ballet Company, in London, Malmgren had a serious hip injury. He stated to me that whilst he was an expressive performer he had never become an extremely strong dancer and that the lifts required in classical ballet had put strains on his body. The International Ballet Company made the offer to Malmgren to teach in their studio. This was a turning point in Malmgren's life, directing his efforts towards teaching rather than performing. Malmgren joined the staff at Rudolf Laban's Art of Movement Studio in Addlestone, Surrey in 1954 teaching dance.

It was not until shortly after the death of William Carpenter, that Laban approached Malmgren with a set of papers, in June 1954. These were the seminal writings on Movement Psychology, consisting of a loose set of documents termed 'The Six Tables' as well as a 'Glossary of Terms'. Laban asked Malmgren to comment on them and help him with his research. It is these papers which outline only briefly Laban and Carpenter's collaboration.

Malmgren relates this historical encounter dramatically.

> What he handed me was loose papers of the *Inner Attitudes*, what was called 'The Tables'. They were not called the *Inner Attitudes*. They were called 'The Six Tables.' ... But what he said now that Carpenter has died ... "And now he has died and now all my life's achievement is lost" And I said "Mr. Laban that can't be possible. You have had so many people ... And so he said, "And you are the first man." And so I said, "but Mr. Laban, there has been Kurt Jooss and there has been so and so" And he said "Oh, but they have not understood my work as you have understood it ... There stood little me, but you understand ... of course I would be interested ... So, they are all in all the papers, you see. So when I

started to read them ... I spread them out on the floor, you know, and I started reading. And then something very strange happened to me I got too shocked, that I started to completely shake. I shook and I couldn't stop shaking for hours, for hours, for hours, for hours and it was as if I saw something that this is ... This is something incredible, incredible and to think that the Laban people had never been able to do anything about it (Malmgren 2000).

It is clear that with these new insights and questions, Yat Malmgren understood that Laban had shifted away from the investigation of dance itself, towards a far more complex notion of how human action, viewed as movement, is constructed. Whilst Laban has been remembered primarily for his understandings of dance, Malmgren directed this latter section of Rudolf Laban's work to constructing a theory of action, based on personality types for the use of actor training.

2.3.3 Malmgren's actor training[9]

After first receiving Laban's papers, Malmgren continued teaching movement at Addlestone. Malmgren was one of the few teachers who penetrated the privacy that separated all students and staff at Addlestone from Laban himself. Referred to ironically by students as 'the iron curtain', Lisa Ullmann and Laban kept a section of the property separate from the rest of the school. Malmgren, however was allowed into Laban's private space and spent many hours discussing with him the future of movement of psychology. It was Lisa Ullmann who terminated Malmgren's teaching at Addlestone in 1955, which Malmgren attributed to Lisa Ullmann's jealousy of Malmgren's involvement in Laban's new theories of movement psychology.

In 1954 Malmgren and Fettes set up the Actor's Studio in West Street, Cambridge Circus, London. Malmgren taught movement for actors but also later Movement Psychology to a select set of interested performers. Many successful actors and directors attended these classes, including Peter Brook, Tony Richardson, Sean Connery, Harold Lang, Diane Cilento, Fenella Fielding and Anthony Hopkins. In 1954 Malmgren, at the invitation of George Devine, took up a teaching position at

---

[9] The information in this section unless indicated otherwise is taken from personal interviews with Yat Malmgren on the 28th and 29th November 2000.

the English Stage Company at the Royal Court. Then in 1960 Malmgren joined the staff of the Central School of Speech and Drama, invited there by John Blatchley. In 1961 Malmgren taught as well at the Royal Academy of Dramatic Art (RADA). In 1963 Yat Malmgren and John Blatchley together left the Central School of Speech and Drama, after Malmgren's work was rejected there. Joining forces with Christopher Fettes they lead a set of students from the school, who wanted to be taught by Malmgren, in order to establish Drama Centre London in 1963 (Fettes 2002). Malmgren and Fettes became the founders and with Blatchley, the Joint Principals of Drama Centre, London. It was Fettes who saw the possibility of housing the new theories of movement and acting that Malmgren was developing in a new actor-training centre. It was also Fettes who provided Yat Malmgren with examples from literature, both novels and plays, of the character types that Malmgren needed to demonstrate his theories of character and action to English speaking students (C Fettes, 2005, pers. comm. 10 March). For although Malmgren had created and danced solo characters with a depth of understanding about dramatic action, Fettes understood that characters from drama and literature had a longevity to which the newly developing method could readily be applied. Fettes complimented Malmgren's developing technique through always using its terms and in particular those of the *Inner Attitudes* to analyse the texts that he directed at the school. Other directors at Drama Centre often followed in this convention.

Malmgren aligned all his acting classes in his studio with Laban movement classes taught by him usually at the start of each day. He continued these classes until he was well into his seventies and even then continued to run Laban *space* classes until he retired in 2001. However in the mid 1980s Malmgren changed the name of the developing actor training technique away from Movement Psychology, heralding a major shift of intention, disassociating the technique from its links with Jungian psychology and to Laban's name for the technique's origins. Malmgren linked his technique firmly with Stanislavski's system as taught by Doreen Cannon (see Chap 3, p. 64). After Cannon left Drama Centre London, Malmgren termed his technique simply 'Action'. He wanted to highlight the differing ways in which performed characters instigate action.

Malmgren's presumption, from Rudolf Laban's previous work, is that differing character types perceive and interact with the world in different ways; that differing intentional desires, lead to very differing bodily movements. Malmgren's actor training system enables performers to investigate their own and others' behaviours in the light of Malmgren's typology. Malmgren's technique aims to establish the means by which actors can reflect the differing intentional actions of characters through their bodies. He often reiterated that his technique was not a therapy but was to be used solely for training actors. Although Rudolf Laban's terminologies in the developing technique remained, Malmgren directed their use specifically to dramatic action. The concept of *Inner Attitudes* (see further pp. 51-4), of *Flow* (see Chap. 8, pp. 257-261), of *Externalised Drives* (see p. 54), all of which terms appear in Laban's writings, take on differing meanings in Malmgren's actor training technique aimed at refining the performing of text based characters. Finally in the mid 1990s Malmgren settled on terming his technique Character Analysis. This thesis however places Malmgren's name in association with his technique to emphasise the man, Yat Malmgren, as the initiator of this sophisticated actor training process.

Yat Malmgren, like Laban, believed in the life-enhancing qualities of his theories of movement and behaviour. Malmgren stated that his actor training technique assisted the development and organisation of an actor's 'inner life'. He also spoke with me about the evolutionary nature of the work. Malmgren intimated that a character's *Inner Attitude* changed throughout an individual's lifetime as his/her consciousness of environment grew, and that the study of his technique could enhance changes of this manner. The growth and development of Malmgren's technique was structured to continuously challenge actors in this direction.

Until his life's end on June 6th 2002 Malmgren directed himself towards enabling actors to discover the *Effort* or inner life of their characters. His obituary in the *Times* (June 15, 2002) states,

> Character Analysis, ... is a fully worked-out theory of acting that places transformation – vocal, physical, and emotional at the heart of the process. He [Malmgren] devoted his life as a teacher to conveying the profound understanding of the laws governing transformation, the means whereby the chaos of an actor's raw material is converted into the logic and focused energy of character. Malmgren's work stands with the great acting theories of the 20th Century, those of Stanislavski, Meyerhold, and Artaud...

Malmgren used his actor training technique to provoke, inspire, and challenge actors and directors, through illuminating the perceivable interconnections between bodies and their lived worlds. In my last interview he stated:

> I think that what, what I have come near, is what Laban definitely dreamt about ... he started from nothing ... and it is not so difficult to start where somebody left off ... but I turned it into something quite different through Carpenter's glossary (Malmgren 2000).

2.4 *Effort* in Laban's model

I am in Room 2, Yat's room, or so it has always been. I have returned again, after years, to learn more whilst Yat is still teaching. He is 84 now and yet seems as bright as ever.

Yat is being magnanimous. He lets me lead a set of student performed scenarios, allowing me to offer comments and give notes on each. I am overwhelmed and eager. I sense his recognition of my commitment to his teaching and my many years of teaching his work in Australia. However, whilst commenting to a student, he intercedes. "Of course you know Janys here was very depressed when she first came to Drama Centre." I blush. I stammer, "But Yat ... I didn't even know I was depressed until I came here."

The words are out of my mouth before I can think. The class roars with laughter. Drama Centre is renowned as the "trauma centre" throughout London's theatrical trainings. The psychological probing is known to be intense. I blush again. I hadn't meant to reflect on the institution, rather I wanted to convey my own confusion. Yat picks the situation up quickly. "Well of course, Drama Centre teaches what you have never known before".

Researcher's Journal 2.2 February 1998, Visiting Drama Centre, London.

The following section of this chapter establishes an investigation of Laban's notion of *Effort*, which is a fundamental basis for his model of movement. Malmgren too based his teachings on the principle of *Effort*, placing a definition of it on the first page of his lecture notes (1979). 'Effort: The sequence of INNER ATTITUDES and EXTERNALISED DRIVES which activate an ACTION'

According to Laban (1948), sequences of *efforts*, moving in directions of *space*, create *shapes*. Laban conceded that any set of *efforts* can be combined to create performed patterns of movement. However, he believed that certain *effort sequences* combine more efficaciously in particular *directions* (Laban, 1948, p38). He consigned areas of the *kinesphere*, in other words regions of the body, where each *effort* is more 'naturally' performed.

> The easy performance of certain *efforts* into definite *directions* or along stretches of free *shapes* or regular patterns makes the movement harmonious.

Jean Newlove (1993, p. 23) echoes Laban's implicit belief in the natural harmony of certain movement sequences when she writes,

> The comprehensive study of logical *spatial forms* within the *kinesphere* and their link to the moving body is called choreutics. Some prefer to call it a study of Space Harmony ... Natural growth in nature is based on the principle of "crystalline structure". I am no scientist but I believe that man is an organic part of this wonderful world of molecules, protons, neutrons and atoms, ...Our bodies not only displace space, they also move in space and motion in space exists within us. In all this movement there is a relatedness.

Harmony and relatedness of movement are essential qualities in Laban's vision for human development. Laban in *The Mastery of Movement* (1971, p. 25) says that, 'dance can be considered to be the poetry of bodily actions in space.' As dancers or students move in combinations of *efforts*, Laban (1971, p. 96) believed that moods or feeling states are provoked, of which the dancer or student may only be partly aware.

> Words expressing feelings, emotions, sentiments or certain mental and spiritual states will but touch the fringe of the inner responses which the *shapes* and *rhythms* of *bodily actions* are capable of evoking ... Sequences of movement are the sentences of speech, the real carriers of messages emerging from the world of silence.

In Laban's (1971, p. 115) understanding, the *shape* or sequence of a set of movements carries with it an indissoluble connection to the person's inner state.

> The *shapes* and *rhythms* which are formed by *basic effort actions, movement sensations, incomplete effort, movement drives,* give information about a person's relation to his inner and outer world.

This notion of the symbolic nature of dance and its connection to an inner imaginative world is in Laban's (1948, p. 48) understanding vital as a pathway for the modern person to find meaning and refreshment in a world that is dominated by primarily functional movement.

> The final success of a well-developed and well-ordered effort-life for which the baby starts to strive can be achieved and the pupil leaving school will have acquired that poise of personality which to-day is often lacking because of the lop-sided development of intellectual faculty, balanced only by a rough-and-ready impetuosity of movement or by exaggerated self-consciousness and rigidity.

Betty Redfern in *Concepts in Modern Educational Dance* (1973, pp. 25-57), devotes a substantial proportion of the book to investigating the meaning of Laban's use of the term, *effort*. This necessity arises partly from Laban's acknowledgment that it is the action emerging from *effort* that is discernible. In using the term *effort* in an all embracing manner Laban opened himself to criticism that his statements,

> illustrate Laban's apparent readiness to ascribe "*effort*" to practically the whole of the natural world, inanimate as well as animate. It then turns out to be some Life Force pervading the whole universe ... and the term is stretched to such limits as to lose any useful purpose (Redfern 1973, p. 29).

Laban's use of the term *effort* to refer to bodily exertions or bodily expressive movements has had more success. Ullmann, in the revised editions of *Mastery of Movement* (1960, 1971), after Laban's death, clarifies this confusion by always referring to these rhythmic, energised movements as *effort-actions* (Laban 1971, p. 78). It is these *effort-actions*, in particular the *eight basic effort actions* – of *punch, slash, press, wring, dab, flick, glide* and *float,* that are most readily associated with Laban's teachings, being used in educational dance and drama, in Art of

Movement or Laban tertiary dance courses, and in drama courses, as well as in movement therapy circles (McNiff 1981, p. 125).

However, Laban's premise that 'The impulse given to our nerves and muscles which move the joints of our limbs originates in inner *effort*' (Laban 1948, p. 26) is a more contentious concept. Although the developmental aspect of Laban's theories have been taken up by educationalists in the form of modern dance and educational dance, the more holistic understanding of Laban's work has been followed through the therapeutic arts (Chodorow 1991; Stanton-Jones 1992). The model of inner *effort* reflecting outer *effort*, of an indissoluble link between feeling states and movement sequences, has often been lost by arts educationalists transmitting only the more categorical aspects of his work. Malmgren's actor training technique transmits this more phenomenological dimension of Laban's theories to actors.

The restrictions within the dance educational world, which impacted on theatrical educationalists, are reflected in Betty Redfern's (1973, p. 123) study of Laban's principles,

> it is possible to dispense with the notion of "*effort*" as an inner function or faculty which can be trained, together with the related concepts of "*effort* balance" and "*effort* harmony" where these carry metaphysical implications, yet appreciate the significance for dance of Laban's codification of so-called "*effort-elements*" ...

and again,

> Similarly, it is not necessary to subscribe to the idea that through certain *spatial configurations* one can achieve unity with the cosmos, in order to recognise the usefulness of Laban's system of "space harmony" (or "choreutics"). Through this there is available to the dancer a means of sorting out and developing *shapes* and patterns ... (Redfern 1973, p. 124).

Moreover Laban's model of the *icosahedron* has been criticised due to its complexity, as a major stumbling block in the understanding of Laban by students both of dance and movement (Foster 1977, p. 64).

The problem of whether dance is a direct expression of feeling or a symbolic form of feeling, also became a stumbling block for the continuation of Laban's theories. Susanne K. Langer (1953, p. 187) criticised not only Laban's mystical metaphysics but also his concept that bodily gesture emerges from actual feeling. J. L. Hanna, an American dance theorist, discards Laban's concepts of inseparable links between 'motion, emotion, form, content, mind, and body' (1983, p. 35), on the basis that Laban and his followers' works were over-generalised, based on the universality of bodily expression of emotion, and cultish. Yet Hanna, herself, retained the use of Laban's categories of movement as indicators of emotion in her own investigations of perceived emotion in particular dance works (1983, p. 228).

By the latter part of the twentieth century Laban's theories were sustained by his immediate followers and the dance establishments that they coordinated. The Laban Centre for Movement and Dance in London, which emerged from the Art of Movement Studio in 1975, became a hub for the teaching of Laban's movement theories as applied to dance (Laban Centre London 2007). The International Council of Kinetography Laban/Labanotation was set up in 1959 to interconnect practitioners of Laban's movement and dance notation (International Council of Kinetography Laban Labanotation 2007). Both this organization and the Laban Centre have become international forums through which research into Laban's movement theories have been collated. However, as Preston-Dunlop states, Laban's 'notation and analytical methods became more prominent within education than his experiential work' (Preston-Dunlop 1998, p. 272).

It is through the work of Yat Malmgren that Laban's experiential discoveries have been offered to actors; Laban's concepts about the functioning of human bodies are offered by Malmgren through an explicit actor training technique. Malmgren's technique locates the human body, as both a source of emotionally based gesture and also as a symbol-making entity. In Malmgren's system Laban's principles are used, not only for the categorisation of action, but also for the full development of the performing artist.

2.5 The development of Malmgren's technique

> I am back at Drama Centre again. Amazing how sensations realign with memory. The contour of the worn stone steps to Yat's upstairs

office fling me back to my years here, as if I have never left, as if I have always known this winding staircase.

Christopher and Yat greet me as a long lost compatriot – arms wide, their grins genuine in their warmth. Christopher draws from behind his back a photograph, one of my Drama Centre third year headshots. It is of a girl in me that I have almost forgotten. I felt so vulnerable, so unsure at the time – and yet the image smiles winningly back at me.

"Group 18! Group 18!", he is teasing and Yat is laughing. Thirty-four groups of students have passed through this battered old church premises and my group has been remembered more for its resistance than its talent. I return a sheepish smile.

Researcher's Journal 2.3 February 1998, Greeting Malmgren and Fettes at Drama Centre.

As his actor training system developed, Malmgren began to use Laban's terms in new and significantly different ways. A key example is the notion of *Inner Attitudes*, which were not much emphasised in Laban's own work after the death of his collaborator William Carpenter.

Laban writes of *Inner Attitudes* creating *incomplete actions*. These are small unconscious movements that are often transitional states between more decisive actions (Laban 1971, pp. 86-87). In Newlove & Dalby (2004, pp. 185-195) these transitional moves are termed *incomplete efforts* and they refer to unconscious moves made in the process of achieving a task. The tasks outlined are specific and mainly physical. However, in Malmgren's system, the term, *Inner Attitude*, developed into a nomenclature synonymous with personality type. The *incomplete actions* that Laban spoke of became in Malmgren's technique *shadow moves,* 'movements of any part of the body made without conscious will' (Malmgren 1979). *Shadow moves* are outward unconscious gestures of pre-reflective motivations. In this new system, the Stanislavskian notion of *actions* performed to achieve *objectives* is matched with Laban's *eight efforts* performed as aspects of a character's *Inner Attitude*.

It appears from Lisa Ullmann's revised editions of Laban's *The Mastery of Movement* (1960) that, for a short period, Yat Malmgren's developing Movement Psychology system, as used in his teaching of actors at his West Street studio, mirrored Lisa Ullmann's continued teaching of Laban's work at Addlestone. As previously stated, Ullmann (Laban 1960, p. 127), names *Inner Attitudes* as the combination of two *motion factors* and gives them the six distinct names but different names to Malmgren: *awake, dreamlike, remote, near, stable* and *mobile*. She also links Laban's *motion factors* with the Jung's personality functions of *Sensing, Thinking, Intuiting* and *Feeling*. Ullmann states that Laban, before his death, had communicated clearly to her the new directions of his findings and on this basis she made substantial revisions to his published work (Laban 1960, Preface by Ullmann).

It is noteworthy that *The Mastery of Movement* (1971) was first published before Laban's death as *The Mastery of Movement on the Stage* (1950) and that in it Laban refers to theatrical acting as being, 'the artistic enhancement of human action' (Laban, 1950, Preface). This use of the term *action*, rather than movement or *effort*, as well as the all-embracing nature of the statement places it clearly within the Movement Psychology system. In doing so Laban aligns himself with Stanislavski's (1973, p. 1) position, 'There is only one system – creative organic nature. There is no other system.' Laban, perhaps through his association with Michael Chekhov recognised the affinities of his own movement concepts with theatrical concepts of *action*. Malmgren's actor training technique reinforces this. In Yat Malmgren's Movement Psychology, later termed Character Analysis notes (1979), action refers to:

> a bodily movement expressed through the *Motion Factors* of *Weight, Space, Time* and *Flow*, performed for a functional purpose, with a measure of conscious volition (Malmgren 1979).

Newlove (Newlove & Dalby 2004, pp. 196-201) also sets out *incomplete efforts* in groups of three as part of Laban's Drives. She calls these *incomplete efforts*, 'modes of *Awake, Near, Stable, Remote, Mobile* and *Dreamlike*'. Newlove's concepts are a reflection of her training with Laban. Malmgren however, takes this embryonic understanding of *incomplete efforts* or *shadow moves* as they are termed in his actor training and differentiates a system whereby *Inner Attitudes* precede or activate *actions*. An individual expresses her *Inner Attitude* and intentions through movements and language that are interconnected with the ways in which she perceives her world, including others in it. Each *Inner Attitude* is a combination of two of the *Motion Factors* and each *Inner Attitude* is also a combination of two of the *Mental Factors* of *Sensing, Thinking, Intuiting* and *Feeling* (See Table 2.3 p. 30). Each *Inner Attitude* creates a set of *tempo-rhythms* for a character, sixteen for each *Inner Attitude*.

In Yat Malmgren's (1979) notes, the *Inner Attitudes* are set out as:

> The sub-conscious states of
> *STABLE (Sensing/Thinking)*
> *MOBILE (Intuiting/Feeling)*
> *NEAR (Sensing/Intuiting)*
> *REMOTE (Thinking/Feeling)*
> *AWAKE (Thinking/Intuiting)*
> *ADREAM (Sensing/Feeling)*
> which are normally motivated in the sub-conscious mind
> but which can be activated by bodily movements

Each of these *Inner Attitudes* results in differing basic *effort sequences*, which are mirrored throughout the body, in language, posture, gesture and intentional movement. Just as Laban's use of the term *effort* implies an inner or hidden dimension to movement, so Malmgren's use of the term *Inner Attitude* implies an unseen aspect of character. The investigation of *Inner Attitudes* in Malmgren's technique is in fact an in-depth investigation of *action*, with the belief that performative action stemming from an activated motivational or pre-linguistic state is more expressive than purely functional movement.

Action lies at the heart of performativity and yet few systems of acting investigate it through differentiation, categorisation, and nomenclature as the Malmgren system does. Performed *action* is shaped by text, but as Alice Rayner says in *To Act, to Do, to Perform* (1994, p. 31),

> Character is a textual function that is performed by an actor, but the substance of a character is absent except as a linguistic construct.

Through text a character is constructed, however it is through performed *action* incorporating text, delivered through the actor's body, for the audience, that flesh is added to the initial textual image. *Action* becomes the keystone to the performance, whilst also being linguistically bound by it. The audience views the actor's *actions* within the confines of the text, reading the *action* as a narrative that both suggests motivation as well as projecting possible consequences. Malmgren's *Inner Attitudes* are an investigation into the way performative *action* defines character as much as an investigation as to how character defines *action*. Each *Inner Attitude* carries with it differing modes of perceiving other characters, differing non-verbal communication, and differing motivational goals.

> The character that aims toward a goal is also one that is created by that goal. In doing something [the character] is being done, that is, he is making a self as he appears to be doing other things (Rayner 1994, p. 44).

Malmgren, through the introduction of the concept of *Inner Attitudes*, plays with a self-reflexive examination of the actor's *action*, begging the question, at any moment in time, of what narrative is being constructed through a performer's *action*. This *action* is both verbal and non-verbal and requires the performer to be precisely aware of their bodies as the expressive medium of their motivations. Through the concept of *Inner Attitudes*, Malmgren constructs an all-embracing model for the investigation of character.

2.5.1 *Externalised Drives*

From 1969, Malmgren, as well as using *Inner Attitudes* to investigate performative *action*, also developed the concept of *Externalised Drives*, as a means of stimulating expressive *action*. Malmgen utilised this concept in particular for the analysis of text and the interpretation of text into performed *action*. Four *Externalised Drives* are mentioned by Laban (1971, pp. 87-89) as combinations of three *Motion Factors*: *Action (Weight, Space & Time), Vision (Space, Time & Flow), Spell (Weight, Space & Flow) & Passion (Weight, Time & Flow)*. Preston-Dunlop (1963, p. 144) refers to these as *Effort* drives. She interestingly conflates all of Laban's *efforts* under the heading of Laban's drive of *Action*, so that all *effort-actions* in this context are lacking *Flow*. She suggests that educationalists teaching movement will be better suited to restricting *effort-actions* by this means and that the other *Drives* can form the study of human movement for actors or movement therapists or dancers. Newlove (Newlove & Dalby 2004, pp. 196-201) refers to the *Drives* as simply 'the four *Drives*'. Newlove (p. 197) also suggests that, '*Vision,*

Spell and *Passion Drives* cannot be so precisely determined as the *Action Drive*.' The extension of Rudolf Laban's work in the latter part of his life, with his growing interest in a range of expressive *actions* stemming from differing psychological types has been minimalised within the educational dance field. The more functional *effort-action*, or action formed through the *Externalised Drive* of *Doing*, as Malmgren termed the *Action Drive* has been the only type of *effort* explored.

In Malmgren's technique the emphasis for trainee actors is on the performance of characters with recognised *Inner Attitudes* formed by the conjunction of two *Externalised Drives*. The four *Externalised Drives* in Malmgren's technique are termed *Doing, Passion, Spell* and *Vision*. In speaking with Malmgren regarding training actors, Malmgren (2000) regarded his role as being:

> to definitely waken the activations of the actions from the *effort*, that is done by the connection between the *Externalised Drives*. It is very difficult for [actors] to understand an *Inner Attitude* is the combination of something – two drives – that most people self indulge in what is called the *Inner Attitude* and they do not in life play an action ... they don't have objectives. So they never come out of the *Inner Attitude* into life into action, and without the two other *Externalised Drives* it's impossible to come out or to produce an inner and an outer.

Malmgren here suggests that it is only through a drive towards an objective that an *action* is stimulated. He used the concept of the *Externalised Drives* to bring this to life for acting students. He required students to be specific about which *Externalised Drive* they were being moved by for any particular section of text that they performed. Malmgren (2000) referred to this when speaking of the relationship that a character has with another character on stage.

> My relationship with that one person ... that person has its objective and I must create a relationship with a problem of that person ... that is then an obstacle for me. Right, and so I must be in constant contact with the person, outside of me.

Here Malmgren refers to his concept that other characters on stage need to appear as *obstacles* for any performed character, so that *action* is always directed towards *objectives* that encounter these character/*obstacles* and that specific *externalised drives* are used in these encounters. This is a concept that has clear connections with Stanislavski's theories of a character's through-action (Stanislavski 1973, p. 71). The through-action represents the direction of all the character's activities and represents a clear ruling or super objective for the character. Malmgren requires specificity in *how* a character plays the *actions* towards the *objective*.

2.5.2 The body/mind

In the 1950s and 1960s in American actor training, the Stanislavski System as taught by Sonia Moore (1979, p. 34) and others was emphasising the mind's control over the body's actions.

> It will take time to learn control over your emotions and all your organic resources, but you will learn it if you have the will to learn and to overcome the difficulties. You will become actors when you control your physical and psychological nature to build characters in a play.

Malmgren in the same period was attempting to bridge the 'body/mind dualism' so prevalent in the interpretation of Stanislavski's system in the USA. His method emphasises that action can be stimulated equally by physical or mental means and that a two-way interaction is constantly in flow between imagination and movement.

In Malmgren's technique, *effort* is expressed through *Inner Attitudes* and *Externalised Drives*. That is, the shape of our imaginative *effort* creates an *Inner Attitude* and we extend in action through *Externalised Drives*. Our bodies reflect our *Inner Attitudes* in muscle shape, freedom of movement in the joints, *directions of movement, shadow moves* and much more. However *Inner Attitudes* are themselves influenced by environment and so *Inner Attitudes* are movable and changeable.

Malmgren's work on Character Analysis classes at Drama Centre was aligned with his movement classes (Malmgren retired from leading movement classes in the mid 1990s) and corporeality is central to the training. Experiential reflection in Malmgren's Character Analysis classes was matched with Laban *effort* training, to expand movement choices. So in the teaching, possibilities exist to retrain bodies and, through reflection to reshape *Inner Attitudes*.

These notions are not uncommon in the fields of movement and dance therapy. McNiff in *The Arts and Psychotherapy* (1981, p. 111) concurs with these possibilities of transformation when he states,

> Traditional psychotherapies have stressed the importance of unconscious imagery and thought, whereas I feel that equal attention must be given to unconscious movement and kinesthetic conflict ... Because of the advances being made in the understanding of how the body stores tension, how the muscles have emotional memories that restrict the functioning of the whole organism, how the body and muscles block the flow of creative and spontaneous thought in all modes of expression and how all thought is dependant upon muscular sensation.

In the 1970s the closest Betty Redfern (1973, p. 34), a leading Laban dance proponent, could come to conceptualising Laban's view of *Effort* was to suggest that

> Laban is perhaps leaning towards yet another theory ... that mental phenomena are one and the same thing as states and processes of the body.

However this is too materialistic an explanation for what Laban was striving to express with his poetic and contradictory language. Now in the twenty-first century a new sensibility of the interchanging nature of matter and energy has led to clearer understandings of the body/mind, so that Berger (Berger & Leventhal 1993, p. 253), a New York dance therapist can state,

> One of the most powerful realities of the human condition occurs when feeling and the symbolic expression of this feeling find a match in the forming of the felt thought into the expression/reaction ... The body is simultaneously the working instrument and the symbol.

There is a difference in this statement in comparison to Redfern's. Redfern's is reductionistic, inner *effort* and outer *effort* are reduced to nerve functionings. However Berger straddles the two perceptual worlds of experience of one's self and the awareness of movement suggesting that at heightened moments there is a synthesis. This notion of synthesis or unity is implicit in Malmgren's work. The struggle to allow the body to reflect the inner state begins with the scenarios from the actor's personal life.

Yat Malmgren often turned to movement itself to bridge the dualism or simplification that his students wished to impose on his technique. A dance could speak more eloquently than words. His words, however most of which have never been recorded or documented, still echo with the knowledge of human motivation and movement that he so faithfully taught.

> We speak into six distances inside and outside of us, the
> *Inner Attitudes*
> Muscles by themselves express liking or disliking
> (Malmgren 1988).

CHAPTER 3

ACTING TECHNIQUES, MALMGREN AND EMBODIMENT

> Drama is conflict. If I have an objective, immediately, I am in conflict, for better or worse, because for every objective that you ever want there will be an obstacle and what I can do to come through the obstacle. The excitement of having an objective - students can't understand at all. They think of it as a sort of anger. It is conflict inside of me, so I risk something. So immediately I am *Mobile*. The importance is this insecurity inside of one, while one presents the action, quite outside.
>
> Malmgren November 2000.

3.1 Introduction: the second ripple of contextualisation of Malmgren's technique – actor training for theatrical realism

As argued in the previous chapter, Yat Malmgren's actor training technique developed at a time when theatrical psychological realism was challenging modes of performance in the theatre. By examining the context of Malmgren's work, both in terms of the times in which it developed as well as in terms of its relevance to performance theories regarding embodiment and by referring once more to my metaphor of the pebble's ripples in the water, this chapter may be viewed as the second ring of contextualisation of the embodied meaning in Malmgren's methods.

The first half of this chapter looks at a set of acting techniques that surrounded the development of Malmgren's actor training at Drama Centre London in the 1960s to 1980s. My aim is to differentiate Malmgren's view of the actor's body in comparison to the view of the actor's body offered in the other actor training techniques taught at Drama Centre London at that time for the purpose of training actors in realism. The second half of this chapter aims to examine the Malmgren technique in the light of postmodern performance theories about embodiment, in order to establish the author's view of the commonalities that Malmgren's technique has with late twentieth and twenty-first century discourses on embodiment. These commonalities are pertinent to the contemporary practice of Malmgren's actor training technique that is reflected in Chapters 5-8. Both parts of this chapter together aim to create a new and documented means of establishing Malmgren's actor training technique, as one among many actor training techniques, developed in the twentieth century, that at the same time offers new and relevant insights into the field of embodiment in the twenty-first century.

Heritage from Laban

Actor Training for Theatrical Rea

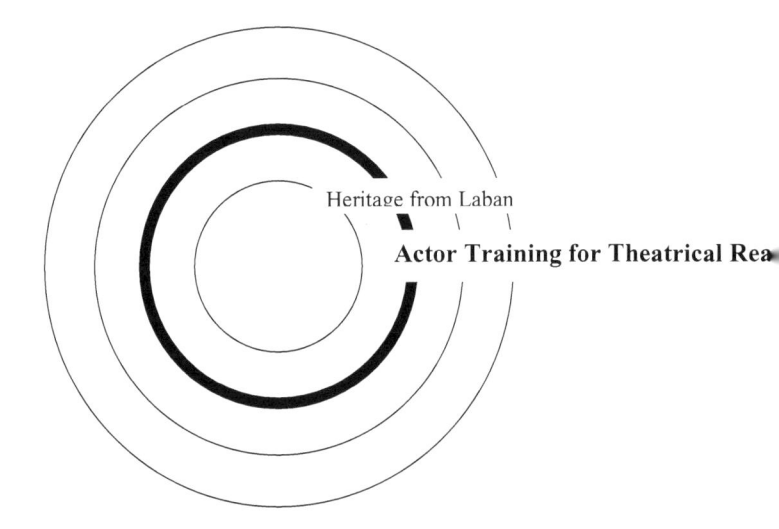

Figure 3.1 The second ripple – Contextualisation of Yat Malmgren's actor training: a system for theatrical realism

Previously, in Chapter 2, the first ripple of contextualisation documented Malmgren's inheritance of Rudolf Laban's expressionist dance techniques and terminologies. The fundamental premises of Malmgren's actor training from that heritage include spatial awareness in expression, the specificity of physical actions and the development of mind/body expression. This latter could be described as the growing mindfulness of psychophysical actions. Malmgren's actor training technique inherited elements of theatrical psychological realism; the Jungian psychological typology of *Sensing, Thinking, Intuiting* and *Feeling* are matched in Malmgren's actor training technique through motivational considerations with

Laban's physical categorization of movement into *Space, Weight, Time* and *Flow*. As Hayes (1996) states Malmgren's technique 'equate[s] movements with intentions and so with psychological ... or personality types' (cited in O'Connor 2001, p. 51).

Throughout the 1940s and the 1950s naturalism championed the search for psychological truth in the theatre. In America, actors skilled in the 'Method' as it was labelled or the 'System' (Clurman 1972), as it was called by those who adhered to it, challenged the styles of acting for stage and film. Their aim was to infuse the theatrical productions of the time, by writers such as Tennessee Williams, Arthur Miller, Lillian Hellman, Clifford Odets and Eugene O'Neill, with new emotional vitality. Likewise in the United Kingdom new theatre companies emerged, such as the English Stage Company, to present radical works. John Osborne's (1956) 'angry young man', in *Look Back In Anger,* created a new space for working-class characters on the British stage. Drama Centre London was formed in 1963 with an aim to equip actors to meet the new demands of the recently created National Theatre through a thorough 'Methodological Approach' to actor training. As Christopher Fettes, the Director of Drama Centre in 2002 writes in Malmgren's obituary,

> the school would never have survived but for immediate support of a council chaired by Lord Harewood, and including George Devine, Glen Byam Shaw, "Binkie" Beaumont, Peter Hall, Peter Brook and Kenneth Tynan. These leading figures knew that the repertory of the recently opened National Theatre, stretching from Aeschylus to Brecht, made increased demands on training. They saw the approach of the new school, closely associated with developments in Russia, the United States, France and Germany, as offering a possible long-term solution (Fettes 2002).

The study of Character Analysis or Movement Psychology as it was first termed at Drama Centre London is placed in Yat Malmgren's obituary in *The Times* as Drama Centre London's pedagogic core (2002). Malmgren viewed his technique as the study of human nature, rather than of constructed characters. My descriptions of actor training in this chapter and my framing of Malmgren's actor training technique in a postmodern setting in the latter half of this chapter, describe it through a questioning of the interaction between any performed character and the actor performing the character. These descriptions represent my own historical progression of Yat Malmgren's actor training processes.

3.2 Bodies of knowledge: acting techniques and differing views of the actor's body

A variety of approaches to acting were taught at Drama Centre London, alongside Malmgren's development of his technique, during the period 1963 – 2002, when Malmgren was co-director with Christopher Fettes. The four director-approved Acting methods taught at Drama Centre London were:

- Stanislavski's system[1]
- Littlewood's improvisational techniques
- Copeau and the French classical heritage
- Malmgren's technique of Character Analysis (previously known as
    Movement Psychology and then Action and taught in conjunction with
    Laban Movement)

Each of these methods of acting was a subject for all students enrolled in the three-year Acting course at Drama Centre London. Each of the first three methods had a presence in the western theatrical milieu of the period, in Europe, the United Kingdom and the United States.

Each of the methods above has unique attitudes towards actors' bodies, established through each method's historical development. In this section of the chapter, I will document the teaching of the first three methods at Drama Centre London. Comparisons will be made between the embodied training processes of each method and Malmgren's actor training technique, in order to differentiate the ways in which performing bodies are considered in differing actor trainings. Performance theories and contemporary perspectives about performing bodies will be taken into account in order to discuss each of these actor training methods.

---

[1] The Drama Centre prospectus and website have used the term The Stanislavsky Method to cover two varying methodological approaches to training actors both derived from American acting schools influenced by Stanislavski's system.

3.2.1 The Stanislavski system

Throughout the years that Malmgren was a co-director of Drama Centre London (1963-2001) the Stanislavski system of actor training, as developed in the USA was a major pillar of the methodological approach to actor training.

Although Stanislavski (cited in Magarshack 1973) decried the codification of his 'system', seeking instead ever-changing and organic responses from actors, the 1923 tour of the USA by the Moscow Arts Theatre stimulated the introduction of Stanislavski's concepts of working with actors to differing acting schools and theatre groups (Hirsch 1984). The Group Theatre formed in 1931 led by Harold Clurman, Lee Strasberg and Cheryl Crawford was one such actors' ensemble. Clurman had made personal contacts with Stanislavski and developed his theatre direction and teachings via these contacts (Clurman 1972). Strasberg viewed Stanislavski's work in Moscow and built his teaching on this plus Stanislavski's writings and information from Richard Boleslavski, a former Stanislavski trained member of the Moscow Arts Theatre (Hirsch 1984). Later in 1947 the Actors Studio opened, becoming the main disseminator of 'the Method', an American version of applying Stanislavski's theories to scene work, based on affective memory work. The Actors Studio was founded by Elia Kazan and Cheryl Crawford. Then in 1949 Lee Strasberg took over the teaching of the workshops.

In contrast, the HB Studio in New York, founded by Herbert Berghof, introduced Uta Hagen's teachings there in 1947 (Hagen 1973). Hagen was Berghof's wife. Whilst Berghof had studied acting in Germany with Max Reinhardt, Uta Hagen was influenced by Harold Clurman. In her seminal text, *Respect for Acting* (1973), she rejects the notion of a 'method' instead she emphasises that Stanislavski had based his concepts on the observation of exceptional actors' work. The exercises that Hagen's develops as an acting teacher are intended to enable actors to work independently.

It was through both of these American actors' studios, HB Studio and The Actors Studio that differing forms of systematic actor training with links to Stanislavski's theories entered the sphere of Drama Centre London. Even in America different acting schools emphasised differing aspects of Stanislavski's techniques. Whilst Strasberg concentrated on emotional memory, Stella Adler's studio was more concerned with actions (Watson 2001). After Drama Centre

London formed, Doreen Cannon became the prime teacher in this area concentrating on the through line of action in any play and the performance of actions. Cannon was recognised for introducing Stanislavskian techniques to British acting colleges. Her training was from HB Studio, where Cannon was taught by Uta Hagen. Cannon moved to London teaching at Drama Centre London for twenty years (1964-84) and becoming Head of Acting. Doreen Cannon was instrumental in the process of dissemination of Drama Centre techniques to a wider British and international theatrical industry. In 1985 Cannon left Drama Centre to teach at The Royal Academy of Dramatic Art (RADA). She also taught in Stockholm, Malmo and Gothenburg, in Sweden. On Cannon's death, on September 18th. 1995, London's *The Guardian* (Barter 1995, p. 16) wrote of her work,

> Like her own teachers, Doreen was gifted at demystifying the technique codified and developed by the great Russian actor and director, Konstantin Stanislavski. ... and she was largely responsible for changing [English] attitudes to what she so resonantly described as "the work".

Cannon's processes of acting are affectionately portrayed in Simon Callow's autobiography, *Being an Actor* (1995, pp. 27-29). The young Callow describes himself as clearly baffled as to how to put his acting coach's teachings into practice. Although, "Play your action!' was Doreen Cannon's catch-cry, understanding what she meant is clearly a problem for Callow, until Cannon's personal ferocity propels him into taking a performative risk. The terms 'having a want', 'having an objective', and 'playing an action' were part of the language used in Cannon's teaching, which concentrated on specific physical actions. In Callow's recounting of this training it is clear that he had no knowledge of what a character might want in a set of circumstances, or how to relate to a perceived objective that he may have been set in an acting exercise or what an action might mean to a performer in those circumstances. Identifying a 'want' and then playing an action through text analysis can remain a mystery for any actor trying to embody an objective.

The text that Cannon most often cited in her acting classes was Uta Hagen's, *Respect for Acting* (1973). 'Object exercises' as established by Hagen underpinned not only Cannon's direction at Drama Centre but also productions directed by Fettes and the student directors in Drama Centre's Directors course. In any 'object exercise' (Hagen 1973, pp. 91-94) an actor works individually to imagine and create a sensate world for a character where 'wants' or 'immediate objectives' propel character's actions through constructed scenes. Cannon formulated these 'wants' as 'actions'.

In contrast to Cannon's background, Reuven Adiv, who taught at Drama Centre London from 1983-2003, and who took over from Cannon as Head of Acting in 1984, studied at Lee Strasberg's Actor's Studio and later taught there. Fettes (2005) in Adiv's obituary in *The Guardian* gives a moving account of this inspiring acting teacher's life. Born in Jerusalem in 1930, Reuven Adiv's father was born in Belarus. He died in a Nazi concentration camp. Reuven Adiv worked as an actor in Tel Aviv before moving to New York. As well as studying at The Actor's Studio he undertook the Director's course there and studied too at the New York University's film school. In 1971 he returned to Israel acting on stage and screen. In his teachings at Drama Centre Adiv emphasised both physical and emotional spontaneity. He introduced affective memory exercises to Drama Centre's curriculum. Adiv's work allowed for a more flexible approach than Cannon's to 'the truth' of a performance. In Strasberg's training, the work on personalisation, finding points of empathy with the character and the situation is paramount (Krasner 2000, p. 134). Relaxation and spontaneity lead to creative performative choices rather than will, Strasberg suggested (Krasner 2000, p. 135). From 1986-96 Reuven Adiv was a guest teacher at the Swedish State Theatre School in Gothenburg.

Yat Malmgren often criticised the teachings of Stanislavski's system at Drama Centre. As Kendall notes (1984, p. 157) 'terminological differences' between Malmgren's acting technique and Cannon's (and later Adiv's) sometimes caused 'confusion and resentment in the students at Drama Centre'. Malmgren regarded 'Method' students, with their constant work on themselves, as 'excessively negative' (Malmgren 2000). In Malmgren's technique the term *negative* refers to when the body/mind is not active in any one of the areas of *Sensing, Thinking, Intuiting* or *Feeling*. In Malmgren's method of actor training a performer must awaken each *Mental Factor* so that she can be: *receiving and transmitting stimuli; putting reflections into action; making decisions relating the past to the present and future;* and *creating actions based on liking and disliking.* Malmgren (2000) asserts that 'the Method' creates a concentration on the personality of the actor. Malmgren's actor training seeks a self-reflection on any dominant mode or habitual mode of expression in an actor. Malmgren went as far as to state that no true bodily transformation can take place when personality is uppermost in an actor's process (2000). The character in Malmgren's technique is not necessarily the same personality type as the actor and may interpret her world in a completely different way to the actor. However as Watson (2002, p. 70) has documented the demise of Stanislavskian training in acting schools, at least in the USA has had as much to do with the emergence of 'alternatives to psychological-based theatrical realism', rather than criticisms of the Method itself.

3.2.2 Littlewood's improvisational techniques

Improvisational techniques of Joan Littlewood have been a consistent element in the Drama Centre London curriculum, although Littlewood never personally taught there. Christopher Fettes however had been an actor in Littlewood's Theatre Workshop at the Theatre Royal in Stratford, London joining it in 1953. Fettes' over-riding organization of Drama Centre's curriculum resulted in many of Littlewood's principles influencing the direction of the school. Most importantly Littlewood and subsequently Fettes believed in the theatrical creativity of the ensemble (Holdsworth 2006). In a joint interview with Pierce Brosnan in 2002, *The Independent* (Thompson 2002) quotes Fettes as saying, '... he [Brosnan] chose the Drama Centre. We trained people in a different way: as part of a group, an ensemble. When you came to the school you were treated just like everybody else.' Joan Littlewood's ensemble of actors, established firstly in Manchester in 1945, became known as the Theatre Workshop. Committed to left-wing ideology, the Theatre Workshop, which moved to The Theatre Royal in Stratford East in 1953, devised and commissioned plays about Britain's working class. In 1955 Littlewood directed and performed in *Mother Courage*, creating a landmark of the first professionally produced Brecht play in Britain (Holdsworth 2006).

By promoting the techniques of Littlewood, Christopher Fettes and Yat Malmgren placed themselves and Drama Centre as a provider of a radical and socially pertinent training. Just as Littlewood's ensemble had rebuilt the dilapidated Theatre Royal in Stratford East, so Fettes and Malmgren set the students to work in renovating Drama Centre London's first premises at 176 Prince of Wales Rd. in

Chalk Farm. Students were expected to clean studio spaces and the theatre at the school, based on Littlewood's principles of everyone assisting with work in her theatre ensemble (Holdsworth 2006). Littlewood had accepted untrained actors into her company to perform, preferring the dynamics of bodies that had not undergone the social constrictions of training for the theatre of that period[2]. Drama Centre in a similar approach accepted auditionees from all class and ethnic backgrounds, many of whom at that time (1960s and 1970s) would have been unlikely to gain places at more conventional drama schools. Previously in 1961, East 15 another radical actor training college was established particularly 'to ensure the retention of the working method and inspiration of Theatre Workshop' (Holdsworth 2006, p. 43), indicating that Drama Centre London was not the only British acting school of its time promoting these practices.

Littlewood's approach to improvisation was used to heighten spontaneity. Actors' voices and bodies were allowed to retain the habitual sounds and stances of their cultural heritages. More conventional trainings of that period required actors to speak with a particular accent. Body shapes often predicated the castings that an actor could expect both in an acting school and in the theatre industry. In other words normative pressures resulted in theatrical space being a physically constricted and gender regulated environment (Hayes 1999).

Rudolf Laban's movement techniques were employed by Littlewood's Theatre Workshop (Warburton 1993). Littlewood also utilized 'Laban's ideas on 'efforts' to develop vocal characterisation' (Holdsworth 2006, p. 51). Movement and vocal exercises were worked at daily in the same way as they were at Drama Centre, where each day started with Yat Malmgren himself, teaching Laban movement[3]. The flexible and expressive abilities of the actor's body were regarded as paramount, both in Littlewood's company as well as at Drama Centre. Littlewood's Theatre Workshop relied on making theatre 'accessible to a wide range of audiences'

---

[2] In 1995 I met Joan Littlewood when she visited the University of Wollongong. She spoke then of the deadening effects of actor training and humorously insisted that she would rather invite the University's canteen workers to perform than the students that I was training.

[3] Yat Malmgren taught Laban movement daily until the mid 1990s. Until his retirement in 2001 Malmgren continued to teach Laban space classes.

(Barker 2000, p. 116). This was often achieved through incorporating dancing and singing. Littlewood's techniques of improvisation were used at Drama Centre to bring complex texts into a more understandable light through allowing young trainee actors to imaginatively extend the lived worlds of their performed characters through improvised scenes.

Littlewood's improvisational processes have increased their share of the curriculum at Drama Centre London since Malmgren's retirement in 2001. Improvisation, which is now generally listed as one of the Methodological Approaches of the school (Drama Centre 2009) is aligned with political awareness.

> Following in the footsteps of great originals such as Joan Littlewood and Mike Leigh, Drama Centre adopts an eclectic approach that fuses the contributions of the modern masters, Vakhtangov, Brecht and Grotowski, placing at the heart of its work the exploration of character, story and dramatic relationships through improvisation. This approach also involves actors, directors and writers in active research into the social background of the dramatic text and places political awareness at the forefront of their work.

Currently, Bertolt Brecht's ideology, which influenced Littlewood, has increased in Drama Centre's curriculum, in comparison to when Malmgren was co-director. Improvisation is practiced as a creatively expansionary means to performance at Drama Centre, whether the actors' representation of characters is through realistic, Brechtian, farcical or Shakespearean modes. Each of these are theatrical genres[4] emphasising differing aspects of representation for an audience. In Malmgren's time, however each genre relied on the actor to embody the character with a dedication to exposing 'the truth', whether of a psychological, political, social or historical nature.

Drama Centre's initial vision was to materialise new social possibilities through offering new and radical modes of performance. The combination of the

---

[4] Genre here refers to historical styles of theatrical performance, noting the definition of genre from critical analysis in Fairclough (2003, p. 11), where genre refers to a mode of social practice that shapes or organizes communication.

Stanislavski system's exercises, plus Littlewood's emphasis on improvisation plus Malmgren's technique created a new dimension of self-direction for performers in a British acting school. Malmgren's technique, at the centre of the school's training, producing an examination of the habitual physical embodiment of the actor and was viewed as the beginning point of Drama Centre's radicalisation of theatrical training.

3.2.3 Copeau and the French classical heritage

Jacques Copeau's actor training, as refined by Michel Saint-Denis, was the third acting process at Drama Centre during Malmgren's years there.

Copeau founded the actor training school of the École du Vieux-Colombier in Paris in 1923. His contribution to performance practice supports the fundamental focus of Drama Centre's approach to physical practices. Étienne Decroux and Jacques Lecoq, as Copeau's students, disseminated Copeau's physical techniques and theatrical styles through teaching European as well as international students. Whilst Decroux was taught by Copeau and with Jean-Louis Barrault developed the mime exercises from the École du Vieux-Colombier into Decroux's own revolutionary Corporeal Mime, Jacques Lecoq and Copeau's nephew, Michel Saint-Denis, developed the neutral mask exercises taught at the École du Vieux-Colombier into each of their own physical trainings for actors. Saint-Denis' techniques concentrate on character masks to illuminate text and action. Lecoq's technique develops the notion of a 'neutral state' for the performing body where actors evolve economical use of their muscles (Eldredge & Huston 1995, p. 121). John Blatchley, the Deputy Director of Drama Centre at the time of its formation in 1963, worked as Saint-Denis' assistant at the Old Vic Theatre Centre and School before joining the staff at the Central School of Speech and Drama (Fettes 2000). Blatchey's contribution to Drama Centre's curriculum was to establish a rigorous training method based on Saint-Denis' mime exercises.

Copeau was a reformer of French bourgeois theatre. He wanted to strip back the staging and gestural acting style common in the theatre of his time. His actor training was aimed in the same direction, to strip the actor bare of superficial habits and to establish a still, silent, calm but energised state from which to create action. This required work on the actor's relationship to herself and her body. Barba

(1995, p. 107) compares Copeau's studio processes with Stanislavski's early work with Vakhtangov, in that 'They discovered that work on oneself as an actor often became work on oneself as an individual.' In Copeau's training the work was primarily physical. Barba (1995, p. 108) discerns in Copeau's physical exercises, ' a complex set of practices whose purpose was to transform the performer's daily body-mind into a scenic body-mind'. This transformation of the body/mind was accomplished through the repetition of sequences of movement. Copeau (quoted in Cole & Chinoy 1995, p. 220) in speaking of the bodily awareness that he was seeking in the performer said,

> What is needed is that within them [performers] every moment be accompanied by an internal state of awareness peculiar to the movement being done.

This awareness assists integration of body and mind rather than domination by will of the body. The actor has to learn a readiness 'to be possessed by what he is expressing and to direct its expression' (Copeau quoted in Cole & Chinoy 1970, p. 220). As a training, Copeau's physical exercises and those of the proponents of Copeau's work were seeking integrations of body and mind similar to those used in Malmgren's acting technique. Through the liberation of the expressive body, Copeau and Malmgren both seek to elevate the performer's awareness beyond the Cartesian duality of mind and body and provide a more holistic state of being for the actor and her interaction with the audience. Thus the body/mind is free to respond imaginatively because a newly integrated actor is involved in each moment of action. The actor may be viewed as a conduit of both the conscious and unconscious, both, to use Malmgren's terms, the outer and inner, in an interconnection with the audience.

The four acting techniques, taught at Drama Centre throughout Malmgren's and Fettes' co-directorship (1963-2002), contributed to a growing development of the embodied 'self' of the actor: an integration of emotional presence through the Stanislavski Method, an integration of social relevance through Littlewood's approach and an integration of body/mind connection through the French physical techniques. These techniques surrounded Malmgren's actor training technique, probing the expressive possibilities of each individual trainee actor. Together the techniques provided a framework within which any actor could broadly question the purpose and extent of their expressive 'self'. The four approaches placed the actor as the agent of the practice. They embodied discourses encoded through bodily acts. The 'expressive' actor that Malmgren and Fettes wished to develop can only be investigated through viewing Drama Centre in an historical context.

3.3 The ambiguous site of the performing body: the fragmented 'self'

From the 1970s onwards as Malmgren developed his actor training technique at Drama Centre, many diverse disciplines were contributing to research in performance (see Schechner 1985, 1988, 2003) – anthropology, theatre studies, literature, communications, cultural studies, to name a few. Philosophical re-interpretations of the fundamental assumptions that govern the production and reception of cultural products, including performance, formed a basis for research in the arts. Even though academic modes of inquiry had little place in Drama Centre curricula, the impact of poststructuralist philosophy on performance, provides a niche for this thesis through which Malmgren's method and its development can be contextualised through poststructuralist performance discourses.

Performance is now recognised as an intricate web of significations that is both reflective of culture, as well as inventing culture in each performative moment (Zarrilli 1992, p. 42). With this re-evaluation of the process-orientation of performance, uncertainties have arisen as to the position of the performer herself. If one of the main structures of authority in modernist performance is the concept of the presence of the performer, then deconstruction and critical analysis as it impacted on performance questions this presence. Numerous theatre directors, including Brook (1972), Chaikin (1972), Grotowski (1975), Schechner (1985) and Barba (1995), resisted attempts to deconstruct the presence of the actor. Jerzy Grotowski (1975, p. 37), moving beyond the theatrical problems of representation of character on stage, emphasised the archetypal psychic impulses made accessible via the actor's physicality. Schechner in an early essay, 'The politics of ecstasy' (1968, p227), elevates the performer and audience participation and cites the theatre as being 'more authentic than the civilization – the specific inhibitions – it opposes and frequently obliterates'. The assumption behind these experimental theatrical practices is that an essential presence can be accessed through the actor's spiritual capacities. The spectator, whether passive or actively involved, as in the Happenings of Anna

Halprin (1995), or as in Brook's famous production of Orghast (Smith 1972) in Persepolis, is communally swept up in an embodied ecstatic experience.

Postmodernist understandings of performance (Huxley & Witts 1996) have become a means through which not only the presence of the actor is rejected but also all the structures of authority within theatre are rejected (Auslander 1994, p. 44). The aim of deconstruction is to expose the ideologies underpinning the theatre. Robert Wilson's theatre works may be considered as early examples of this. Here the spectator's viewing of theatre in a conventional manner is disrupted, so that no attempt is made to construct a linear narrative, to depict characters or to reflect on social or political issues (Roose-Evans 1984, p. 118). Postmodernism is able to accept the simulated nature of culture and eschews any claim of 'truthfulness', whether through the position of the text, the position of the performer or the position of the performer's body. Each is seen as encultured, pluralistic and contingent on the viewer. Performance trainings or practices likewise can no longer be understood as occurring in isolation. In fact being aware of these positions is part of the artistic milieu that performers are educated to consider. It is in this context that this study is undertaken.

3.3.1 Malmgren and postmodernism

Malmgren was largely insulated from postmodern influences through his own rigorous attention to the development of his training technique and through his separation from academia. Drama Centre became affiliated with the University of Central Lancashire as a partner college in 1995, then in 1999 it became a part of the Central Saint Martin's College of Art and Design, within the London Institute. This association resulted in Drama Centre becoming affiliated with the University of the Arts London in 2004, when the Central Saint Martin's College of Art and Design became a constituent college of the university. The integration of Drama Centre into the academic realm did not interrupt its curriculum. Drama Centre remained separate and distinct from all that was being taught about Performance Studies at that time. It was, however, Malmgren's theories of Character Analysis, a systematic and theoretically analytical subject, which became the recognised theoretical component in an otherwise practical course. This influenced the recognition and approval of Drama Centre's course in Acting as a degree course.

Malmgren's theories of the human body in action, as outlined in Chapter 2, presume the existence of an historically and circumstantially placed 'self'. Each of Malmgren's *Inner Attitudes* is a category of personality type. The technique presumes that these character types are 'selves' which have been constituted both genetically as well as culturally. Each personality type, or *Inner Attitude* is understood psychologically as being only partly conscious to the individual. That is, the typology is formed primarily in the unconscious and manifests as a *drive* (hence the *Externalised Drives* of Malmgren's system) or as fields of intention. Actions, proceeding from *Inner Attitudes*, are defined in the Malmgren technique as being 'for a functional purpose with a measure of conscious volition' (Malmgren 1988). The intentionality of an action is understood as being only partly conscious. Whilst systems of bodily encoding have been generally outlined through literature on body language (Lamb & Watson 1979; Pease 1987), Malmgren's system of *Inner Attitudes* extends bodily coding into the specificities of psychological types. It is the actor who is required to think more deeply about any character's motives, history or context and who takes account of the character's *Inner Attitude* in action. O' Connor (2001, p. 59), in his brief overview of Malmgren's technique as taught in Australia, calls this 'placing the actor in charge of the creative process'.

What were the effects then of this essentialist training, from the 1980s until Malmgren retired in 2002, given that the students living in London at the time were surrounded by the melee of postmodern eclecticism? What areas of experience from Malmgren's techniques, amongst the juxtaposing cultural messages, were pertinent to those that encountered this actor training system? What circumscribed fields of tradition of learning or actor training were maintained, authorised or challenged by this practice?

Malmgren's technique can best be investigated through taking account of how the training has developed through time to shape the practices of trainee performers and what they perform. Convergences between Malmgren's practices as instituted by the author and current discourses of embodiment in performance from the literature indicate ways in which the author situates Malmgren's technique in the context of contemporary performance practice. Current ideologies of the performer's concept of self reflect an interdependence of critical discourses that span this field. Butler (1988, 1990) in speaking of the performative body is at once taking a phenomenological stance as well as a feminist stance. Through proposing that gender is constructed through performative acts, Butler has opened discourses about the extent of the constructed body, revealing that performativity is a means of reiterating or materializing social norms and constructs. Diamond (1997, p. 46) defines a feminist perspective of the female body as viewed in performance, where performance reveals a fragmented subjectivity, 'the body as effects of discourse(s)'. Her writings are also informed through psychoanalysis. Peggy Phelan in *Unmarked* (1993), takes a Lacanian, psychoanalytical, feminist approach to the intersubjective meeting of the performer and her audience and yet more recently has placed her analysis of performance in more cultural and anthropological contexts (Phelan 1998). Blau, who defines performance in a cultural context (1982), includes the broader analysis of Marxist critique and psychoanalytical theory in the investigation of the actor's being in rehearsal (1992). The following review of the literature, regarding embodiment and agency in performance, is then of necessity, an eclectic one considering the field from a number of ideological perspectives.

3.3.2 Embodiment and the limits of the constructed 'self'

The investigation of performance as a representation of cultural identity has burgeoned since the application of textual analysis to performative events. Aspects of performance, written text, staging, lighting, costumes, style of acting, may each be decoded as cultural signifiers. However, whilst instructive in a political, cultural or socioeconomic context, textual analysis throws little light on the experiential nature of performance to those enacting it. Malmgren's technique centres itself on the experience of the performer, through its emphasis on the concepts of *Inner Attitudes* and *Externalised Drives*. Whilst textual analysis views the performer as a set of signifying systems, the understanding of the performer's sense of 'self', in her own performance, is not accounted for. Stanton B. Garner Jr. (1993, p. 444), a phenomenologist, criticises deconstructionist analysis of performance as being 'materialist' and as having 'furthered the "depersonalizing" of experience'. Garner posits that contemporary literary and performance theory position 'consciousness (is) dispersed within the field of the externally constituted'. A performer in Malmgren's training may not initially consider herself as being externally constituted by an audience. In fact considerations of her body as a signifying system may undermine the most fundamental aspects of her performing process, destabilizing her breath or her ability to remain present to the people around her. Even if the performer in the Malmgren training becomes or is aware of transmitting certain embodied signifiers she may not experience herself as being compatible with the coding that is being read.

> I stand. My hips are aligned beneath me. They're slightly tilted because of my high heeled shoes. My hand carries a document. I breathe, slightly shallowly. My breath releases uneasy as yet. I smile fleetingly. I am being watched. I can feel my cheeks beginning to relax. My breath sinks slightly deeper in my body. I am observed but I am also the observer. See. My arm is reaching up now passing the paper from one hand to the other. I shift my weight. I am a performer but I am also the performed. What do you see? Is it the same as what I think I am giving? There is a connection. But what is it?
>
> Perhaps this moment of observation has made you reconsider your surroundings, the carpet, the windows, the rest of the audience. I am a body in space. What is it that I am representing for you? Perhaps there is a discourse formulating in your mind. But of what? What is it that is foregrounded for you by this 'performance'? Is it a discourse on education, perhaps or gender or elitism, or middle age? There are elements of each of these discourses present here. They are placed here.
>
> In fact you could say that in 'performance' my body has become a myriad set of discourses of which I am only partly conscious. I am a performing body. I am a set of conceptual bodies.
>
> If I am conscious of my multifarious conceptual bodies do I 'act' more clearly? If my conceptual bodies present such contradictions to one another my split self is quite incapable of stepping into action, of acting at all!
>
> Now my breath quickens. My heart races. 'Oh my god! Should I be here at all?' I see an audience observing me. My hands prickle with sweat. What right have I to represent these words? Do I even believe in them? My performance falters.

Researcher's Journal 3.1 June 9th. 2000, Presentation at the Postgraduate Colloquium Program, Centre for Contemporary Performance, University of Western Sydney.

What then of the body of the performer as it is experienced? In his book, *Bodied Spaces: Phenomenology and Performance in Contemporary Drama*, Garner (1994, p. 26) proposes that poststructural criticism with its linguistic and textual interests limits the field of inquiry in performance. He regards critical analysis as reflecting 'an attitude symptomatic of a deeper uneasiness with the body – in this case, with the body as a site of corporeal and subjective elements that always resist reduction to the merely textual'. Csordas (1999, p. 146) reiterates this problem,

> textuality has become, if you will, a hungry metaphor, swallowing all of culture to the point where it ... has ... gobbled up the body itself – certainly we have all heard phrases like "the body as text," "the inscription of culture on the body," "reading the body." I would go so far as to assert that for many contemporary scholars the text metaphor has ceased to be a metaphor at all, and is taken quite literally.

Garner stresses (1993, p. 444) that he is not referring to any 'metaphysics of presence' but rather a consciousness, which by its nature is embodied. He suggests (1993, p. 445) that 'the second generation' phenomenology of Maurice Merleau-Ponty, 'by foregrounding the body as the ambiguous site of subjectivity' is able to provide a discourse for investigating the 'embodiment we call "theatre"'. It is this position that I have taken as being useful in the investigation of Malmgren's technique in a postmodern setting. A performer may be aware of herself as encoding certain signifiers, however at the time of performing, and in this case training, she may be primarily regarded as an expression of her embodied consciousness.

Merleau-Ponty's phenomenology of bodied subjectivity presents the ambiguity of the embodied subject who is at one and the same time grounded in and of the world, but who is also able to reflect on that very condition. The body can reflect on itself as an object in its field of perception, and yet the reflection will never be congruent with itself. As Garner (1993, p. 448) puts it,

> Merleau-Ponty's language oscillates between a discourse of belonging and an equally pronounced discourse of subversion and contingency, whereby subjectivity becomes both that point from which the world arises into meaning and the seat of non-coincidence, "that gap which we ourselves are".

Garner considers Samuel Beckett's plays, particularly his latter works, where bodies on stage are fragmented, dismembered or partly absent, as being dramas of the impossible pursuit of identity by a subjectivity that can't escape its embodiment and yet is constantly self-estranged from that embodiment (1993, p. 450). Beckett's diminished bodies are the dispossessed, the characters who can no longer believe in their own agency or purpose of being. Terry Eagleton (1998, p. 160) writes engagingly of the problem of the subject and embodiment:

> It is not quite true that I have a body, and not quite true that I am one either. This deadlock runs all the way through psychoanalysis, which recognizes that the body is constructed in language, and knows too that it will never entirely be at home there. For Jacques Lacan, the body articulates itself in signs only to find itself betrayed by them. The transcendental signifier which would say it all, wrap up my demand and deliver it whole and entire to you, is that imposter known as the phallus; and since the phallus does not exist, my bodily desire is condemned to grope its laborious way from partial sign to partial sign, diffusing and fragmenting as it goes.

This ambiguous corporeal position is, for the actor, and particularly for the trainee in the Malmgren technique, who is often required to perform 'herself', always acutely present. Any performance by the trainee actor, even if performing 'herself' in an exercise or improvisation never encompasses a total expression of her 'true self'. The desire to reveal all that she has to give is never satiated. Yet, it appears that the literature has not dealt with the performer in the way that Garner has been able to deal with Beckett's characters, or the way that Jacques Lacan has been able to deal with his concept of the ego's 'meconnaissance' (Miller 1988, p. 170).

The experience of the actor has become even more complex, as the influence of poststructuralism may dispel her belief in her own corporeality as a site of being. As a 'text' the performer is first and foremost a material object in the spectator's field and is able to reflect upon that. Awareness of fragmentation of subject positions is a daily experience for the actor in the act of representation. No matter how conscious a performer may become of her representation in the act of performance, it is only a part of whatever the actor understands herself to be. The ancient Greeks understood the peril of this position. The masked performer always stood on sacred ground, guarded from fragmentation of the psyche through the paying of honour to the gods. Yet actor training schools appear to enter this territory paying little respect to the experiential demands made on actors through daily encountering the fragmenting psychic effects of acting.

Bert O. States (1985, p. 20) has looked at theatre with the double vision of the phenomenological view and the semiotic view. He pinpoints the way that 'the vitality of theater' is created 'not simply by signifying the world but by being *of* it.' In speaking of the actor and the audience he refers to the audiences' sensory delight in their bodily reception of signs as images. States includes amongst these the sensorial reception of the image of the actor, both the visual and the auditory. States (1985, p. 125) suggests that the audience marvels in the actor's embodiment of representations (in this case States is talking about characters in realism), which in every instance do not encompass the totality of the actor. 'It is visible in the effortless hard work that produces on the actor's brow beads of perspiration that do not belong to the character.' The corporeal presence of the actor is consumed, by the audience, as it absorbs imagery from a lived process (1985, p. 26). States' emphasis on the sensory aspects of embodiment in performance points to a perhaps less conscious aspect of the understanding of bodies watching bodies. It is possible that there are fundamental elements of this experience of performer and audience, which are not consciously apprehensible.

Wilshire (1991, p. 232) speaks of the self as being 'an occasionally conscious body that displays itself in a theatre-like way to others, and the first-and third-person points of view on it are deeply intertwined'. This view of the performative body is decidedly similar to Malmgren's image of *Inner Attitudes*. Wilshire emphasises the partial consciousness of action, as does Malmgren's definition of action initiated by any *Inner Attitude*. Wilshire inter-relates the nature of bodies in theatre to broader human behaviour similarly to Malmgren's conflation of the use of *Inner Attitudes* as an acting technique with a broader understanding of human bodies. Although not grappling directly with the problem of the body as 'text', and the problem of displaced subjectivity, Wilshire is able to position the partly conscious performing body in a web-like interconnection of mimesis between bodies. These reflective actions structure the performative acts of any body. This seeing and responding to others through reflection has similarities to the modes of learning in the Malmgren technique, where students learn as much through observation of others' performances as through performing. Wilshire (1991, p. 157) uses the term 'engulfment' to describe 'the absorption of the experiencing body in the experienced object', where there is a merging with the other. This too is similar to Malmgren's notion of being dominated or surrendering to an object, a person or an idea, through Malmgren's concept of an *Externalised Drive* of *Spell*.

Zarrilli (1995, 2001, 2002, 2004) is one performance theorist who has written about the actor's embodiment from a phenomenological perspective. In a 2004 *Theatre Journal* article, Zarrilli offers a methodological approach to understanding the embodied work of actors. Not only does he highlight embodiment as 'a process of encounters' but he also pinpoints the problem of 'the absent body' (2004, pp. 655-656), where consciousness is directed away from the body itself. Zarrilli notes four modes of embodiment: the Surface Body, which both receives sensory information and acts in its lived-world; the Visceral Body, where the corporeal processes and functioning of internal organs take place, of which any person is only partly aware; the Inner Aesthetic Bodymind, where the engagement in psychophysical practices of breath, action and attention are linked; the Outer Aesthetic Bodymind, where the actor's body is in action that is viewed at the same time as being inhabited. The latter two modes of embodiment are beyond the everyday experiences of embodiment, and may be viewed as the modes in which performers in particular are in training.

Viewing the actor's body through the phenomenological perspective of embodiment offers unique ways, over and above representational views of the body, to contribute a broader understanding of the actor's experience of performance. The phenomenological framework for this thesis' investigation will be discussed more fully in Chapter 4.

3.3.3 Feminism and performance/agency

Malmgren's technique not only positions the body of the performer as the experiential centre from which performative expression springs but as taught by the author it also predicates an embodied agency capable of transforming that expression from one habitual mode to another. Malmgren's technique presumes that habitual expressions of the actor can be transformed by the actor into differing modes of mind/body expression. The nature of the embodied agency of any performative act has been investigated, by feminist theorists and academics in gender studies engaging in postmodern discourses of subjectivity and the body. From Kristeva (1987), to Butler (1990), to Irigaray (1993) to Braidotti (1994) the problem with the framework of textual analysis of sexual identity is its inherent determinism; there is an inability for 'the text', which is the gendered cultural identity of the subject, to be defined by anything other than a patriarchal discourse. As Butler (1990, p. 143) has stated,

> to be *constituted* by discourse is to be *determined* by discourse, where determination forecloses the possibility of agency.

Butler, here, reflects a generally held feminist unease with the loss of agency in the linguistic model of representation of behavioral acts. If experience is constituted by discourse then experience is reduced to language. This by extension covers textual representations of performance as well, and the viewing of the female body on stage.

Agency in Malmgren's technique, however, is a pre-linguistic yet physically expressed phenomenon. This will be discussed further in Chapter 8, however, through perspectives of embodiment, either via a phenomenological epistemology (Butler 1988) or via a psychoanalytical epistemology (Kristeva 1987), pre-linguistic modalities of corporeality can be assimilated into mainstream theories of subjectivity allowing feminists to elaborate strategies subversive of cultural codes. These perspectives predicate the means through which agency can alter identity, via 'an instability at the heart of gender identity that refuses to surrender the possibility of contestation' (O'Connell 1999, p. 65). Butler's early work in this field used performance as the metaphor for a means of transformation of gendered identity (1988). Malmgren's technique suggests that performance can be an experiential site of contestations of identity, including gender identity.

Feminists have both criticised and used Merleau-Ponty's phenomenological insights on embodiment. Irigaray (1993, p. 151) in her rereading of Merleau-Ponty's, *The Visible and the Invisible*, whilst critical of his essentialism, sees the necessity to:

> go back to a moment of prediscursive experience, recommence everything, all the categories by which we understand things, the world, subject-object divisions, recommence everything...

Only in a return to the body, as a site of the intersection of the biological, the social and the linguistic, as a field of intersecting forces, can an agency be predicated that may precede or interact with any symbolic or linguistic system of culture. This is not harking back to an essentialist or biologically determined subject, but rather a construct of the subject as a corporeally situated process, enabling multiple codes to be inscribed through the body. Identity and subjectivity may be viewed as different but interrelated moments in the process of defining a subject position (Braidotti 1994, p. 196). Agency by consequence may not be congruent with consciousness.

Through this fractured, or rather, multiple identity, as ascribed to the body of the performer, it is possible to conceive of acts of transformation of consciousness and most importantly acts that transgress the already structured definitions of gender identity. Malmgren's technique, through highlighting processes of *Flow* in action, correlates with these feminist concepts of subjectivity and identity being temporally shifting processes. In the Malmgren technique, performances of differing *Inner Attitudes* reflect the fragmentary nature of the performer's subjective relationships with varying aspects of her identity. *Flow,* either *Free* or *Bound* is used in Malmgren's technique to describe an affinity with or a resistance to an identification with the behaviour or actions manifested by the performer. This may be aligned with notions of identity and subjectivity shifting and at times being congruent and at other times being oppositional.

Similarly Butler (1990) and Kristeva (1987) both use the possibilities of desire as the means of asserting that whilst sexuality is constructed it is neither a 'free' construction of a pre-existent subject, nor that it is immutably fixed (O'Connell 1999, p. 65). Desire or the concept of a psychological drive is the interconnection of the constituted subject with what has been delimited by entry into the symbolic, cultural domain. The subject position is constantly in the process of 'becoming' as it reaches towards or is driven towards what has not yet been named, 'the unsayable'. Notions of 'becoming' may be framed then wherever this concept of reaching towards the yet 'unsayable' occurs.

Whilst Kristeva (1987, p. 6) uses the word 'symptom', Butler (1990, p. 143) uses the term 'excess' to describe the gap between an embodied subject's alignment with her culturally constructed sense of self and her non-alignment. Irigaray (1993, p. 176) hypothesizes 'the interval' to shape that moment between which the world is perceived and the moment when the world is reacted to, between anticipation and retroaction. This interval becomes a temporal bridge through which the foundations of language, or through which the entry into the symbolic, can be altered. Malmgren's technique concentrates on the differences rather than the commonalities between an actor and any performed character. This produces an awareness of subtle performative shifts in embodying identities, using feminist frameworks of identity formation. Malmgren stresses a movement away from self-recognised modes of embodiment allowing the possibilities for new modes to be enacted. These may be culturally transgressive, perhaps liberating, perhaps alienating, each offering radical questioning of how an embodied self is performed or enacted.

Olkowski (2000) relates Irigaray's interval to that of early phenomenologist, Henri Bergson's conceptualization of the interval as the moment between a received stimulus and an executed movement. Bergson (1913) has hypothesized that there is a two-pronged response of consciousness to perception. One line of sensory perception leads to the storage of memory, the affective connection of the subject with the world, and the other line leads to an intentional action that perceives, in the interval, what is of interest to the subject, so as to enable action. Bergson's model of this two-pronged affective and intentional response to reception as well as his notion of the interval may offer new ways to view Malmgren's *Weight* and *Flow,* where *Weight* refers to the modes in which a character impacts on circumstances and *Flow* refers to a feeling of synthesis or fragmentation associated with those actions.

Feminists Kristeva, Irigaray, Butler, Braidotti, Phelan and Tait have turned to the body to seek the means to hypothesise an embodied agency that can reach beyond the foreclosed cultural encoding of any performative action. Phenomenologists such as Merleau-Ponty, Bergson and Olkowski, writing about the body, have illuminated bodily processes which when added to feminist theory have elucidated the processes where this may be possible. These feminist and phenomenological discourses provide a new means of reflecting on the practical and embodied processes in the Malmgren training, which enable trainee actors to reshape their expressive actions.

3.4 Conclusion

The intention of contextualising the meaning of Yat Malmgren's actor training technique by comparison with the techniques of other performance makers or acting teachers, has situated its construction at Drama Centre in a wider perspective than its role as an actor training technique for the creation of realistic stage and film characters. The movement underpinnings of the technique align it more closely with French physical trainings, which negate Cartesian mind-body dualism. The technique has been associated with concepts of transformation, both cultural and embodied, through its association with political theatre, Laban movement and Jungian psychology (Mirodan 1997).

In order to view Malmgren's theories of bodily action in the light of postmodern discourses on performativity, it has been necessary to reference a broader field of literature, encompassing the understanding of embodied concepts of subjectivity and affectivity. The works of feminist psychoanalytical researchers and feminist phenomenologists have provided discourses, which resonate with specific practices in Malmgren's acting technique. These synergies will be pursued further in Chapter 8. More particularly, the field of embodiment through the perspective of phenomenology has provided a unique means of considering the performative body as an ambiguous site where agency and identity are viewed as fluctuating processes. It is in this field that this thesis will pursue a deeper investigation of what the Malmgren technique offers to understandings of performative action. Phenomenology both as a methodological framework for this thesis' research and as a theoretical frame for considering embodiment in Malmgren's actor training is the third ripple of contextualisation of meaning of the technique and will be considered in the next four chapters.

This chapter by considering the second ripple of contextualisation of meaning of the Malmgren technique, through a literary review, has enabled a distinct placement of Malmgren's technique within actor training methods. The chapter has elucidated postmodern discourses of phenomenological embodiment, and feminist phenomenological and psychoanalytical discourses of agency and affectivity, which provide confluences with particular practices in the contemporary Malmgren training established by the author. These discourses offer a new means for elucidating the practical and embodied modes in which actors in training in the twenty-first century may be able to utilise Malmgren's technique to recontextualise performative expression.

CHAPTER 4

USING A PHENOMENOLOGICAL METHODOLOGY

Everything we touch or deal with is a point outside of ourselves and the strongest energy productions must be motivated by things we are moved towards or away from strongly.
We think we are just dealing with people. No. What is the idea?
Malmgren January 1988.

4.1 Introduction

This chapter describes how a qualitative research design is used to investigate Yat Malmgren's actor training system, in particular its impact on actors in training and their understandings of themselves as performers. Chapters 2 and 3 examined the Malmgren training technique, firstly as a technique for actor training translated from Laban's movement theories and secondly the evolution of a technique during the 1960s and 1970s, for realistic acting on stage and screen. This chapter presents a research methodology and methods used to investigate the meaning of Malmgren's training to actors in the twenty-first century. Amongst the plethora of acting traditions that a young performer encounters in a tertiary actor training institution, how does Yat Malmgren's method of actor training add to or shape a performer's journey? The first section of this chapter sets out an argument for and exposition of the methodological framework of hermeneutic phenomenology for this investigation. This tradition of enquiry is directed towards phenomenological concepts of embodiment in order to develop a detailed analysis of the experiential impact of Malmgren's training on actors as a means of investigating the major question of the thesis:

In what way does Malmgren's actor training contribute to understanding the performative body?

The latter part of the chapter defines the parameters of the methods used, which have on the whole been developed in the field of nursing research and which are newly applied here to performance research.

4.2 A methodological framework for research on Yat Malmgren's actor training

David Kendall, who taught Yat Malmgren's work at the Centre for the Performing Arts (CPA), Adelaide from 1987 and then consequently at the Centre for the Arts, Adelaide until his retirement in 2006, stated in *Meanjin* (1984, p. 157):

> In my opinion this 'work' cannot be explained or described; it must be experienced.

Since Yat Malmgren himself wrote nothing of his work beyond a series of tables, definitions and diagrams, the Yat training, as it has been known at the University of Wollongong's Performance course, is characterised by its heritage of being passed from one practitioner to another. My experience, as one of Australia's principal Malmgren trainers, has initiated and shaped this thesis, and is a crucial aspect in defining the influences I bring to this study. For instance, I have placed the locus for the investigation of the experiential journeys of actors in training in Malmgren's technique as the 'performative body' of the trainee actor, emphasising the concept of lived engagement or embodiment, from within an understanding of my own experiences in this training. The use of Butler's term, 'performative' (1988, p. 521; 1990, p. 139), in reference to bodily acts, positions, performativity as that which 'materializes' possibilities, via action. The experience of undertaking an actor training program may be primarily recorded through sensory processes rather than through conscious reflection, however the term, performativity, or my term, the 'performative body' encompasses both those bodily inscriptions that are conscious as well as the less conscious. The argument for taking a phenomenological as well as emancipatory approach to Malmgren's techniques is set out below. Defying the notion promulgated by Kendall (1984), that Malmgren's experiential tradition is unable to be investigated, I inquire into the experiential systematic journey of trainee actors through Yat Malmgren's method of actor training.

4.2.1 The body in performance

In Malmgren's technique, as outlined in Chapter 2, the emphasis is on the actor's body, which is placed in the spotlight not only of the audience's perception but also of the actor's consciousness. Zarrilli (1995, p. 72) contextualises the actor's body in action when he states,

> Particular modes of training and particular genres of performance demand specific bodies fashioned in a particular environment for a particular set of performative expectations.

In this study, when I refer to the actor's body in action, I frame the limitations of my enquiry to encompass only actor training at tertiary institutions. Whilst the mode of training being investigated is Yat Malmgren's technique, the genres of performance that actors in training in this method then perform, vary widely, more widely that the realism for which Malmgren's method was first fashioned. However, it is true to say that Malmgren's technique emphasises the development of character and the training enables the construction of character for stage performance. By locating the actor's body as the site of the actor's experiential journey through Malmgren's method, it is possible to place Malmgren's work not only in the sphere of performance theorists who have considered bodily action and its meaning in their trainings (Artaud 1958; Barba 1985; Feldenkrais 1972; Grotowski 1968; Laban 1948, 1966, 1975; Stanislavski 1973, 1989; & Zarrilli 1995), but also in the realm of researchers interested in conceptualisations of human action and/or movement (Butler 1988; Chodorow 1991; Foucault 1977; Grosz 1990a, 1994; Merleau-Ponty 1965; Pradier 1990).

As set out in Chapter 3, feminist theoreticians in considering the body have made it possible to see how:

> Social, economic, psychical and moral relations... are not just experienced by subjects, but are, in order to be experienced, integrally recorded or corporeally inscribed (Grosz 1987, p. 7).

Chapter 3 has examined a number of constructivist models of the body in performance, as well as throwing light on some less conscious aspects of bodily action, including phenomenological considerations of affectivity and the French feminist psychoanalytical concepts of desire and psychological drives. It is in the materializing of performed action that this study locates itself and in particular the performed action of conscious reflection about the Malmgren training by trainee actors. My study is situated in this domain of postmodern discourses on the body and embodiment.

4.2.2 Assumptions

Crotty (1998, p. 4), a Melbourne social researcher in the field of nursing, suggests, in order to outline any selection of a methodological framework and a pertinent methodology for this undertaking it is necessary for me to plumb the depths of not only my philosophical stance in this study, but also the epistemological basis for that theoretical perspective.

My goal is to move outside the domain of objectivist social science research, for I do not wish to assume that a found world will appear from the research to 'legitimate' (Van Maanen 1988, p. 23) Malmgren's actor training. The experiential nature of any acting technique predicates multifarious ways of understanding that technique by those involved in it. Neither do I wish to assume that I will find a communicable 'theory' about this method of acting. Qualitative research acknowledges that the philosophical stance of any qualitative study sets the means of judging that study (Patton 2002). Readers may have their own interpretation of the data presented (Whitehead 2004), as this research study's interpretation of the data is a temporally set understanding. However what can be made clear in this research process are the decisions through which the research is propagated and how these reflect the theoretical framework of the methodology used. Malmgren, like Laban, trusted movement before words, as a means of opening the imaginative capacities of his students (Laban 1960, preface by Lisa Ullmann). The epistemology, or basis of knowledge in this project, is through the construction of the consciousness of the subject to whom Malmgren's method is taught. Consciousness is understood as being an embodied process (Leder 2005). The emphasis on the experience of the trainee actor, places this basis of knowledge in the body of the performer, who is herself immersed in a wider milieu of relationships.

Performance by its very nature can never be viewed objectively and defies the traditional 'objectivist' values of western science. Any audience to a performance is immediately an element of the performative process. As Peter Brook (1972, p. 11) says,

> A man walks across [an] empty space whilst someone else is watching him and this is all that is needed for an act of theatre to be engaged.

Consequently, it is the unenviable state of the performance researcher always to be immersed in the many subjectivities of performance.

The approach to this research, a study of a particular actor training technique, recognises that knowledge about performance is socially constituted, historically embedded and value-based. Although there is a distinct mode in which Malmgren's technique is formally taught, how it is received and understood will vary from subject to subject. This research is aimed at an interactive engagement with the research participants, allowing for their voices, their passionate understandings to be acknowledged. Through disclosing my value-base, I can invite joint participation in the exploration of my research issue, the lived meaning of a particular actor training system, in order to disclose an understanding of the body in performative action.

Barbara du Bois (1983) speaks of passionate scholarship being a feminist method, however I think that such approaches to research may now be regarded as post-feminist, and fundamentally hermeneutic or, in other words interpretive; it is post-feminist in that it assumes that emancipatory objectives may be part of a researcher's motivations, and hermeneutic because interpretation is always a necessity whenever knowledge is understood as contextualized (Laverty 2003).

To describe the experience and realities of the performer being trained through Yat Malmgren's method is for me to move into a complex web of contextualities. It means moving out of realms of discourse that rely on linear conceptions of reality, or dualistic models of human nature or dichotomous modes of thought and inevitably the web includes me, the researcher in my attempting 'to know'. Since I teach Malmgren's method and have already indicated how deeply it has shaped my life, I cannot be an objective researcher. Each group of subjects who are interviewed in this research, whether students at my institution (The University of

Wollongong, Faculty of Creative Arts) or at other actor training institutions, know of my involvement. Consequently my presence as a teacher of Malmgren's method is implicit in all my investigations.

My aim in placing this research within hermeneutic social science (in this case Performance) research is to create a space for the voicing of the experiential, to allow corporeality to speak. This tautology might be regarded metaphorically as 'the voiced body' or as 'the knowing body'. However, since consciousness is that which reflects on what is known, my understanding is that I am searching for reflection on those almost pre-conscious moments of the body being made aware of itself in action, due to the demands of Malmgren's acting exercises. I am aware that each person who has trained with Malmgren, or with a teacher trained by Malmgren, may comprehend their experience differently, for each will bring their own 'lifeworld' (van Manen 1990) to that point where they meet with Malmgren's work. As Patti Lather (1991b, p. ix) has so clearly stated,

> We must shift the role of critical intellectuals from being universalizing spokespersons to acting as cultural workers whose task is to take away the barriers that prevent people from speaking for themselves.

4.2.3 Qualitative research

From the aims that I have delineated for this study it is apparent that the methodological approach necessary to answer my questions lies in the realm of qualitative rather than quantitative research. Qualitative research has arisen from the understanding that researchers, themselves, bring with them diverse beliefs and assumptions that influence their ways of seeing; the criteria used to assess data, the contexts in which the data is viewed, the involvement of the researcher herself, all are influences on the research outcomes. As Denzin and Lincoln (2005, p. 3) define it,

> Qualitative research is a situated activity that locates the observer in the world...qualitative research involves an interpretive, naturalistic approach to the world. This means that qualitative researchers study things in their natural settings, attempting to make sense of, or interpret, phenomena in terms of the meanings people bring to them.

Since the growth of the use of qualitative research methodologies in the 1980s, a range of research designs and traditions have developed for a more widespread use by social scientists. A qualitative researcher studies qualities, contexts, processes and meanings that are not easily measured, is involved through her viewpoints, biases, intentions and values and uses a variety of methods to capture a 'bricolage' of representations of a phenomenon (Denzin & Lincoln 2005, p. 4). The research methodologies or paradigms of qualitative research follow basically the traditional processes of research procedures of asking a question; collecting data to answer the question; analyzing the data; and answering the question. However, in qualitative research there may be a number of phases to data processing; collection, reviewing, immersion, reduction or editing, preparation or coding, and analysis (Kumar 1996). Coding in particular and even the data collection itself will depend on the researcher's initial question, and the philosophical stances of the researcher. Grounded theory, feminist theories, critical theory, poststructuralist theory, Frierian theory, neo-Marxist theories, can each provide a methodological framework that will stipulate a different approach to the research material. Higgs (1998, p. 140), for instance, includes in her interpretive methodological qualitative research framework the theoretical stances of phenomenology, ethnography, hermeneutic phenomenology, and constructivism.

It is essential that a researcher choose an appropriate methodological paradigm or framework for the research, comprehending the underlying philosophical stance initiated through the inquiry.

Lather (1992, p. 89) uses the term paradigm to outline possible holding-forms to contain ideas of how reality can be defined, investigated and reported in educational research. She has listed four paradigms: Predicting or Positivist, Understanding, Emancipatory and Deconstructivist. Like Higgs, Lather places phenomenology in a paradigm which aims to understand and interpret reality. Guba and Lincoln (2005, pp. 195-196), however, revise their previous tabling of 'inquiry paradigms', extending them to include Positivism; Postpositivism; Critical Theory; Constructivism and Participatory. Participatory has been added here to acknowledge that realities may be viewed as jointly constructed, where subject and participant positions coalesce in conscious consideration of any apprehended reality. In this latter tabling of the modes of acquisition of knowledge, the phenomenological methodological framework articulated in this chapter fits within Guba and Lincoln's Participatory category of inquiry paradigms.

Recently concern has been expressed as to the rigour needed in using phenomenological methodologies and for the necessity of clear understandings of the philosophical underpinnings of any research methodology (Maggs-Rapport 2001; Laverty 2003). Consequently a more detailed background of the philosophy of hermeneutic phenomenology, its contemporary use in research and in particular nursing research and how this research paradigm will be applied in this study is an important factor in maintaining the rigour of using hermeneutic phenomenology to inquire into the meaning of Malmgren's actor training technique in the twenty-first century.

4.2.4 Phenomenology and lived experience

Phenomenology arose as a philosophical resistance to the dominant objectivist scientific approach to research inquiry. In phenomenology human consciousness or awareness is philosophically understood as bringing reality or realities into existence. Fundamental to phenomenology is its defense of the 'role of subjectivity and consciousnesss in all knowledge' (Moran 2000, p. 15). Edmund Husserl (1859-1938) through his eidetic tradition used description and clarification of lived experience in order to reveal how things or objects become constituted through consciousness. Phenomenology has, since its formal emergence in 1900, shaped philosophical enquiries into the nature of experience. It has become an approach to research; creating research frameworks that are concerned with the manner in which lived experience presents itself to consciousness.

> Anything that presents itself to consciousness is potentially of interest to phenomenology, whether the object is real or imagined, empirically measurable or subjectively felt (van Manen 1990, p. 9).

Michael Crotty (1996) acknowledges the diversity of contemporary phenomenological research proponents as well as their philosophical distance from the initial development of phenomenology. He claims that even with the new awareness of postmodern discourses, phenomenology has a relevance and usefulness to modern social research, due to its basic approach to inquiry. As Crotty (1996, p. 3) states,

> It is a study of phenomena, i.e. of the *objects* of human experience. It elucidates *what* people experience. If it inquires into how certain subjects experience this or that, it is not for the sake of learning and describing how these particular people feel, perceive and understand ... (instead it) wants to elucidate, first and foremost, the phenomena to which people are attaching meaning.

Ray (1994) cautions social science researchers, that to achieve excellent research in this methodology, it is necessary to understand key philosophical notions that are traditions within phenomenology. Cohen and Omery (1994), writing about the use of phenomenological research in nursing, insist that it is necessary to be aware of the claims of phenomenology and the history of its development.

Husserl, in 1913, came to the position that consciousness was, in itself, the one absolute (Moran 2000, p. 10). How phenomena impinged on the mind was his interest. Experience was his means of investigation. Husserl's notion that philosophical reflection should begin not through theory or history but through direct experience has some similarities to Kant's 'transcendental philosophy', in that both are concerned with the mode of knowledge of objects, an epistemological approach (O'Brien 1999, p. 2). Both attributed this mode of knowing to a structure, existing a priori to experience itself, in Husserl's case, the structure of the mind, a consciousness. Husserl endeavoured to formulate a method for revealing the meaning and essence of things, 'the true and genuine form of things themselves' (Ray 1994, p. 119), through revealing their structures as they appeared to the mind. In his method, in *Ideas* (1913; English translation 1952), he formulates the necessity to 'bracket off' pre-suppositions or judgements of phenomena, so that their essential elements can appear through intuition.

Whilst Husserl's phenomenology was essentialist in its philosophy, Martin Heidegger (1889-1976) developed phenomenology to diverge substantially from his teacher. Heidegger succeeded Edmund Husserl in holding the Chair of Philosophy at the University of Freiburg. In his development of phenomenology, bracketing became redundant as he acknowledged the historical and socio-cultural aspects of any expression of human consciousness (Ray 1994). Phenomenology as Heidegger conceived it strives to interpret the meaning of phenomena as they present themselves to individual consciousness, which is always situated in socio-historical time and space. The concept of essences remains a Husserlian construct.

Heidegger's text, *Being and Time* (1996, originally published 1927) became a turning point in philosophical thinking, struggling with the ontological question of the meaning of 'Being' (cited in Moran 2000, p. 194). For, as Heidegger understood, even human reflection about Being (*Sein*) is itself embedded in the world. He coined the term 'being there' (*Dasein*) to signify this inseparable nature of our Being from our world (cited in Cohen & Omery 1994, p. 140). Phenomenology, through Heidegger, became less about description and more about understanding (*Verstehen*) of the Life-world (*Lebenswelt*), through the interpretation of human experience. This method of interpretation of lived experience, Heidegger termed hermeneutics. Through hermeneutics Heidegger believed it was possible to uncover or disclose the hidden meaning of Being, or the hidden phenomena that constitute Being (cited in Cohen & Omery ibid). For as Hans Jonas (1994, p. 819), a German phenomenological philosopher has so eloquently stated it, 'Dasein is that form of being which in its being is concerned with this very being.'

In other words, it is human nature's innate essence to reflect upon itself, as only consciousness makes possible. Heidegger termed this earnest questioning in a temporal setting as care (*Sorge*) (cited in Ray 1994, p. 121). This direction of Heidegger's philosophy has resulted in the development of various, differing schools of phenomenological research. Cohen and Omery (1994, p. 149) outline three such schools. Eidetic phenomenology is based on Husserlian beliefs in essential structures and uses his descriptive methods, which employ Husserl's famous notion of 'epoche', where researchers suspend all pre-conceptions about the matter that they are studying. Interpretive or hermeneutic phenomenology is based on Heideggerian philosophy and in particular his concept of *Dasein*. Hans-Georg Gadamer (1900 - 2002) extended Heidegger's interpretive directions, emphasising language as the fundamental means to interpret modes of being-in-the-world. Gadamer (1989) placed understanding as the shared means through which humans encounter their lived worlds and through which the meaning of language is shared. Understanding for Gadamer occurs through shared practices, which are historically and culturally placed. Gadamer coined the phenomenological concept of 'horizon', (*Horizont*) where previous experiences and shared languages shape the meaning of temporal events. However, any horizon formed from past traditions, Gadamer conceived as being in constant dialogue with new possibilities of understanding. Where people share horizons through this heumaneutic dialogue, Gadamer refers to this as the 'fusion of horizons', *Horizontverschmelzung* (cited in Rosen 1997, pp. 207-218). Hermeneutic phenomenological research now rests primarily on this linguistic approach, using the concept of fusion of horizons for 'uncovering the presuppositions' of understanding a phenomenon (Ray 1994, p. 120).

Cohen and Omery point to a third school of phenomenology, arising from the Dutch, or Utrecht School of phenomenology, which combines features of the other two schools. Its emphasis is on the contexts in which meanings of words arise (Cohen, Kahn & Steeves 2000). Description, thematic interpreting and metaphoric insight are means with which this school of phenomenology works (Morse 1994). More recently Laverty (2003, p. 17) has limited the phenomenological research methodologies to two. She separates Husserlian or eidetic phenomenological methodologies, on the basis of its use of 'bracketing' the presuppositions of the researcher, from all interpretive phenomenology termed hermeneutic, which position the presuppositions of the researcher as the 'embedded and essential' basis for interpreting of the phenomenon. This is the approach that is adopted in this thesis.

The focus of interpretive phenomenology as a research methodology is on the structures of experience, which precede language. So that language too is investigated:

> not just as a medium or a tool for the designation of meaning, or as a means of representing something, but as that which is also a source of meaning and of expression. Language is...that which makes meaning and expression possible, ... (Rothwell 1998, p. 24).

Rothwell (1998) emphasises the context in which individuals or groups of individuals use language and that the language used may remain unclear except to those who belong to the group. Interpretation is required to elucidate what that group of people mean given their circumstances. Lawler (1998) takes this further, indicating that the hermeneutic phenomenological researcher must firstly reveal how individuals have interpreted an experience and then secondly interpret those findings as a researcher. Geanellos (2000, p. 112) underlines the 'interrelationship between epistemology (interpretation) and ontology (interpreter)'. She refers to the work of Paul Ricoeur (1981) in offering an understanding that humans create narratives about themselves in order to encompass meaning. A researcher is required to sensitively atune herself to the meanings embedded in the narratives. As van Manen (1990, p. 18) suggests,

> The basic thing about our lifeworld (such as the experience of lived time, lived space, lived body, and lived human relation) are preverbal and therefore hard to describe. For this subtlety and sensitivity are needed (by the researcher) ...

It is through the consciousness of the interpreter that the hermeneutical circle of understanding continues. The hermeneutic circle, a concept that is common to all hermeneutic phenomenological research approaches, suggests that in order to understand the meaning of a phenomenon, it is firstly necessary to understand pre-existing understandings of the phenomenon. The interpreter moves from a naïve to a more explicit understanding of the data. The commonalities that a phenomenologist is looking for are in culturally grounded meanings rather than in abstractions or abstracted elements of a situation. Phenomenology seeks for the distinctions and differences that arise through differing histories of the participants (Benner 1994, p. 104).

This brief overview of the philosophical foundations of phenomenology underscores my intention to explore Yat Malmgren's method of actor training as a lived experience and directs this study towards the methodological framework of hermeneutic phenomenology. The experience of the human body in performance is a lived experience, which can be elucidated through conscious reflection. Malmgren's theoretical categorisations of the performative body, which structure his method, have synergies with Heidegger's concepts of Dasein. At their core, Malmgren's actor training theories promote an investigation of being-in-the-world, whether onstage or off. Malmgren's *Inner Attitudes*, *Externalised Drives* and his interpretation of Laban's *Motion Factors* are all texts, directed towards enabling consideration of the nature of human behaviour. Malmgren's knowledge has been directed towards the trainee actor in order to provoke a set of ongoing questions about the full range of human intention and how it is expressed physically.

My aim is to explore this phenomenon, the Malmgren acting technique. I intend to investigate the human body in action in performance, the being-in-the-world (Lebenswelt) of the trainee performer. Hermeneutic phenomenology, consequently provides a unique methodological framework to enable this, where my own understandings of Malmgren's categories of action will assist in the interpretation of the trainee performers' narratives. As in the Dutch phenomenological school (van Manen 1990), I seek descriptions, gained from the participant performers, I use thematic interpretations, which require a sensitive attunement to the participants' meanings and I aim to facilitate a richness of possibilities of understanding of the emergent phenomena.

Moreover, my own conscious perception of the Malmgren technique, from having trained with Yat Malmgren, formulates or raises the questions of inquiry. In order to probe the underlying conscious negotiations of actors with their bodies, I plan to use my own understandings of these very processes.

As the phenomenological researcher, Crease (1994, p. 215) written,

> the meaning of a dramatic work for each individual has do with the experience of the work as it is occurring...

4.2.5 Merleau-Ponty and the phenomenal body

Jocalyn Lawler suggests another school of phenomenology, which she calls, 'Existential phenomenology' (Lawler 1998, p. 52). Characteristic of French phenomenologists, including Gabriel Marcel (1889-1973), Jean-Paul Sartre (1905-1980) and Maurice Merleau-Ponty (1908-1961), embodiment and the ways in which corporeality shape the lived social world are this school's major concerns. Merleau-Ponty's insights into the nature of the body are particularly pertinent to this investigation.

Merleau-Ponty emphasised the vital role that the body plays in constituting any perception of reality. He rejected the notion that sense perception or judgement, shapes the concepts of the world but rather, that meaning, which permeates action through intention, creates a lived-through-world.

> Consciousness is being towards the thing through the intermediary of the body (Merleau-Ponty 1962, p. 146).

> He [Merleau-Ponty] posited a consciousness caught up in
> the ambiguity of corporeality, directed toward a world of
> which it is inextricably and materially a part (Garner 1993,
> p. 448).

This conceptualisation of the body in intentional action correlates clearly with Malmgren's models of action, as structured through Malmgren's *Inner Attitudes*. It is through an intentionality that is already embodied in particular ways of viewing the world that the performer in Malmgren's technique conceptualises the *Inner Attitude* and the action of the character. The performer, through considering the intentions of the character, 'shifts' her perception of her own lived world, to take up the world of the character. Space, time, status, direction, motivational stances all constitute the world lived-through the actor's body. Moreover this body, the body in performance is subjected to scrutiny both by the actor, herself, and the audience. From Merleau-Ponty's perspective it is intentionality or effort that formulates our habitual perceptions (Reynolds 2002). This 'habituality' is understood by Merleau-Ponty as 'knowledge in the hands, which is forthcoming only when bodily effort is made, and cannot be formulated in detachment from that effort' (Merleau-Ponty 1962, p. 144). The similarities between Merleau-Ponty's effort and Malmgren's effort are clear, both emphasise the body or body/mind, rather than any Cartesian conception of mind, in creating intentional action.

In phenomenology as influenced by Merleau-Ponty, the 'phenomenal body' (Garner 1994, p. 99) is expressed in how we experience our body subjectively in the world. In comparison the material body is how we can view our body objectively as an entity in the world. As Merleau-Ponty understands it, the latter is a subset of the former; 'this material Other, at the heart of the One' (Garner 1994, p. 109).

In *The Phenomenology of Perception* (1962, p. 198) Merleau-Ponty grapples with the intertwining of these two, the phenomenal and the material aspects of the body.

> The experience of our own body, on the other hand,
> reveals to us an ambiguous mode of existing ... I am my
> body, at least wholly to the extent that I possess
> experience, and yet at the same time my body is as it were
> a "material" subject, a provisional sketch of my total
> being. Thus experience of one's body runs counter to the

reflective procedure which detaches subject and object from each other, and which gives us only the thought about the body, or the body as an idea and not experience of body or the body in reality.

Again it is clear that this is the heightened experience of the performer in action, at once an experience of the body, embedded in the reality of the performance and at the same time an awareness of the material body, belonging to the performer and perceived by the audience as well as the performer herself. This ambiguous placement of the body, to which I have referred at length in Chapter 3, is the position at which I begin my study, a position posited by Merleau-Ponty, and emphasised through Malmgren's training, the liminal position of the body in performance for the performer (Wilshire 1991).

It is clear, through his writing, that Merleau-Ponty establishes the body-subject as embedded and interactive with every other body-subject, creating as it were 'phenomenal fields' of experience (Merleau-Ponty 1968). His concept of 'the *chiasm*' (Merleau-Ponty 1968, p. 143), that is, the relationship of the seer to the seen, of speech to the listener, of touch to the touched, opens the vision of a web-like world of reflexivities. Through the reflexivity of bodies, one person has access to the reality of another through their bodily expressions. Embodiment means that there is no privileged access to oneself, and other people are equally not closed to oneself. Despite this Merleau-Ponty precludes any notion of a unity of subjectivities that might create a 'reality' but rather posits a network of provisional adjustments, always open to reformulations. Hadreas (1986, pp. 141-2) writes that, 'Being is not a circumscribable concept.' It is the participatory aspect of the life-world that Merleau-Ponty emphasises. We are 'of it' and we cannot help but play some part in it.

It is from these positions then that this research proceeds:

> he who sees cannot possess the visible unless he is possessed of it, unless he is of it (Merleau-Ponty 1968, p. 134).

Yat Malmgren's work is as much a part of my way of perceiving the world of the performer, as I am an expression of his teaching. Likewise my students are participants in this field of phenomenal perception, sharing insights with other students taught elsewhere but in the same method. The aims of this study are more than simply reiterating the Malmgren method, but rather through investigating the experience of the actor in training, to unearth some of the fundamental formulations of being, always open to negotiation, that form the world of being-in-performance in the Malmgren training.

4.3 A methodology for research on Yat Malmgren's actor training: phenomenological collection of data

My phenomenological approach to the investigation of Yat Malmgren's method of actor training places its emphasis on allowing the participants, all trainee actors, to reveal the meanings that they have constructed around their experiences of Yat Malmgren's actor training technique. Plager (1994, p. 75) indicates a process of encouraging dialogue with research participants. Whilst this could be considered as an interview, this study as phenomenological research places its emphasis in seeking distinctly open and respectful means of eliciting information from participants. My biases are required to remain open to being critically challenged (Benner 1994, p. 105). Narratives about events and experiences of the participants are then recorded as the research texts and these texts form the basis for interpretation in the hermeneutic phenomenological study. Although Plager's (1994) process of narrative gathering is constructed for nursing research and is directed at family members in a family health study, it will be applied here in a similar way to groups of trainee actors in a common course of training. Plager identifies three important conditions from Taylor (1985, p. 33) in interpreting the data,

> (a) there is an object or field of objects (the Text) about which we
> want to make some sense
> (b) there are meanings in the text that can be distinguished
> from the expression of the meanings, that is, how they are
> expressed or embodied in the everyday practices, and
> (c) there must be a person or persons (e.g., the family) for
> which these meanings and expressions are significant.

Plager here refers to the family members having modes of expression about events that are meaningful to them. In the same way in my experience of teaching acting in numerous acting schools I am aware that students in full-time acting schools develop their own ways of speaking of their trainings. The text in this case will be the taped dialogues with groups of students as well as individual students, as explicated below. The meanings extracted from the texts via the hermeneutic practice requires insight and openness on my behalf as well as an awareness of the joint understandings of the participants created through their acting practices, histories and cultural heritages.

Identification of general themes of the phenomenon and comprehension of the relationships among the themes form the basic processes through which this phenomenological research will proceed (Benner 1994; Creswell 1998; Willis 2004). In seeking to hear and understand the voices of my participants in this project, I acknowledge that their lived-worlds can never be fully grasped, given the finite and situated nature of each of their worlds. Even the interpreter cannot escape all of the assumptions predicated by her background. However through empathy, sensitivity to the participants' unstated assumptions or unarticulated meanings, through imagination and through reasoning, interpretive phenomenological research predicates that it is possible to draw a set of valuable findings from the research (Benner 1994).

In comparing gathered data, whether from group discussions or from interviews I will be searching for commonalities, the cultural categories and assumptions through which a participant construes the world (Benner 1994, p. 104). I also will be searching for differences arising from the acting students' different cultural backgrounds, and the different orientations to their actor training.

Since phenomenology is based on the premise of the role of intentional consciousness in coming to know the world, it is the depth and richness of the participants' responses that is sought rather than any quantitative element of the responses. Using quantitative terms with respect to the informants' information, such as observing that 'all' or 'some' or 'more than half', has no part to play in this study, instead it is about entering and throwing light on a complex web of contextualities.

4.3.1 Methodological rigour

Laverty (2003, p. 23) speaks of three ways in which the rigour of any hermeneutic phenomenological research can be enhanced. Following the concept of the hermeneutic circle, she suggests that multiple stages of interpretation are necessary to allow for a fuller meaning to emerge of the phenomenon being studied. In addition, discussions of how interpretations arose from data need to be comprehensively set out and the interpretive process and the steps involved need to be fully described. Whitehead (2003, p. 512) sets out five principles for quality research in hermeneutic phenomenological research. She terms these credibility, referring to the researcher situating their own experience within the research; dependability, where readers consider that the research is transferable to another context; confirmability, where the researcher shows clearly how the interpretations are arrived at; clarity in the steps being taken to reach interpretations and finally reflexivity, where the researcher takes account of her background and experience and how these have informed the enquiry.

Each of these issues has been factored into this study and is described at each step in the methods used, including the data collection and the numerous levels of analysis

4.3.2 The settings and participants

Three training institutions were chosen as the sites of my data collection:
- The Theatre Performance course at the Faculty of Creative Arts at the University of Wollongong, New South Wales, Australia
- The Acting course at the Adelaide Centre for the Arts, TAFE[1] South Australia, Adelaide, South Australia, Australia
- The Acting course at Drama Centre, London, a Centre in the Central St. Martin's College of Art and Design, University of the Arts London, United Kingdom

Each of these institutions train actors for entry into the performance industry and each utilises the Malmgren training, as one of a number of actor training techniques. Students are accredited academically in differing ways at each institution. In the Faculty of Creative Arts at the University of Wollongong, the training of actors is housed within a Bachelor of Creative Arts degree, where half of the credit points are accrued through practical components of the course aimed at training actors and where the other half of the course is comprised of academic

---

[1] TAFE is the generic term for Australia's Technical and Further Education system. Each Australian state government funds post-schooling vocational training through TAFE colleges.

subjects. TAFE South Australia's three-year Acting course is accredited as a TAFE diploma course and is primarily a practical course to train actors. At Drama Centre, London, students are engaged in a Bachelor of Arts degree three year course associated with the University of Arts London, although all the subjects offered are essentially practical subjects and all directed towards actor training.

In the first of these institutions the researcher, that is myself, is also the Malmgren trainer. In the second institution, David Kendall was the Malmgren trainer at the time of the interviews. In the last of the institutions Yat Malmgren, himself, was teaching second and third year Drama Centre students, whilst James Kemp had taken over the Malmgren training at a first year level.

Ethics approval for this project was sought and gained from the University of Western Sydney Nepean Human Ethics Review Committee on the 28th August 2000 (Application Protocol No. HE 2000/043). Ethics approval to interview Performance students in the Faculty of Creative Arts was also sought through the University of Wollongong's Human Research Ethics Committee and was gained in March 2000. Information forms were distributed to all students in the final year of each institution outlining the research project, its aims, its procedure and giving information about the researcher. At Drama Centre, second year rather than third year students were chosen for the study. This alteration in the chosen level was due to the greater intensity of classes devoted to the Malmgren technique at Drama Centre, where students have three Malmgren classes per week as well as Laban movement classes which supplement Malmgren's method. At the University of Wollongong's Faculty of Creative Arts, the students chosen were third-year Bachelor of Creative Arts students who had studied Malmgren's work for four semesters with one class a week. At Drama Centre London, the students were second-year acting students in their third semester of their three-year training. At the Adelaide Centre for the Arts, the students had studied two semesters of the training, as an intensive course in first year, in their three year course. The University of Wollongong students thus had studied the Malmgren technique for four semesters, Drama Centre participants had studied the technique for only three semesters, and the Adelaide participants had studied the technique for two semesters. A consent form was also handed out to these students. Each group was asked to volunteer their willingness to join the research project.

A total of 17 students, based on voluntary self-selection from each of the three institutions, signed consent forms acknowledging that they were willing to be involved in two separate interviews about their Malmgren training. Unlike other methods, the small numbers of respondents is adequate for phenomenological research. Ray (1994, p. 127) suggests that a group between 8-12 is an ideal size. The final group of 17 participants consisted of seven from the University of Wollongong's Performance course, four from Drama Centre and six from the Adelaide Centre for the Arts.

As outlined in the description of the methodological framework my subjective stance, through being a Malmgren trainer, is a factor in this investigation. My experience shapes the objectives of this study, and may impact on this study in unpredictable ways (Guba & Lincoln 1981, p. 128-152; McCracken 1988, p. 18). It is necessary to take this involvement into account, as much as is possible, both when interviewing and analysing the data. To this end a trial group interview was conducted, with the participation of 5 University of Wollongong, Faculty of Creative Arts students, in order to foster the development of non-directive and non-hierarchical interviewing techniques, particularly with my own students.

4.3.3 Interview design

Phenomenologists often approach their investigations through three frames; the experience of place, the experience of events in time and the ways that participants talk about their experiences, although even these divisions are recognised as being artificial (Cohen, Kahn & Steeves 2000, p. 46).

Malmgren's acting technique employs its own specific language in order to analyse and investigate performed action and also to investigate character 'types'. So this investigation set out to study how actors in training experience this language, as well as investigating the frames of reference just mentioned.

Based on Crotty's (1996, p. 20) description of phenomenological nursing research methods, I chose to use unstructured or open-ended interviews, where the interview develops in a spontaneous fashion and where the researcher adopts non-directive techniques such as active listening, repetition of statements, and refocusing of responses. This was a choice that would enhance pursuing the meaning of statements in greater depth. It was also a choice to allow the participants to direct the interviews towards their own intentional lifeworlds. I applied Morse's (1991) method of interactive interviews, where phenomenological researchers share their own stories about the experience under investigation. This was aimed at information being exchanged in both directions so that conversation became another means of eliciting information. Holstein and Gubrium (1995) describe these as active interviews.

Throughout the process of the interviews, I reflected on and honed my abilities to listen carefully, drawing out further comments rather than surmising. I also took note of and allowed for silences. Developing skills in these interactive interviewing techniques became an important procedure for the project, in order to elicit meaningful dialogues amongst participants. The ability to resist leading the participants, the ability to stay open to what was said without having pre-formed judgements, became important considerations. Listening for those moments when important information was either being proffered or elided became vital in opening out rather than closing down the focus group discussions.

In particular, in the interviews with the Faculty of Creative Arts students from the University of Wollongong, it was crucial to be aware of moments where I was steering the dialogue. This role, being a habitual one in my relationship with my students as their Performance Lecturer, could be easily and unconsciously assumed. Rather than leading the dialogue I needed to stimulate the willingness of the participants to contribute openly. Even at the other two institutions, care was needed in interviewing procedures. My introduction there as a Malmgren trainer could, in itself, have meant creating a hierarchical relationship with the trainee actors. To avoid this I attended classes and rehearsals at each institution, mingling with the students in their training locations. The research interviews and focus group discussions were also held in the institution's premises, heightening both the familiarity of the process but also drawing on the immersion of the participants and researcher in the world of the training.

The other area that needed particular attention was in the preference for eliciting narrative constructions. The hermeneutic phenomenology tradition holds that informants have already interpreted the meaning of their lives in the very act of turning their experiences into stories that can be told (Cohen, Kahn & Steeves 2000, p. 61). Character Analysis, since it provides a new language system for the young performer, requires, from the performer's perspective, an interpretive stance to apply the language to performance in the first place. It was important to direct the participants towards descriptions of this performance process rather than encouraging them to form abstractions about Malmgren's theories.

4.3.4 Step1: Focus groups

In choosing to respect the students as collaborators in the research, a focus group discussion was chosen as the first formal meeting with the researcher in each site and an atmosphere was engendered in which students' experiences could be heard and acknowledged openly. The focus groups were videotaped, enabling a recording of participants' body languages and physical interactions with each other. These visual recordings assisted in the understandings of meanings being generated.

A broad based question designed to elicit rich descriptions and/or understandings of the training was offered to the participants when they volunteered to join the focus groups, in order for them to fully engage in describing and/ or reflecting on the training as they encountered it. It is important to note here that in this hermeneutical phenomenological research the question posed to the participants is not the researcher's question of the thesis. The participants' question is rather a general open-ended question that is able to elicit narrative responses about the participants' experiences of the phenomena. This question was:

In what ways has Malmgren's training shaped your understanding of yourself as an actor?

It was suggested that students present a written response to the question in the focus group, although this was merely encouraged and not insisted upon. The group meeting consisted of up to two hours of open discussion about Malmgren's training. Each focus group was allowed to keep interacting until everyone felt that no more could be added to the dialogue, that the participants and researcher felt 'saturated'. In all three institutions the group met inside the training institution itself. Theatre students at each of the colleges often spend up to 60 hours a week in their institution. The college rooms and studios form an intimate setting for trainees, where thoughts on theatre and acting are intensely experienced. These settings became a means of encouraging the open sharing of former experiences encountered in the participants' training. Each videotaped focus group discussion was later transcribed, with notes taken as to gestures used in discussions and physical interactions between the participants noted. Pseudonyms were used for each participant, for ethical reasons.

4.3.5 Step 2: Individual interviews

Later, each participant was asked to view the video recording of their group session and to clarify or add more to any of the responses that they or others made to the topics under discussion about the Malmgren training. The negotiated reflection on their previous focus group discussion became the substance of the individual research interviews. These were audiotaped interviews between myself and individual participants (van Manen 1990) and later transcribed using pseudonyms for the participants. Each interview lasted up to an hour. Techniques of active or interactive interviewing were used and where possible narrative constructions of experiences were sought, especially in relation to the initial question of the research posed in the focus groups.

4.3.6 Other sources: field notes, participants' journals

Observations by the researcher of both the participants and the settings, that are the three institutions at which the interviews were conducted, form part of a set of field notes (Cohen, Kahn & Steeves 2000, p. 65). These notes provide a context for the interviews and assist in sensitive considerations of the data. The field notes became the first written means of considering the hermeneutic circle of understanding (Moran 2000, p. 237). This term may be considered as a metaphor, which can guide the investigation. A researcher can only understand what is being revealed in the context of what he or she already knows. Through reflexive consideration of parts of the incoming data in relation to its whole, the researcher is led into a deeper consideration of the data, allowing more sensitive and aware data collection to follow. So in this respect the beginnings of data analysis was occurring as data was being collected.

It was also possible to elicit written responses, in the form of journals, from several of the Wollongong students, allowing for what Taylor (1996, p. 43) terms, 'crystallization'. This is the possibility of developing multiple perspectives on the phenomena being examined. Several of the students, who formed the research group at the University of Wollongong, were participants in a preliminary trial group interview, which was taped and transcribed. The data from this trial group became part of the hermeneutic considerations.

Van Manen (1990, p. 67) stresses that for the phenomenological researcher to gather the right amount and kind of material it is necessary for the researcher to stay strongly oriented towards the notion they wish to explore. In this case I had to keep orienting my respondents towards descriptions, perceptions, anecdotes, and understandings about their bodies in reference to Malmgren's training.

4.3.7 The researcher's journal

The idea of inserting particular field notes, written memories of encounters with Yat Malmgren, and personally written material, into the body of the thesis developed during the writing period. It was chosen as a means of reflecting on the concept of fragmented subjectivities, in this case a fragmented set of narratives embodying my personal meaning of meeting with Yat Malmgren. As he has stated, an action, in his method, 'must send someone else on a journey' (Malmgren 1998). Extracts from my Researcher's Journal appear throughout this thesis as a reflection of my journey on which Malmgren sent me. It is a journey of *Flow* and intends to capture through description and personal narrative the intense feelings that have propelled this thesis. The Researcher's Journal is my testament to the methodological framework or paradigm of the thesis, which places subjectivity as the substratum of all objectivity. The Researcher's Journal appears as a subjectivity that is fragmented and at times chaotic and yet which, through embodying meaning that is at once personal and interactive, creates a participatory or shared set of understandings that have and will move into further embodied action. I have separated each Researcher's Journal entry, through shading and a differing font as well as listing each entry numerically in order to differentiate it from the body of the academic text. Similar to a set of figures it is a differing text, illuminating the text through a non-linear and felt means of communication.

Mrs. Russell shuffles into Room 1. We are in Yat's second year Movement class, after lunch on three days a week. I am observing after years of being away from here, but nothing seems to have changed. Room 1, the old Methodist church is slightly shabbier, with its high ceiling and long windows. The paint is beginning to peel. Yat stands on a dais in front of a set of arches in the wall in his dance gear. This is the room that Drama Centre uses as its theatre, the only room really that has enough space. The piano sits at the side of the room. Mrs. Russell is Yat's accompanist for his dance classes and she plays with the certainty of years of repetition. A minute old woman she totters in a determined manner in a straight line to the piano, whilst the already assembled class face Yat. He is directing students to stand in particular rows and spaces. "Hello Mrs. Russell", Yat intones and then grins knowingly at the students when Mrs. Russell makes no response, knowing full well that Mrs. Russell hears nothing of his greeting. The class laughs. Yat is clowning for them. Mrs. Russell is extremely deaf. She sits now with half-mast black trousers at the piano and begins playing, straight into it. Yat starts demonstrating the various dance exercises making much of clapping vigorously at Mrs. Russell when he needs her to stop so that he can speak in more detail to the students. It is a kind of game that these two act out, but Yat's is definitely a performance for the students. He seems to relish it. Mrs. Russell travels all the way from Brighton to play for these classes. It is her life's work. In years to come I find out from Yat that she dies not long after retiring, a premonition of Yat's own fate, but today the two of them, Yat and Mrs. Russell are playing together. Two elderly figures in the room dancing with one another.

Researcher's Journal 4.1 January 1988, Drama Centre London, Movement Class, Group 25.

4.3.8 Malmgren and trainers

Yat Malmgren, himself, was interviewed as a major contributor to this research project. His transcribed tapes throw light on the understood meanings of his training for the performative body and have formed part of the hermeneutic circle of research that I have been engaged in. Through outlining his own life history I have structured a shortened biography into Chapter 2. The interviews have also contributed to Chapter 5, which describes the Malmgren method as it has been traditionally taught by trainers. I have included numbers of Malmgren's statements about his actor training technique in this thesis, both from Malmgren's taped interviews as well as from notes taken from Malmgren's studio classes when I have visited Drama Centre. Two other trainers were interviewed, David Kendall, the principal teacher of Malmgren's work at the Adelaide Centre for the Arts, and David Tyler, another Malmgren trainer at the Adelaide Centre for the Arts.

4.4 A phenomenological analysis of data

Data analysis in an interpretive or hermeneutic phenomenological study recognizes that lived experience by its very nature is an interpretive process (Cohen and Omery 1994). Moreover, the participants in engaging in descriptions or narratives about their experiences are once more interpreting. The disclosure of the meaning of their 'being' rests on the researcher's understanding. Understanding of the meanings in the 'texts' examined is linked to cultural norms.

Gadamer (1989) put forward two basic ways in which one human being, the researcher, understands another (Ray 1994, p. 121). Firstly the researcher's understanding is based on 'prejudgement' – the preconceptions and prejudices that the researcher brings to the study. This encompasses common linguistic contexts that the researcher and participant share, the horizon of meaning of both researcher and participant. The second means of the researcher understanding the participant is that of universal or common human consciousness, the concept of which lies at the heart of phenomenology. Data analysis as Ray (1994, p. 129) describes it is ' a sensitive attunement to opening up to the meaning of experience both as discourse and as text.'

Crotty (1996, p. 22) clearly outlines procedures to identify themes in hermeneutic phenomenological data.

> By reflecting on the data, the researcher expects to uncover common themes that stem from 'the significant statements' or 'meaning units (Crotty 1996, p. 23).

This reflection began during the collection of data. In the midst of interviews as a researcher I was structuring questions based on my understanding of the meaning of previous replies. It became important to return to the data gathered from the first interviews with the participants, in order to check the validity of emerging 'meaning units' (Georgi 1985, p10). Moreover in each new set of interviews the emerging themes intuitively established from previous data formed the basis of probings for new interviewees. It became apparent even from the trial interview carried out in Wollongong in August 2000 that clear meaning statements were emerging.

Immersion in the data is an important phenomenological process that takes place in terms of analysis (O'Brien 1999, p. 6). In this case the preliminary 'meaning units' were established in relation to the researcher's own experiences of actor training and of Malmgren's actor training in particular. Added to this first movement of the hermeneutic circle were the differing historical and social contexts in which the interviews were taking place in comparison to the researcher's own experience of my Malmgren training (which took place over twenty years ago, in the early 1980s in London, when Yat Malmgren was 64), the differing understandings of performance in that place in time and the differing social and cultural meanings of studying Malmgren's technique for the participants.

Phenomenological analysis, like many qualitative analysis processes begins by the locating of these 'meaning units' as textual passages. The 'meaning units', grounded in the text, are words, phrases, sections of dialogue that jump out at the researcher as being significant. They are on a common 'horizon' to the researcher's 'horizon'. However, unlike other qualitative methods, these significant texts may not necessarily be linked by similar words or phrases. The 'meaning unit' is dependant on the context in which it is spoken and not necessarily on vocabulary. Diekelmann, Schuster and Lam (1994, p. 131), give the example of a researcher using a computer word search for data using 'the words fear, trepidation, anxiety, dread, foreboding, misgiving, uneasiness, and all of their variants'. They then proceed to indicate that the following transcribed conversation, clearly indicating an implicit unease, could not be located by search software based on vocabulary.

A: I didn't want to.
B: Why didn't you want to?

A: (Laughing) I knew the needle would be this big (holding hands far apart).
(Diekelmann, Schuster & Lam 1994, p. 131)

Although there are no words here that are synonymous with the searched for words, the entire conversation, added with the gesture of speaker A, is clearly about anxieties surrounding an injection, a common experience. Given the need for this kind of scrutiny, data analysis was carried out manually, separating meaning units and only later regrouping them. This identifying of 'meaning units' (Lindholm, Uden and Rastam 1999, p. 103), Creswell (1998, p. 147) calls the 'horizonalization of the data'. All the statements at this point are considered of equal worth.

The next step was to identify and ascribe the segments of text to 'named sub-themes' (Creswell 1998, p. 144; Lindholm, Uden and Rastam 1999, p. 103). It is this layer of analysis that identifies meaning (Carpenter 2003, p. 84). The clustering of statements into sub-themes begins the interpretive process. In this research the clusters chosen for the groupings of meaning-units reflected the various structures of experiences in acting training and in the Malmgren training in particular that students returned to throughout the interviews. From these clusters it was possible for me to label a set of shared experiences. I included verbatim examples or 'exemplars' as Benner has called them (Benner 1994, p. 117). An exemplar is viewed as a piece of text from one participant seen as expressing the heart of a sub-theme in that participant's language or voice. The aim of including exemplars is to allow a reader to distinguish the separations of experiences into subthemes that the researcher is making.

The third analytical step was to weave these sub-themes into an understanding of 'the major themes' of the research (Carpenter 2003, p. 64; Creswell 1998, p. 144). This is the next interpretive step, reaching beyond the sub-theme clusters to consider a more holistic meaning of the sub-themes. Overall my writing of the participants' explications needs to read as a good narrative, rich in felt meaning, deep in understandings of the body perceiving itself in action and the search for 'authentic' or 'expressive' action.

O'Brien (1999, p. 5) states,

> Hermeneutic Phenomenological writing is a creative process with the aim of making some aspect of lived experience understandable

Writing and rewriting is an essential part of interpretive phenomenology (van Manen 1990, p. 32). Only through understanding the participants' experiences as revealed through their exemplars and through the comparison of themes in writing will an overarching coherent picture emerge.

In order to create the descriptive chapter (Chapter 5) of the experience of a Malmgren studio, I engaged in data transformation, where I made decisions to reorganise data, linking discussions of the same topics, editing digressions, and hesitations. In Chapter 6 and 7, this data transformation results in revealing the essential themes of the phenomenon (van Manen 1990, p. 106). Drawing the gathered sub-themes into a set of existential understandings about the Malmgren technique, as experienced by trainee actors, in the twenty-first century, can reveal the overall meaning of the phenomenon. In Chapter 8, using the participants' words I use the creation of the 'narrative text' to allow the reader to participate more fully in the experiences of those interviewed (Cohen, Kahn & Steeves 2000, p. 76). Georgi (1985, p. 15) calls this 'the consistent statement of the structure of the experience' This is, then, a multi-voiced description of a learning process through Malmgren's technique.

Writing the experiential was my task; metaphor, narrative, anecdotes and written images supplied my need and the totality presents itself as a multi-voiced crystalisation of meaning.

4.5 Research participants

The following information about the seventeen research participants has been gathered from the group and individual interviews, from speaking informally to these students, whilst at their institutions and in the case of the University of Wollongong students, from prior knowledge (having previously taught them) and in some cases from the trial discussion group that I organised.

Group 1 Participants
Faculty of Creative Arts, University of Wollongong
Wollongong, New South Wales, Australia

Seven third-year students in the Bachelor of Creative Arts course at the University of Wollongong, majoring in Theatre Performance, volunteered to take part in the focus group discussion. It took place on 5th September 2000 in the Blackbox studio – G18, in the Faculty of Creative Arts complex on the university campus from 7pm to approximately 9pm in the evening. The Blackbox studio is the principal teaching space for the Malmgren technique, although this studio is also accessed for other performance course classes.

Each of the participants had been trained for four semesters in Malmgren's acting technique. It is vital to recognise that each of these participants had been taught by the researcher in acting classes and had further contact with her through being directed by her in numerous theatrical productions. These relationships had existed for either two and a half or three and a half years. Each participant has been given a pseudonym.

Individual interviews took place in studios and lecture theatres in the Creative Arts Faculty from $5^{th} - 18^{th}$ October 2000.

James

James had enrolled in the BCA at the University of Wollongong when he was twenty-six years old. He had specifically moved to Wollongong in 1998, in search of the Yat Malmgren technique in order to improve his acting. When he was seventeen and living in Melbourne he had started applying to be admitted to a professional acting course. Each year he would return to the Victorian College of the Arts in Melbourne in order to audition for a full-time acting course and each year he was rejected. For several years he was reaching the final stages of the audition process but always being excluded from a placement in the course. Finally, one of the staff at the college spoke to him about his vocal problems, suggesting that, rather than these being about 'technique', they were in fact part of his 'makeup' and that he would need to seek a more probing and holistic acting technique to address these matters. The staff member suggested James either move to New York or perhaps audition at the University of Wollongong to study Yat Malmgren's technique.

James had left school in Year 10 and was dyslexic. He had gathered a substantial amount of stage and screen experience since leaving school, but had not been able to create a career from his performance work. His entrance to the BCA at Wollongong University had been problematic due to his low levels of academic achievement. James' abilities in the practical components of the degree course exceeded his academic abilities. James was twenty-eight at the time of the interview.

> I started with what I perceived as sending me on this journey and that is when I auditioned for the VCA. They suggested that to move on as a performer - to progress and grow as a performer - I needed to nail myself down or to get to know myself better as a performer. This confused me hugely at the time. I had no idea what to make of that at all.

Alex

Alex was nineteen when she began the course. She had taken a year off after a successful completion of Year 12 in order to travel to South America and in particular Chile, where her mother was born. She had been interested in acting from an early age and whilst at school, in Sydney, had attended classes at one of the better known youth acting groups. She had felt drawn to further study in this area and came to the University of Wollongong to take a double degree in Arts and Creative Arts. Her major in Arts was in Communications. In the Bachelor of Creative Arts she had applied her knowledge gained in Communications to excel in the particular area of Devised Theatre. However in other sections of the course, Alex was not achieving the kind of results that she had been hoping for. In the Malmgren training in particular Alex was feeling uncertain of her progress. She had been reconsidering her commitment to performance as a career option when she embarked on this research project. At the time of the interview she was twenty-one years old.

> I thought acting was the thing for me at the beginning of the course, whereas now I don't. But that could also have been just having had a history of being involved. I don't know.

Megan

Megan was one of the younger members of the course for her year. She had started university and in particular the BCA course in 1998, when she was seventeen. Megan had grown up on a commune on the south coast of NSW. She had attended a high school in Nowra and had participated in annual summer pantomimes with a community theatre group in Nowra. She had also taken youth theatre classes there. Her life up until moving from her home to Wollongong had revolved around her family and the commune members. Megan was an academically high achiever and maintained high grades in both the academic and practical components of the course. Megan was nineteen at the time of the interview.

> [Studying 'Yat'] was so scary and so new and so exciting, that it was more alive than anything. It's like a pinnacle, like it's the most alive. It just obsessed me and I would lie awake and every day I would have to allot time when I was allowed to think about it because I wouldn't think about anything else.

Gina

Gina came from Sydney and had already completed a Bachelor degree in Psychology from another university before embarking on her actor training. Coming to the Faculty of Creative Arts course in 1998 at twenty-three, Gina was the most mature female in her year. She had enjoyed major roles in productions throughout the course. At her previous university Gina had been involved in student shows and had come to hear of the Wollongong course through a student theatre festival held at Wollongong in the year prior to her auditioning. Already having a degree, Gina was in the course primarily for its practical subject offerings. Gina was twenty-five when interviewed.

> For some people it must have been so amazing to do Yat, because I know a lot of them were straight from school and they had just, not even really thought about themselves. Whereas, I think because I'd done a psychology degree I was more – It wasn't so much a shock. It wasn't such a watershed for me, whereas for them it was.

Gary

Gary had come to the Faculty of Creative Arts course straight out of high school, from a small country town in the west of NSW, where his family owned property. Gary was nineteen when he entered the course in 1997. He had decided to spend four years finishing his degree and majoring both in theatre performance as well as theatre production. In this final year of his course, Gary had already completed a set of theatre production subjects, allowing him to work professionally as a theatre technician. In this final year he was now concentrating on his acting. Academically Gary had struggled with various subjects but in his practical work he was a competent student. Gary was twenty-one when interviewed.

> I think a lot of actors spend more time than the average population analysing themselves because they're given the tools to.

Rick

Rick had also begun his studies at the University of Wollongong in 1997. He was seventeen at the time. He had enrolled first as an Arts student. He had wanted to study Theatre, however had missed selection into the course, through audition. In 1997 Rick had taken an elective in Theatre and had auditioned again in 1998 in order to transfer courses. Although he had made the transfer, his status within the course had remained questionable. Several members of staff had made it clear to Rick that they saw his potential as an actor as limited. In his first year in the Faculty of Creative Arts he had been advised to study Theatre Production rather than taking the Malmgren training class. He had been involved in numerous stage management roles. He joined the Malmgren training a semester later than the majority of his year. At the time of the interview Rick was nineteen.

> I don't think getting on the stage will ever get easy – it's never going to get easy but you know what to expect after a while.

Andy

Andy was a mature aged student, twenty-five years old, when he came to study at the Faculty of Creative Arts in 1998. He had already completed a prior Arts degree at a Sydney university in which he had achieved good results. In his audition

Andy had outlined a set of clear goals in relation to a career in theatre. He had stated then that he intended to set up his own independent theatre company in Sydney. Over the ensuing years he moved determinedly in this direction, setting up a small theatre in a hotel in Balmain, Sydney, where he worked as a hotel manager. Andy had played in a number of leading theatrical roles in his training and had applied his Malmgren training to an understanding of each of these. He had been attracted to the training at the University of Wollongong primarily because he felt it trained actors to create their own work and take responsibility for their careers. Andy was twenty-eight when interviewed.

> My parents are teachers and I was always in the humanities. Dad's a big Joyce fan - so I suppose that language is the best way I've always approached things. I always thought - "Well you just say the words!" and that's the way to approach it.

Group 2 Participants
Drama Centre, London, A Centre in the Central St. Martin's College of Art and Design, University of London, United Kingdom.

Four second-year students at Drama Centre, London volunteered to participate in the focus group discussion and the subsequent individual interviews. In 2000, whilst Yat Malmgren was teaching at Drama Centre, the institution ran only one course, a specialist course in Acting. The group interview took place on the 6th of December 2000 from 1pm to approximately 3pm in Drama Centre in Room 2, Yat Malmgren's studio.

Each of the participants had studied Malmgren's technique for three sessions. In their first year, the participants had been taught by James Kemp, Yat Malmgren's assistant. From August until December 2000 the participants had been trained by Yat Malmgren, himself.

Individual interviews were held in a separate room at Drama Centre and took place from the $7^{th} - 9^{th}$ Dec. 2000. All interviewees have been given pseudonyms.

Roger

Roger was twenty when he was interviewed. He had chosen to do a year's preparation course in drama after finishing his A levels because he had been unsuccessful in gaining a place in a major drama school straight after leaving school. Roger was straight forward about his ambitions to become an actor. He had left his home in Surrey to attend a preparation course in Paddington, London. It wasn't until his second year of auditioning for drama schools that he had heard about Drama Centre. He was intrigued by the reputation of the school as one that 'break(s) you down' and had auditioned successfully after hearing about this. Roger had a clear confidence in his work. In class Yat complimented him on his 'heroic' qualities but at the same time criticised him for using these qualities to attempt playing a speech of Shakespeare's Richard II. Roger finds it amusing that Yat teases him by calling him, ' Mr. Cool man'.

> Half the challenge is to try to marry what you are doing intellectually and what you're trying to express physically. I am a sympathetic person, although I maybe use a lot of thinking.

Danny

Danny had studied drama throughout his schooling. Although British by birth, he traced his ancestry to an Italian background from the sixteenth century, 'all that way back to a merchant ship, shipwrecked off the coast of Cornwall'. He had grown up in Essex, moved to Oxford and then at sixteen he had moved with his family to Germany. His international school had had excellent theatrical facilities and Danny had been involved in musical theatre and in choirs as well as in school tournaments where he often performed in duologues. Danny had a strong academic background and was still uncertain as to whether he could earn his living as a professional actor or whether he would become a businessman. Danny felt that he needed to attempt to be a professional actor or he would regret never having tried. Danny had applied to a range of acting schools before being accepted at Drama Centre. His acceptance happened on the day that he had auditioned, which had surprised him. Danny had not as yet excelled at Drama Centre. He was aware that as yet Yat confused him with other students in the year. Danny was nineteen at the time of the interview.

> I tend to look at everything from that perspective (academic) and I do get caught up in a lot of head work as opposed to the organic side of stuff.

Bella

Bella was twenty years old at the time of the interview. She came to Drama Centre straight from school. When asked she says that her ethnic background is Persian, however she was born and brought up in a northern city in the UK. Her mother wanted her to study medicine and her academic achievements at high school were leading her in that direction. However during her A Levels she changed from the sciences to the arts. This caused a rift with her mother, which at the time of interview was still on Bella's mind. Bella chose to audition for Drama Centre because she wanted to retain and develop her skills as a playwright. Bella was passionate about Drama Centre and her acting, whilst as the same time extremely critical of her own performances. Her passion attracted both open praise and criticism in classes and rehearsals. Bella was concerned about the pressures that Drama Centre was exerting on her. In particular the director of Drama Centre asked her to lose weight. This criticism and her passionate response made her question her position within the school.

> My Mum always drummed it into me that I was going to be a doctor. And I thought that that was what I was going to be. But then I wrote a short play and the director of it told me she thought I should go to Drama Centre. She said it was the only drama school that would let me continue to be a writer, that it would actually help me in my writing.

Donald

Donald was German and was one of a number of international students at Drama Centre. Academically, he failed the equivalent of A levels in Germany. His interest had always been with the arts and performance so after his schooling he attempted to find work as a performer. Donald came to live in London when he was twenty-one, in order to attend a course on performance that had no entry requirements. He studied for two years. In the course he was introduced to Rudolf Laban's work. After the course he again attempted to enter the theatre industry and again found that he couldn't earn a living from it. He decided to opt for further training. Drama Centre appealed to him as a drama school because of its Eurocentric perspectives on theatre and because of the emphasis on Rudolf Laban's theories. Donald was a dedicated, hard working student. When not engaged directly in rehearsals he studied his text, preparing himself for classes.

> I am from a school where we did lots of eurythmics and that kind of movement. I was always interested in ballet. One of my main aims is to understand body language and body movement, so that's why I'm interested in Yat's work and Laban's work.

Group 3 Participants
Adelaide Centre for the Arts, TAFE South Australia, Adelaide, South Australia, Australia.

Nine third-year students volunteered to be part of the focus group discussion, which took place at the Adelaide Centre for the Arts, in the rehearsal studio, where at the time David Kendall still taught the Malmgren technique as part of the course in Acting. The group interview took place on the 12th May 2003 from 3.30–5.30pm approximately. Of the nine volunteers only six advanced to the individual interview, which was audiotaped. The three who did not continue in the research cited as their reasons, the time consuming nature of their rehearsal schedule and their reluctance to put aside the necessary time for the interviews.

At the Adelaide Centre for the Arts, acting students are trained in Malmgren's method in the first year of their study. This teaching is structured as an intensive course. Students are then encouraged to use the Laban technique, as it is called, throughout the rest of the training by applying the technique to rehearsal exercises or to productions. Laban theory is emphasized through movement classes in the course and Malmgren's language, established in the first-year classes, is used by all permanent members of staff.

Individual interviews took place on the 13th and 14th May 2003 in a rehearsal studio at the Helpmann Building. All participants have been given pseudonyms.

Lliam

Lliam grew up in a country town, not too far away from Adelaide, where he had lived with his mother on a small farm, since his father and brothers had left when he was seven. Then in high school, in Year 12, his mother moved to another state. Lliam had lived independently. Although he had not enjoyed the Year 12 drama course, he had moved to the city to study acting. Lliam aspired to being a music theatre performer, but hoped first to further his acting studies, through applying to another training institution after he graduated. Lliam was 20 at the time of the interview.

> This intensive training course, it's the first one I'd come across, so I can't say for sure whether this is the method that works for me, but it is my first step. I think because it is the first one I've come across, I'll always have that to refer to.

Carmel

Carmel had already worked as a professional actor in the film and television industry. Over four years, whilst working professionally she had taken evening classes in acting from a NIDA graduate, who had taught some basic Stanislavski exercises. Although she enjoyed working, especially in film, she had wanted to study, intending to take one year out of professional acting to undertake just the first year of the course, which included the intensive Laban course. Instead Carmel had stayed to complete her three-year Diploma. Carmel was 25 at the time of the interview.

> Another couple of people, men who I really respected in the industry, said to me not to do it and so I kept putting it off, but in the end I realized that it was what I wanted to do ... Now they're saying it's the best thing I've ever done.

Douglas

Douglas had studied medicine for five years before deciding that he no longer wanted to become a doctor. He had also, over those years completed an Arts degree. His mother in particular had been disappointed by his decision to leave medicine. His father, who was himself a doctor, however advised Douglas not to continue 'unless you're going to be happy doing it…because doing the first ten years or so you've really got to dedicate everything you've got to it.'

At school Douglas had never really liked theatre, he had never seen any theatre that had appealed to him, until in Year 11 he saw Peter Weiss' 'Marat'. He read plays, however, then started to write poetry and short stories when he left school. Douglas had become interested in the Adelaide Centre for the Arts, Acting course, as his brother had trained as an actor there. His brother had encouraged Douglas to audition, but it wasn't until after his brother had graduated that Douglas did, primarily with the thought that the course could encourage his writing. Douglas was 28 at the time of the interview.

> In a way, I always say that the theatre found me … I felt like I almost dropped out into it.

Gillian

Gillian had learned ballet from the age of five until she was nineteen. After finishing Year 12, Gillian auditioned for the Adelaide Centre for the Arts, Dance course. At that time the Dance course had sent out letters to ballet schools in Adelaide hunting for dancers with reasonable skills in ballet and contemporary dance to join their Dance course in the second year, accelerating through first year. Gillian joined, completed the last two years and graduated. She then joined the Adelaide Centre for the Arts, Acting course. Gillian was 22 at the time of the interview.

> I think I thought too much, but at the time I didn't recognize it. We'd get a mid-term assessment. We'd sit with the lecturers individually and they'd give us some feedback for 15, 20 minutes, and that kept coming up, whether it was in relation to being in class or to an approach to choreography - generally thinking too much and analysing things too much.

Michael

Michael was one of the younger members of the group. He was seventeen when he joined the Acting course. Michael had first wanted to be an actor because he wanted to be different. His friends from high school were all heading into careers in computing and IT. They hoped for stable futures and to make good money.

Michael looked at applying for the Air Force when he was at high school. He joined the air training corps and the cadets, but ultimately he followed his creative bent, finding he was good at Drama and English. Michael was 20 at the time of the interview.

> I don't want a stable future. I want an unpredictable future, you know, and I wanted to be something that was totally out of left field and so different. I love creating, whereas my friends, my old high school mates aren't creative. They're very, very practical or mathematical.

Suzi

Suzi was a Japanese international student. English was her second language. She had left Japan to study in Australia at the Adelaide Centre for the Arts, in particular, with the intention of establishing herself as an Australian film and television actor. However, over the two years of her training she had come to understand the limited number of roles available to Japanese actors in Australia. She was considering her future. In Japan, Suzi had worked arduously at her academic studies. Each level of her schooling had required her to pass a rigorous entrance exam. Suzi had been very stressed. Yet despite this, she had sought to study at an overseas institution. Suzi was twenty at the time of the interview.

> I think I wanted to put myself in a hard situation and then see what happens. I wanted to go to another country since I was really little, six or seven.

Group 4 Malmgren and Malmgren trainers

Yat Malmgren

I interviewed Yat Malmgren over two days, the 28th and 29th November 2000, at the Drama Centre, London. Malmgren related his biography, particularly his career in dance, and his meetings with Laban, including working for him at Addlestone, Surrey in 1953 and 1954. He also related quite precisely the setting up of the original Drama Centre, London. Only portions of the interviews refer generally to Malmgren's training methods.

> It was after all twelve years of work before I dared to teach *Inner Attitudes*. And before I came so far as I am, I just saw the *Inner Attitude* as an activity, which was wrong. But it worked very well on people who had talent, because then for the first time, they find some organisation of their inner life.

David Kendall

I interviewed David Kendall on the 14th May 2003, in Adelaide. David spoke about his years in Melbourne, in the early Carlton theatre scene of La Mama and the APG in the late 1960s. He spoke at length of the impact of Yat and Drama Centre on his acting and training of actors. David also spoke of his teaching of Yat Malmgren's actor training technique at the Centre for Performing Arts and now the Centre for the Arts, Adelaide.

> Everything that Yat said and everything that Christopher [Fettes] said remains in my memory... Everything that I teach and that I do comes from those two years, where I never broke my concentration for a second on what either of them said or did or looked at or commented on. And I realised that the more scenarios that I did the more I was discovering about the very nature of acting, what it

David Tyler

I interviewed David Tyler on the 13th May in the Centre for the Arts, Adelaide. David spoke at length of his 'Laban' training with David Kendall and of how much he valued this particular method in relation to other actor training techniques that he has used as an actor.

> I turned up to do one year retraining [in acting] and I just stayed and I spent the next two years at the Centre for Performing Arts [CPA] learning and discovered that I actually really liked teaching. And that was when I actually managed to admit to myself that what I really wanted to do was to teach actors, to become an acting teacher, to be in an institution which was directly aligned to the training of actors for the industry. The problem with acting has been the puzzle and the interest and the fascination with me even right from the beginning.

4.6 Conclusions

This chapter proposes a phenomenological research framework to investigate Malmgren's actor training technique as set by the research question: **In what way does Malmgren's actor training contribute to the understanding of the performative body?**

Through researching the experiences of actors undertaking the training, the research will move beyond a description of Malmgren's technique. Instead, the emphasis in this research is the embodied understanding of the worth or meaning of the technique to a set of actors in training. The aim is to elucidate an understanding of the embedded practical knowledge located in the Malmgren training through implementing an appropriate research methodology.

Heidegger's philosophy of hermeneutic phenomenology has initiated contemporary research approaches to fields where lived experiences are under investigation. The nature of such an approach is fundamentally interpretive. The concept of the hermeneutic circle, which is common to all Heideggarian phenomenological research approaches, suggests that in order to understand the meaning of a phenomenon, it is firstly necessary to understand pre-existing understandings of the phenomenon. This in particular is established through the researcher's own pre-existing 'fusion of horizons' with the research subjects about the phenomenon. From considering the phenomenon in this light, enhanced understandings can proceed through a spiral of investigation, where the original considerations are returned to and are deepened or expanded. Hermeneutic phenomenology rests on the interpretation of and understanding of text, where text through Ricoeurian philosophy is viewed as the material of the participants' subjectivities. The hermeneutic phenomenological methodology outlined in this case refers to the text generated by trainee actors in the Malmgren technique in dialogue with the researcher, where the impact of Malmgren's technique of actor training on the participants forms the basis for the dialogue.

This chapter sets out a series of hermeneutic phenomenological methods, all of which have been previously applied to research participants in the field of nursing research, which will be used in this research on actor training. It is recognised that actors in training through the Malmgren acting technique establish familiar and common terms in reference to their training. Not only does the Malmgren actor training technique establish a set of common terms but acting trainings in general also inherit a set of languages established through western trainings for realistic character development. Chapter 6 will examine the drawing out of meaning units from the data, as well as the establishment of subthemes reflecting commonalities of meaning about the actor training the participants are undergoing. In Chapter 7 thematic analysis will be used to search for more holistic ways of viewing the participants' understandings about their training. In Chapter 8 a wider contextualisation of the Malmgren actor training technique in relation to affective communication between actors' bodies and their audiences will be considered in light of the data presented in Chapters 6 and 7. In Chapter 9 a narrative text will be offered as a descriptive and empathetic means of elucidating the meanings of the Malmgren training for participants to the reader.

Issues of methodological rigour have been taken into account in designing the research methods. The immersion of the researcher in the research settings, and the sharing of the researcher's stories and hence perspectives with the participants form particular and consistent research processes within the epistemological approach.

Overall the chapter sets out to demystify and offer a hermeneutic phenomenological approach to research in the field of actor training, in order to investigate Malmgren's training from the trainee actor's perspective.

CHAPTER 5

EXPERIENCES IN A MALMGREN STUDIO

You must be in relationship to something. Everybody dances 7, 12 & 5, [using the articulation of the 7 vertebrae in the neck, the 12 vertebrae in the thoracic section of the spine and the 5 lumbar spinal vertebrae]. That very relationship [of each section of the spine in movement] is an expression [of a relationship with an object, a person or an idea]. It's specific information.

Malmgren November 2000.

5.1 Introduction

This chapter outlines the specifics of the actor training encountered in a typical Malmgren Studio from the experiential perspective of the trainee actors. In using the term, Malmgren Studio, I am referring firstly to the three research sites where Yat Malmgren's method of actor training is taught. I am also referring more generally to the teaching of Yat Malmgren's method of actor training as it has been propagated through Malmgren's appointed trainers. This chapter establishes the traditions of the conventional ways in which Malmgren's acting technique has been taught, providing the context in which the practices and languages occur. The chapter also acknowledges however that the pedagogical methods described here may not be the only ways in which Malmgren's technique is disseminated. This chapter is the precursor to the phenomenological research on embodiment in Malmgren's technique, formulated in Chapters 6, 7 and 8. This chapter reveals the systematic actor training processes initiated by Yat Malmgren and undertaken by actors training in his technique.

The descriptions of the training process are illustrated through data from transcriptions of interviews with actors in training, Malmgren trainers and Yat Malmgren himself, in order to create rich and empathetic images of these experiences. The actors in training quoted in this chapter are the research participants, with names protected through the use of pseudonyms[1]. The narratives offered are from both the focus group transcripts and the individual interview transcripts as outlined in Chapter 4, using an ethical practice as set in the ethics application approved by the University of Western Sydney. In offering experiential descriptions of the workings of a Malmgren Studio, this chapter adds to Chapter 3 in distinguishing this Malmgren actor training technique from other systematically taught actor trainings. This chapter adds to the over-arching metaphor of understanding of Yat Malmgren's work offered in Chapter 1, that of a pebble dropped into a body of water creating ever widening circular ripples. A first ripple of contextualisation of meaning of Malmgren's technique was set out in Chapter 2, offering the actor training technique as inheriting its language and meaning in part from the writings and practices of Rudolf Laban. A second ripple or circle from the centre of the pebble's splash was established in Chapter 3 (See Figure 3.1, p. 60), placing the Malmgren technique in the context of one of many complex embodied actor training techniques, offered by theatre training institutions. In this context the Malmgren actor training enables actors to develop skills in creating characters for representation in theatre, film and television. References for this chapter, necessary to contrast the Malmgren method with other acting techniques include not only Australian literature referring to actor training, but also literature from the USA and the UK. All three countries share a cultural inheritance where the dominant genre in theatre, film and television is realism and their actor training processes for the development of realistic characterisation are, on the whole, similar to one another.

This chapter begins by outlining the field of performance training in Australia. Then follows a brief description of pedagogical methods employed through Malmgren's actor training and in particular the training directed by the author. Then, with transcript data from the research participants, the chapter charts a sequential development of Malmgren's actor training, through six steps. This six-step process has never been elucidated before. These categories, which emerged from the research and are embedded in Malmgren's teachings are newly developed by the researcher. Acting students' experiences of the Malmgren technique are investigated and compared to theories developed by other performance theorists to augment the

---

[1] Research participant profiles using pseudonyms are available in Chapter 4.

argument that Malmgren's actor training technique offers the possibility of a transformation of action and consciousness in trainee actors.

Heritage from Laban
Actor Training for Theatrical Realism

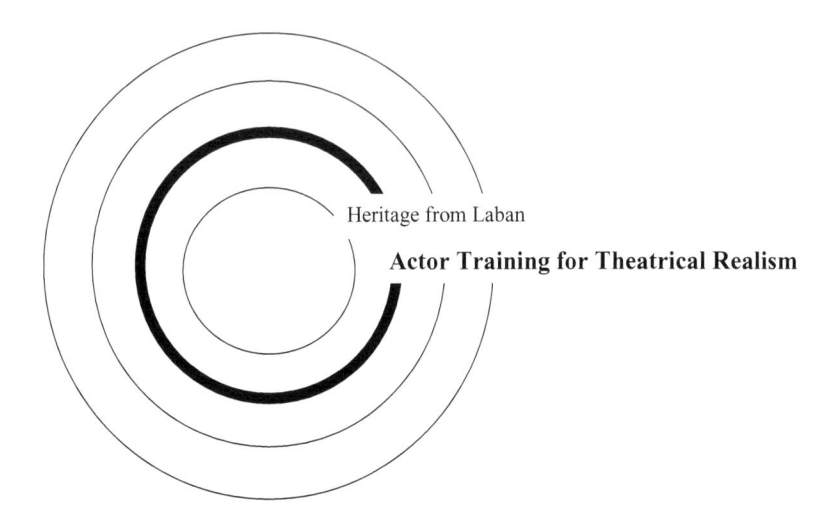

Figure 5.1 The Second Ripple – Contextualisation of Yat Malmgren's actor training: a system for theatrical realism. (See also Chapter 3, Figure 3.1, p. 60)

5.2 Australian performance training

At the post-schooling level, courses in performance and acting in Australia are available through universities and through public and private vocational and educational training institutions, of which Australia's Technical and Further Education system, commonly known as TAFE, is the largest. Students also enter the film, television and theatre industry straight from high schools, including performing arts high schools. Courses for specific skills such as acting or acting for camera are also readily available in major cities for those keen to avail themselves of these skills, whether they are intent on working professionally or not.

The Australian federal government's Department of Education, Employment and Workplace Relations (DEEWR) website (2008) lists 17 universities that offer bachelor degrees in Performance, Performance Studies, Acting, Theatre,

Theatre Studies, Dramatic Arts and Drama Studies. The number of tuition hours in these degree courses dedicated to the acquisition of acting skills varies extensively. Most university degree courses in these areas, apart from those offered through the principal state vocational theatre training institutions such as NIDA, QUT[2], VCA and WAAPA[3], do not offer systematic actor training. The courses offering three years of actor training in degree courses, apart from these at the tertiary institutions mentioned previously, are not immediately apparent. Many, such as the degree at the University of Wollongong in the Bachelor of Creative Arts (Performance) or the Bachelor of Arts (Acting for Screen and Stage) offered at Charles Sturt University in Wagga Wagga, have maintained their practical course offerings in acting through their historic pedagogical development rather than through any systematic federal planning regarding actor training. As Jane Woollard (2002), the Artistic Director of the Union House Theatre at the University of Melbourne, has argued in *RealTime* (2002, p. 43), with regard to actor training in tertiary institutions, including the premier institutions,

> Since these schools are relatively young in terms of the history of Australian tertiary education, their overarching vision and curricula have been formed by their staff.

Woollard speaks of a 'genealogy of method' that is handed from teacher to student actor, suggesting an apprenticeship model. She implies that acting techniques offered at each tertiary institution reflect the ways in which each teacher was trained, either as an actor or as a director. John O'Toole (2002) suggests that another stream of practical knowledge in performing in tertiary institutions has traditionally come from drama educators. However Tony Knight (Mill 2002, p. 16), the Head of Acting at NIDA, who was trained at Drama Centre, London in its Directing course, states in an interview in the journal of the Media, Entertainment and Arts Alliance, *Equity*:

---

[2] Queensland University of Technology, in Brisbane, offers a Bachelor degree in Acting and Technical Production through its Faculty of Creative Industries.
[3] Western Australian Academy of Performing Arts is an institution within Edith Cowan University in Perth. WAAPA offers both diploma and bachelor degree courses. The Acting course is a Diploma course whilst the Musical Theatre course is in a Bachelor of Arts degree.

I don't hold as firmly to "The Method"[4] as I once did. It's a reflection of NIDA's approach which is not dogmatic but more catholic and diverse. There are different types of actors and different types of plays and there are therefore different approaches to acting. I still teach my own method which is based in Stanislavski and influenced by American [based] teachers such as Stella Adler, Uta Hagen and Michael Chekhov. But what the students get the most from me is the work of Yat Malmgren and Rudolf Laban – a European approach. So like most teachers, what I teach is a hybrid of influences I've made my own.

Knight clearly has embraced a wide set of practices rather than holding to his original tradition. This kind of hybridity in the approach to the teaching of acting is common as a mode of synthesising the disparate acting methods that teachers have encountered throughout their careers. Lindy Davies, who was Dean and Head of Acting at VCA from 1995 to 2006, also uses a self-created method. This method blends her experience of the work of Peter Brook, Jerzy Grotowski and Kristin Linklater as well as her work with the Australian Performing Group (APG)[5] in Melbourne in the 1970s (Woollard 2002, p. 43). Professor Julie Holledge, Director of the Drama Centre, Flinders University, having trained at Bristol in the UK, emphasises both analysis of text, which is a standard study in acting schools and an essential element of British actor training, as well as the development of highly disciplined physical skills, an area often less well attended to (Woollard 2002, p. 43). In an interview in *Equity*, on the subject of actor training, Aubrey Mellor (Macauley 2003, p. 14) then Director of NIDA commented that,

> one of the problems is that action-playing has gone out of fashion. Everything seems to be focusing on feeling and *impulse* and I keep thinking, "Well, if everybody's doing that what is actually *happening* in the play?" You know? All this vaguery! ... I can't get away from the necessity of action playing. We need actors who can play actions

---

[4] Knight here is referring to the Stanislavski System, the most prevalent form of systematic actor training offered in Australian actor training courses.
[5] The Australian Performing Group was Melbourne's foremost alternative theatre, developing out of La Mama Theatre in 1970 when the APG as it was known moved into the Pram Factory in Carlton. The APG produced amongst its works seminal Australian plays that helped constitute the 'new wave' of Australian Theatre until the company's closure in 1981.

specifically; actors who can play clearly and cleanly. Too often we just seem to have a lot of things just 'happening' between them.

In essence, Mellor is lamenting the watering down of the Stanislavski system of acting. This point is interesting in itself, indicating that theatrical skills developed for realism have diminished as other styles of contemporary theatre have flourished. Mellor's remarks emphasise that teaching and directing staff at NIDA are often using techniques influenced from popular theatrical forms. In hunting for any uniquely Australian method of actor training it is apparent that as yet major influences on methods of training in tertiary institutions are derivative of international methods.

The Malmgren method has a clear developmental genealogy. In most cases teachers of Malmgren's method in Australia have been taught by Yat Malmgren, himself. The degree of hybridity in the teaching of Malmgren's method, the method's integration with other acting methods, is perhaps less pronounced than in other actor training methods, due to Malmgren's procedures for legitimising teachers of his work. The following section of the chapter outlines a typical way in which Yat Malmgren's actor training technique proceeds. Whilst Malmgren's actor training technique has a place in performance training in Australia it is predicated on the traditions of the individuals who teach it rather than pedagogical imperatives. With lack of written documentation, and despite the Malmgren technique's clearly defined systematic training, the presence of the Malmgren technique in Australian actor training is at this point in time precariously situated.

5.2.1 Teaching Malmgren's technique

In a typical setting for the teaching of Malmgren's technique, students are required to work singly, under close observation by a Malmgren trainer. In each studio class students, whether at a full-time acting school or in part-time acting classes are asked to perform scenes taken from their own lives, or written texts. Scenarios presented must have been written and/or rehearsed previously and any other characters in the scene must be imagined in performance. In other words in Malmgren's technique actors work alone in space with imaginary contacts that, although unseen, have been given their own text and parts to play. This process emphasises the use of the *kinesphere*, characters being related to as ideas, placed in space, rather than sensations. This process demands that students become expressive and selective in their use of the performance *space*.

In my own teaching of Malmgren's method, performed scenarios meet several requirements. Firstly, the actions presented must be recognised as being motivated from a particular *Inner Attitude*. Secondly, within each *Inner Attitude*, the *eight basic efforts* or the *eight working actions* are identified, so that students are required to be selective as to which of the *efforts* they are presenting. The recognition of the *eight basic efforts* is a crucial step in the students' selection of scenarios. Students investigate their functional purpose in a scene and remember their movement impulses. Did they express their actions through *Punching* or *Slashing, Pressing, Wringing, Dabbing, Flicking, Gliding* or *Floating?* The students develop a new movement-based vocabulary to investigate action.

Before performing a scenario, acting students are required to present a physical representation of their chosen effort. As in Michael Chekhov's (1985) approach to creating a character through a 'psychological gesture', Malmghren's technique requires students to create physical *efforts* alone on stage before any text is dealt with. These movement-images are performed by actors and then retained as kinaesthetic memories throughout a scene. Performed as mimed gestures, these sense memories function to inform all verbal and physical action in a scene. These are observed carefully, noting how capable each student is of creating imaginary sensations. The person presenting the scenario performs their chosen *effort* whilst matching a vocal energy production from their text to each effort or mimed gesture. Laban stressed that efforts can be recognised through the voice (Warburton 1993). Malmgren's technique too, stresses the aural quality of differing efforts. Students learn what it might mean to *punch* vocally or to *dab* vocally and remember how they had voiced their action in real life. All this is demonstrated before performing the scenario itself. James Kemp[6], as the current Malmgren trainer at Drama Centre, London, places particular emphasis on these physical and vocal activities performed

---

[6] James Kemp taught at Drama Centre, London prior to Malmgren's retirement. In 2001 Kemp became the sole teacher of Malmgren's technique there.

prior to any scenarios. These *subconscious motifs* are embodied images of the action that is to be undertaken.

For example in the BBC2 programme, *Theatre School* ('Being There' 1993), the viewers are introduced to Stephanie, a third year student at Drama Centre, London in 1993. Stephanie, in a Yat Malmgren class, is working on a performance of a self-written piece of text. This appears not to be a text based on her own life, but rather a character text, for in this particular scene Stephanie has a north-country accent. She stands alone on stage, next to her simple set of a table and a chair. She tells Yat that her psychological action is 'to flatter' and that she will do so by using the physical motif of 'chucking'. We see her 'chuck' an imaginary light object directly forward of herself three times. Next we see her add to these short, brisk movements three short, brisk vocal expressions. The north-country accent affects the delivery of Stephanie's lines making them much more monotonal than they would appear in text. The quick, direct, dab that Stephanie executes matches her quick, monotonal set of lines. "Hey ya! Eh! Are they new? God! They're a bit flash. Aren't they?"

In this exercise, we the viewers see clearly that Stephanie is *dabbing* both physically and verbally. Later, however in the programme Stephanie returns and we see her performing her *Solo* character of which the previous work had only been a small part. Now the *dabbing* is reflected only in the small section of dialogue, which becomes part of a longer sequence of differing *efforts* that create the wholeness of the character. Within the scenario the *effort* is no longer produced as a mimed gesture, rather it remains more subliminal as a motif underlying the text, or informing the action, a symbolic image of the interaction.

As in the Stanislavski system (Stanislavski 1989) action is the emphasis in all the exercises that students are required to present to Malmgren. "Yes. But what are you doooing?" remained one of Malmgren's catch cries. The aim is not to artificially create vocal energy that mimics the movements of the *eight basic efforts*, but to discover that there are *rhythmic* and *shaped images* that are informing human action.

As Malmgren modelled his teaching methods to his students, the systematic study of *Inner Attitudes*, is undertaken through the performance of recognised actions from acting students' lives, leading acting students through a plethora of experiences. Students are required to begin analysing their actions on the basis of common fields of motivation. For example, motivations that address the world of the senses to gain instant gratifications are classified as those within the *Inner Attitude* of *Near*. Motivations towards solving problems of logic are classified as those within the Inner *Attitude* of *Awake*. Over the years Malmgren varied the order in which students studied the *Inner Attitudes*. One order that he retained for over a decade was to teach firstly *Near*, then *Mobile, Adream, Stable, Awake, Remote*, starting with two *Inner Attitudes* that deal with immediacy and leading to *Inner Attitudes* where motivations are more complex. Only after the study of *Inner Attitudes* were students encouraged to create their own characters using this work. Then Malmgren embarked on a programme, *Solo*, where students self-devised characters with specified *Inner Attitudes*.

Malmgren stated that his systematic ordering of *Inner Attitude* study emphasised the possibility of reassessment of motivations by the actor. In my understanding, for example, the study of *Mobile* may alter an actor's ability to work within the *Inner Attitude* of *Adream*, which also deals with *Flow*. This feedback mechanism may result in the alteration of the actor's relationship to their own body both spatially, in how they position themselves amongst others and in relation to their own sensations. Malmgren's method as in Jung's psychoanalytic technique is a process of change for a lifetime.

In the final years of his teaching Malmgren decided to limit the *Inner Attitudes* under study by trainee actors. The three *Inner Attitudes* containing the *Mental Factor* of *Sensing* became legitimised as being the only three performed: *Stable (Sensing* and *Thinking)*; *Near (Sensing* and *Intuiting)*; *Adream (Sensing* and *Feeling)*. The other three *Inner Attitudes* were incorporated in his method only to the extent as appearing as *Action Attitudes*, created in action through *Externalised Drives*. My own understanding of this progression in Malmgren's teaching was his intense determination to keep acting students constantly present in and aware of the physicalisation of imaginative choices. By restricting the *Inner Attitudes* Malmgren was emphasising further the bodily formation of character.

5.2.2 Teaching Malmgren's technique at the University of Wollongong

My own pedagogical imperatives in teaching Malmgren's technique are primarily to instigate transformative performance experiences that assist the pursuit of life long learning objectives. The Malmgren Studio is an environment where I enable students to openly explore performative actions that reflect the students' creative directions. My teaching can be conceptualised as an interactive dialogue between what the students hope to create or communicate to any audience/community and what skills and knowledge I have to share that can shape their directions. In the process new knowledge is created, new forms of performance emerge, new reflections shape both my own and the students' journeys and new audiences are be reached through our actions. I am able to also use the Malmgren terminology in the direction of theatrical events in my University role.

My emphasis is always on audience reception. The journey through enacting scenarios, scenes and monologues directed by Malmgren's *Inner Attitudes* is about questioning whether an audience receives communication via *Weight, Space, Time* or *Flow*. Students may relate this language to themselves, to characters, to theatrical productions or to genres of performance.

My first imperative is one, as this chapter emphasises, which leads actors in training to consider their expressions of *Weight*. I also stress the immediacy of actions. Over the first two years of the training I concentrate on the *Inner Attitudes* of *Near, Mobile* and *Adream*. In the final year students encounter and create actions and characters where *Space* is a major motivation, as in the *Inner Attitudes* of *Stable, Awake* and *Remote*. In each session of training students are required to work through a set of systematic exercises that demonstrate variations of the *Inner Attitude* under study. They then apply this work to scenes, monologues or to *Solo* (ie self-devised) characters.

In direct opposition to Yat Malmgren's later studio work where he restricted the *Inner Attitudes* to the three concerned with *Sensing,* stating that actors always needed to work with 'the body' (Malmgren 2000), I have retained the studio investigations of the *Inner Attitudes* of *Mobile, Awake* and *Remote*. For me it is vital to experientially illustrate how bodies can be absent from their *Sensing* and to differentiate this from being present to actions based in *Sensing*. I establish an investigation of the *Inner Attitude* of *Mobile* where actions stem from emotional reactivity early in the Malmgren training. My principal sphere of research and interest lies in the *Motion Factor* of *Flow*. Through attention to gesture, vocal qualities, bodily stances and shapes through Malmgren's technique trainee actors can reflect on the ways in which they physically link themselves with or separate themselves from others and their own objectives or sense of self. *Free* and *Bound Flow* do not have precise definitions, however the process of being involved in *Flow* is termed in Malmgren's actor training technique as *Adapting*. The definition for *Adapting* is given as, 'The extroverted adjustment of oneself with the outer world and the introverted relating of one's conscious self with the subconscious' (Malmgren 1979). The notion of *Flow* will be considered more fully in Chapter 8 (pp. 257-261). The only definition given by Malmgren of *Flow* was 'the feeling of viscosity of movement' (Malmgren 1979). *Flow* is definitely one of those areas where Malmgren's teaching was through an oral process. However my methodological approach to bringing *Flow* (which will be discussed further in Chap. 8) to a differentiated awareness of the performer establishes new ways in which Malmgren's technique can be applied to a sphere which, whilst encompassing actor training for realism, reaches beyond this to demand a more holistic investigation of the ways in which bodies communicate with audiences.

In all of this training I endeavour to create an environment where all performed actions by the trainees are considered with acceptance, with critical insight that is immediately reflected to the trainees, and with an established set of protocols to ensure that all students are regarded with equal worth and respect. Creating an environment where trainee actors respect each other's work is a vital element in this method of training, where the training demands high levels of shared intimacy.

The next section of this chapter reflects the experiential journey that trainee actors undertake in the Malmgren training.

5.3 The experiential journey of Malmgren's technique

This chapter moves now to a descriptive journey through the Malmgren technique. Malmgren's method has been claimed by its proponents to be a transformative systematic method of actor training. Vladimir Mirodan (1997), the current Director of Drama Centre, London, highlights the structural nature of this transformative process in his thesis, 'The way of transformation: The Laban-Malmgren system of dramatic character analysis'. Mirodan (1997, p. 196) attributes the transformative abilities of the Character Analysis training 'to the way in which all of his (Malmgren's) students have learnt to become conscious of their sensations'. In the following sections of this chapter I propose a six-step systematic process in the Malmgren training of an actor that allows trainee actors to differentiate sensations and to apply this heightened differentiation to the interpretation of characters in text. My argument for this process is grounded in the research data and arises from it. The proposed six-step transformation melds with the throughline of the thesis, examining the Malmgren method of acting training as a means of awakening and enriching an awareness of embodiment, in order to expand actors expressive capabilities. This six-step transformative process is set out below in Table 5.1 (see also Table 9.1, p. 276 where the table is reiterated).

Transformative Actor-Training Processes in the Malmgren Technique (See also Chapter 9, p. 276)
1. Expectations
2. First Steps – *Motion Factors* and their *Elements*[7]
3. Considering *Inner Attitudes*
4. The Awareness of Being Viewed
5. The Beginnings of Transformation through Sensation
6. The Self-Reflexive Actor: *Externalised Drives* and *Action Attitudes*

Table 5.1 Six-step transformative actor-training processes in the Malmgren technique

---

[7] As in previous chapters terminology from the actor training technique of Character Analysis will be designated through italics.

In naming and describing these steps I am aware that components of this experiential journey are not unique to the Malmgren training, nor do they necessarily occur in a linear fashion. However I am also aware that the journey in any actor training is often over two or three years of studying and that these processes create a temporal journey of discovery for the actors about themselves and their bodies in expressive action. This proposed six-step transformation is situated across the years of the actor's training. It begins with student expectations as to what learning acting might be like.

5.3.1 Step 1: expectations

All acting students arrive with expectations about their learning. Malmgren's technique is one of many that a student may encounter. Jewel Walker (Coen 1994, p. 2), from the University of Delaware's professional theatre training program explains,

> To actors, it looks as if their job is to make up a character, and hope that the director can then shuffle them around so that a play may get conjured somehow. That's to some degree their heritage, whether they've ever been instructed in it or not. It's the way everybody thinks.

Walker, a renowned American movement and acting teacher, suggests this expectation is the common approach to acting that he is required to reshape in order to train actors for present day theatre. His alignment with bodily-based processes allows him to lead his students away from this make-believe view of acting. However, it is still common for students of acting to believe that acting, if not make-believe, at least consists of imitation. As recently as 2005, Robert Brustein (p. 1) suggests that imitation of other actors' styles is a legitimate means of learning to act. Walker's point however is that any actor's body has its own integrity. Expression, rather than imitation, may be viewed as emerging from real and imagined stimuli that create unique responses through each performer's body. The Malmgren work situates the processes of acting in the exploration of the actor herself, in her bodily actions.

In the following quote, Alex, an undergraduate Performance student at the University of Wollongong's Faculty of Creative Arts, illustrates the divergence between her romanticised notions of studying acting and the reality of it.

> I did have romantic, idealised visions of what an acting course would be like; it would get intense, and that's something I found appealing. But then when I was here and going through stuff like that, it didn't really click that that had anything to do with my romantic ideas of how positive and wonderful an experience that could be because it wasn't really. It was quite uncomfortable. The training has taught me, experientially rather than intellectually, what it takes to bring your own real self to a performance. It has taught me how specific each utterance, inflection, and gesture must be, or how specific it is, in real life. Previously I had thought acting could be more intuitive a process – a general emotional wash, a loud voice and then an attempt to own the work the text provides (Alex).

In revealing her difficulties in adjusting to the demands of the training, Alex reveals that the mythical world of performing for the stage is often at odds with trainee actor's experience of it. Alex's reflections on her expectations of acting school reveal the effort she encountered in presenting the specificities of action demanded. Although young actors may be aware that their body, being and experiences are the substance of their craft, working with these perspectives may not match their fantasies. Revealing aspects of oneself can be disconcerting and at times disorienting. The risks taken by actors in training are often to do with revealing private actions in public spaces. It is not simply the comfortable part of the performer's range of actions that are required but also the less revealed range of actions.

> I think I've started in the second year now to actually find the enjoyment of being on stage, which I lost [in first studying acting]. I mean when you're in the amateur world you're doing something because you're enjoying it and it's for you. Whereas, I think what they [Christopher Fettes and Yat Malmgren] start to make you understand is that you're giving and it's all about affecting the audience, not just having a good time

> yourself. You've got to give yourself to the audience. You know what you have to do, but when you sit down and actually think, "Shit! I've got to do this, this and this." You start to find the whole process quite upsetting (Danny).

Danny's response is not unusual for a novice in any acting course. In expressing the dislocation between his previous acting experiences and those in his training, Danny highlights the demands of a course in professional acting. Danny's initial loss of desire for performing, having entered the Malmgren training, reflects his confrontation with the deeper considerations of performing a role, rather than it simply being for his own enjoyment.

Kathleen Tolan (2004, p. 1) in examining the training at the Actors Center in New York writes,

> It is in the work of the actor that we experience the careful unpeeling of layers of intention, resistance, identity and desire; the release into one's wildness; the delineation of a gesture; the refining of physical and mental powers to support the leap to Shakespeare's verse or Beckett's silence; the extension of the self to the fictional character who rises from the page to create the alchemy of the theatre.

Malmgren's processes have this 'unpeeling' of actors' motivations in common with other methodological systems of actor training. The concentration on the actor is paramount; the need for reconsideration of action, instinct, resistances to action and sense of self forms the pathway of the training. The act of performing requires both physical and mental skills that test the actor's dedication to the task.

5.3.2 Step 2: *Motion Factors* and their *Elements*

In a Stanislavskian training, which is perhaps the most clearly identified systematic means of training actors for realism in Australia's actor training programmes, students use improvisations to comprehend the experiences of the characters that are studied. Malmgren's technique begins not with improvisation, but with the specifics of re-performing actions taken from the trainees' life circumstances. In a typical Method approach to training, a student actor may begin with a set of imaginary circumstances from which they are then directed to search for realistic responses. Malmgren's technique begins with events from the lives of the performers. Rather than setting the circumstances of a character in order to analyse action, the actions analysed are taken from the performers' lives.

These actions, that students have been personally involved in, are analysed through differentiating motion factors in the physical behaviour of the individual actor. As indicated in Table 5.2 Laban's *Motion Factors* of *Weight, Space, Time* and *Flow*, as first indicated in Chapter 2 (see Table 2.1, p. 29), are investigated through the oppositional elements of *Strong* versus *Light; Direct* versus *Flexible; Quick* versus *Sustained;* and *Bound* versus *Free*. Rather than setting the circumstances of a character in order to analyse action, actions that students are familiar with are analysed according to physical factors viewed by an audience.

MOTION FACTOR	CONTENDING ELEMENT	YIELDING ELEMENT
Weight	Strong	Light
Space	Direct	Flexible
Time	Quick	Sustained
Flow	Bound	Free

Table 5.2 Laban's *Motion Factors* and their *Elements*[8] (See same Table 2.1, p. 29)

As set out in Table 5.2 Laban's descriptive *elements* applied in Malmgren's actor training technique express the following *Motion Factors:*

- *Weight* in Malmgren's technique refers to the impact of an action on another And refers to the dynamic qualities of the performer.
- *Space* refers to the direction in which the body of a performer moves to play an action as well as how the body moves about its own axis. *Directions* in *Space*

---

[8] The information in this table is available in Yat Malmgren's Character Analysis lecture notes (1979-2002) from Drama Centre London.

- are the ideas that send body/minds on journeys.
- *Time* delineates the rhythm in which an actor performs an action.
- *Flow* indicates how interconnected or how separated the action is from any previous action.

Basic training in the Malmgren system of actor training depends on a working knowledge of these terms. However, these particular terms are not unique to Malmgren's technique and are encountered throughout theatrical and dance trainings and through drama teachings wherever Rudolf Laban's theories have been adopted or incorporated. It needs to be acknowledged that this early step in the Malmgren technique of being aware of the body creating particular *dynamics, shapes, rhythms* and interconnections in action is a recognisable process developed in many performance techniques and acknowledged as stemming from Rudolf Laban's movement theories[9]. In Malmgren's technique the process of recognising and producing differing movement elements as physical expressions is considered as the very start of the journey. Yet often these beginnings ignite in the actor both a recognition of the primacy of the performer's body in theatrical expression as well as the sense of difficulty in discovering means of producing these differentiated movements.

> *It's more difficult than it seems. On paper it all seemed very clear, but on stage it's a little bit more difficult. I don't know whether that's my uncertainties as to my understanding of the work and putting it into practice. I don't know if that's where I'm, coming from when I say that. It was really, really, really difficult. I thought I was being Strong, but I wasn't. I was actually... I was very Light. It's quite...quite difficult to see what you yourself, what sort of qualities you have, whether you're a very Light person, whether you have a Light/Quick tempo. Whereas you might actually think you're a lot Stronger. You think, I must be Strong, but you actually come across as being quite Light* (Roger).

---

[9] For example in, Dezseran, L.J. 1975, *The Student Actor's Handbook*, Mayfield, Palo Alto CA. p. 96, a typical description of Laban's *Motion Factors* and *elements* are named as a Character Quality Chart. In, Barker, C. 1983, *Theatre Games*, Methuen, London. pp. 140-141, a section is devoted to Laban's theories of *space*.

Here, Roger grapples with an essential process of the Malmgren technique, which is the emphasis on what an audience receives from a performer. In this description of an early exercise, Roger shares his lack of certainty about how he is perceived and exactly how he is transacting his actions. The vocabulary of the technique begins to have physically understood or kinaesthetic meanings for the performer. The language of this method, relating to Rudolf Laban's notational system for dance, begins to be associated with experiential sensations of being in physical and vocal action. The technique begins by stressing this awareness of how a performer is perceived to be performing an action, rather than who that character is or in what circumstances she finds herself. Establishing a common kinaesthetically based language becomes a journey of discovery for an ensemble of performers who may have been used to thinking of themselves in more narratively-based or psychologically-based constructs.

In the following example Danny, in the company of Roger, attempts to come to grips with the perplexing situation encountered in the Malmgren Studio when the trainer asks for a demonstration of what appears to be a very straight forward element in action. In this case Danny is discussing his effort in expressing an action in *Sustained Time*. He then reflects on how he is perceived in terms of the *Motion Factor* of *Weight*.

Danny:	When you think you're saying something quite *Sustained*,
Roger:	Yeah
Danny:	it's just a lot of very *Quick* sentences.
	(everyone laughs)
Roger:	You start to realise, well I started to realise, I wasn't <u>doing</u> it. I had to go back and rework it. But also you can't help working on yourself if you like. You're told you're not quite right. "You need to find more strength, more *Strong Intending*. So you can try to do this and try to do that." You certainly firstly do realise what your strengths and weaknesses are and where. And you do look at yourself completely differently - completely differently.

So begins the experiential journey of discovery of the interconnecting relationships between an audience and an actor and the emphasis of the audience's perception of the actor via the actor's body. There are often differences between an audience's perception of behaviour and how the actor perceives herself. The two are intertwined. Danny and Roger, students at Drama Centre London, being interviewed in the above example, laugh at commonly held misconceptions about their performances and clearly identify with the stories of each of their early discoveries about their acting exercises. In the early days of their training Danny and Roger agree through laughter that finding out what it takes to create an action in *Sustained Time* is more difficult than it first appeared. They discover how they are perceived by an audience, and that the particular audience in the Malmgren Studio consists of one another on the same journey.

> The training gives a very specific way of owning the words and charting the emotional journey. But to take it into performance, after *energy productions* and *working actions* have been carefully pinpointed, is often a different matter. I've felt it takes practice, courage, and an acceptance of one's self (Alex).

Alex uses the word 'specific' in describing how she came to comprehend the vocabulary of Malmgren's technique in relation to herself in performance. Since she is unable to see herself the way an audience can she is required to relate what she sees in the studio of others' performances and the response from the Malmgren trainer and to relate that to herself to take that into action. In this extract Alex recognises the role of self-acceptance in enabling her to expose aspects of herself.

Just as Roger in his previous extract reports an understanding of the difference between *Strong Weight* and *Light Weight* in relation to a performance that he has shared with his studio colleagues, so each of the eight elements of *Strong, Light, Flexible, Direct, Sustained, Quick, Free* and *Bound*, are encountered in action in the Malmgren Studio. All *eight Motion Factor elements* are at the same time housed in more encompassing structures relating to the motivation of behaviour, termed *Inner Attitudes* (Malmgren 1963-2002). Chapter 2 (pp. 29-31) introduced the term, *Inner Attitude*, relating each one of the *six Inner Attitudes* to a character's motivations in the areas of perception of *Sensing, Thinking, Intuiting* or *Feeling*. Table 5.3 (see also Table 2.3, p. 30) sets out Malmgren's *six Inner Attitudes*, indicating their formation from a combination of *two Motion Factors*. Rather than thinking of the *Inner Attitudes* in terms of personality types, students are acquainted with the concept of the *Inner Attitudes* through the investigation of movement. Whether characters are driven by *dynamic* movements or by ideas that move them in certain *directions*, whether they are *rhythmic* in their movements, *flowing* or awkward, all become a means of exploring action.

Characters may be understood as being primarily concerned with impacting on others (*Weight*) or with the direction that their actions move towards (*Space*) or with an awareness of a time factor (*Time*) or with their interconnection with others (*Flow*). Combinations of *Motion Factors* create the *Inner Attitudes*. Each *Inner Attitude* may be understood as representing a particular type of character, a personality type who functions via particularised movements, in order to achieve certain outcomes. Characters with these various *Inner Attitudes* may also be viewed as being motivated into action for specific reasons.

INNER ATTITUDE	MOTION FACTOR	MOTION FACTOR
STABLE	Weight	Space
MOBILE	Time	Flow
NEAR	Weight	Time
REMOTE	Space	Flow
AWAKE	Space	Time
ADREAM	Weight	Flow

Table 5.3 Malmgren's *Inner Attitudes* and their *Motion Factors*[10]

Early on in the Malmgren training, a student may be wrestling with an understanding of *Motion Factors*, as well as being required to consider the motivations that produced the actions that she is performing. Since the performances

---

[10] The information in this table is available in Yat Malmgren's Character Analysis lecture notes (1979-2002) from Drama Centre London.

are from the students' own lives, the motivations considered are not imaginary but an encounter, a consideration of why they behaved the way that they did. The Malmgren technique invests in a personal comprehension of already performed action. Its emphasis is on revealing behaviours to the conscious apprehension of actors and locating this arena as the wellspring for the actor's development of skill.

5.3.3 Step 3: considering *Inner Attitudes*

The response by trainees to the concept of *Inner Attitudes* is varied. The idea of different character types can be appealing, like a psychological puzzle. On the other hand actors in training can respond to the Malmgren framework of *six Inner Attitudes* as a restrictive category of character types, a set of stock characters. Some performers immediately believe that considering types will restrict their performance, others that the concept will be used to restrict them personally.

For those that openly consider and work with the technique, it presents some immediate means of thinking about texts for performance, about ways of investigating character, action and modes of performing. Like any embodied systematic learning it requires an adaptation of thought, sensation and feelings.

The response to Malmgren's construct of *Inner Attitudes* is illustrated by two differing examples from the data. The first response is from Bella, a student at Drama Centre, London, who is passionately attracted to the construct and then a second response from Megan at the University of Wollongong, who takes a more probingly thoughtful approach to the notion of *Inner Attitudes*.

I straight away just kind of fell for it. I questioned it in terms of thinking about it, but I never questioned whether I actually believed in what - from the start I just instinctively thought - because it's so wonderful and so brilliant! I think a lot of people, we've all thought these things, but he's [Yat] nailed it down. You know people have perception. The fact that you can categorise these things -thinking about psychology and what drives people, and what people want and why they want it, that kind of thing. Just the way he's formulated it just made sense. Just straight away it made sense to me (Bella).

Bella's enthusiasm for Malmgren's structure of the *Inner Attitudes* is typical of many actors meeting this work for the first time. Many find it fascinating, talk of it excitably, speak of it with their friends and family as well as using it in consideration of characters in scripts. The basic essentialism of the categories, intended by Malmgren, often does not present a problem to performers, who are willing to play with a diversity of models of performance. In a time of eclecticism, performers are often willing to use the concept of the *Inner Attitudes* as much as a metaphor as any kind of literal 'truth'.

> The Yat work has also given me a scientific system that can deconstruct and demystify something as seemingly incomprehensible as acting. The language system and the signifiers used by the technique are as arbitrary as any taxonomical system. They are only intended for ease of communication. To name the *Inner Attitudes*, and identify the *Motion Factors* etc. is not to negate the fact that everything always exists in degrees. Each performer will sit differently in each of the *Inner Attitudes* and express each of the *Motion Factors* according to his or her body (Megan).

Megan has rejected the idea of this construct of *Inner Attitudes* as 'truth' and is yet firmly approving of the ability of Malmgren's method in assisting the process of acting. For Megan, the Malmgren system is simply a language to assist an actor in speaking about and comprehending acting. For her, there is no need for an *Inner Attitude* to represent the core of a person, a fixity of a personality type. Instead she sees the *Inner Attitudes* as part of a technique to communicate about degrees of physically expressed *elements*.

In an interview for this thesis, David Tyler, one of the Malmgren trainers in the Acting course at the Adelaide Centre for the Arts, spoke of the Malmgren training's distinct value for directing actors. Malmgren's method provides a common language that can be used between trainer and student, director and actor. At the Adelaide Centre for the Arts, Yat Malmgren's teachings are called the Laban technique, although as indicated in Chapter 2, Rudolf Laban never used the methods developed by Yat Malmgren for actors.

> One of the best bits about Laban is the fact that it is a taxonomy. It is a way of being able to speak, of being able to articulate very precisely. Words can be slippery and ambiguous. A director will say, "Oh. You know what I want." They will talk about the emotional content of the scene. They'll say, "He's very sad.", but what does sad mean? It means so many things. But if you say to an actor, "The character is *Strong* and *Bound*", they know exactly and precisely what that means. At the very base of it the character is *Strong* and *Bound* and there can be no mistaking that. That's a body thing you experience. You don't learn in your head what *Strong* and *Bound* is. It is not an intellectual concept. *Strong* and *Bound* is a physical attitude (David Tyler - Director & Malmgren Trainer).

Actors, themselves, can use the *Inner Attitudes* for clarification of their performances. The *Inner Attitudes* allow an actor to make choices within ranges of actions that provide cohesion. The actor with this degree of self reliance is able to relate in a less dependent way on any director and communicate more effectively with a director by having clear constructs of the character already in mind. The categories of the *six Inner Attitudes*, representing six differing modes of dealing with reality, or perhaps six differing modes of perception, can be seen as a tool or a performance device. The *Inner Attitudes* are useful to delineate the differences between the characters in any one text rather than as a reflection of human behaviour as a whole.

> It's a vocabulary. It's a set of labels. You say that to somebody and they go, "Oh. How reductionist!' I couldn't imagine being confined to that!" But you have no idea what the system is really about if you think it is confining. You don't know how liberating it is. Actors don't often perceive the number of choices that are possible. They make a decision about a piece of text and the way this person is and when the director says that is not what they want, the actor can't see that there's any other choice but the one they've made. They can't even examine the choice because they don't know what the choice was in the first place (David Tyler - Director & Malmgren Trainer).

In presenting the *six Inner Attitudes* to performers in training, it becomes clear that choices are critical in Yat Malmgren's technique. These choices are fundamental to the interpretation of characters in a text. The choices presented in the training, through the *Inner Attitudes*, also create questions about the habitual choices that performers make in rehearsals and in daily behaviour. Playing the same choices of action in characterisations is seen critically, through the study of Malmgren's technique, as opting for easy and instant solutions to acting. However habitual choices are often what actors can use, as Jamie Horton (Tolan 2004, p. 2), a member of the Denver Center Theatre Company states,

> In the ever-shortening rehearsal periods, all too often you make leaps to familiar places.

Andy, a student from the University of Wollongong's Faculty of Creative Arts, recognises the difficulties of extending his range of performative choices. He didn't want his options in performance to be 'the easiest thing' or 'the way Andy always does stuff'. Instead he describes below his choices when under intense rehearsal stress.

> I had to [use Malmgren's technique]. I had five characters in *Lulu* [by Wedekind] and I was in *Twelfth Night* (at the same time). So I was between two rehearsals the whole time. The first thing that I did was to break them down into types - *Adream, Mobile, Stable, Near,* and all that straight away. I always had Orsino as *Adream*. I always looked at them on paper as that. I had to. It was the only thing that helped me to distinguish between them. That helped the physicalisation as well. It was the starting point. I had to use Yat from there, from the start (Andy).

Malmgren's *Inner Attitudes* proved a useful tool for Andy in a demanding and highly stressful performance environment. Apparently Andy feels that he can create a range of differing characters without compromising his integrity as an actor who produces more than stock performances.

5.3.4 Step 4: the awareness of being viewed

Performer and American academic, Shannon Rose Riley (2004), in her article, 'Embodied perceptual practices: Towards an embrained and embodied model of mind for use in actor training and rehearsal', grapples with the duality of the Cartesian model of western performance and the impossible split between the performer's understanding of herself as a creative mind 'inside' a body that is viewed. Riley (2004, p. 446), in her explication of the Japanese movement form of *butoh*, critiques western performance practices as lacking a language to encompass the gap between the mind/body split.

> The question of whether the character is created in the mind or in the body parallels the question of whether the image is located in the mind or the body. The problem of whether the actor's emotion is motivated internally or externally parallels the question of whether the image is inside or out. They are caught in the same bind. Within the Cartesian model of the mind/body split it is nearly impossible to talk about different relationships between image, mind, and body, or to think of images as anything more than representations. Thus, in the West we often continue to describe visualization as a kind of mind over matter.

As described in Chapter 3 the most prevalent western actor training, using Stanislavski's concepts of objectives and through-lines of action, can take this mind over matter approach to the actor's body. Even contemporary versions of this training, as for example in Declan Donnellan's (2002), *The Actor and the Target*, compromise the holistic phenomenon of the body/mind through a Cartesian split where a subject, the actor, is required to be aware of a target, the material objective. However in the Malmgren training, by the fact that actors begin by presenting scenes that have occurred in their life, the problem of playing a representation of an experience is sidestepped. The character is the actor herself, with living images effecting both her movement and her language. Scenarios are presented systematically, working through the combined elements of the *Inner Attitudes* and are watched by the trainer and the other students. It is in this way that trainee actors begin to differentiate differing modes of perceiving reality, and how these affect the whole body/mind.

For instance, a set of *Near scenarios* would start with actions that are *Strong* and *Quick* and then move on to actions that are *Light* and *Sustained*, *Strong* and *Sustained* and finally *Light* and *Quick*. Each of these exercises requires a differing tempo of action from the actor. At the University of Wollongong's Faculty of Creative Arts, scenes involving actions as part of the *Inner Attitudes* are presented, with one or two *Inner Attitudes* explored in depth in each university session. Since the character created is the performer herself at some remembered point in her history, the image the actor is working with is definitely in Shannon Rose Riley's understanding an 'inner' one. The text doesn't exist until the performer brings it to light. The identity of 'the character' is entirely constructed by the performer. However this text is also embodied, allowing the performer herself to reflect on the elements presented. If the image does not translate into precise action then the scenario will not be adequate as an expression of the *elements*. The balance or integration of mind/body allows performers to stand in a remembered place and time and respond kinaesthetically to the imaginary circumstances as outlined in the scenario.

In the next example Megan, the youngest research participant from the University of Wollongong, finds that her relationship to her remembered images of herself are not at all as she expects. Having grown up on a south coast commune, Megan has been unaware of an embodied self that is separate from her previous environment.

I think it's been a big journey for me to recognise that my body is me ... I would produce something and I'd be shocked that I would be crying or that it was not what I thought it would be. I didn't know what I was going to produce. I didn't have the independent thought or action. I just sort of thought everything was part of a group and everything came from somewhere else and I was just part of that ... I find it even weird looking at myself, like watching the video. I know that I wiggle. They tease me. I wiggle. But it's not easy to look at - looking at so much movement, so much unawareness (Megan).

Megan is shocked to find herself viewed by an audience in her training. Identifying herself with the land and with the group of people she shared that land with, she has never considered herself as her body, or as an individual entity viewed by others. She is surprised to find herself crying in exercises when she never intended to do so. She finds viewing herself, even on the video taken to record the participants' responses in this research, as unnerving. She has been unaware of her idiosyncratic movements and awakening to an awareness of these has been difficult for her. In this awakening of being viewed Megan is for the first time encountering herself as an individual entity separate from her previous landscape.

Perhaps the steepest learning curve for the trainee actor in training for performance in the Malmgren technique is the dawning realisation that the audience of peers and friends can read the scenarios presented of the students' life stories as if they are representations. This notion of reading the body as a representation has grown in prevalence in western forms of theatre since the advent of semiotics. The philosopher Terry Eagleton (1998, p. 158) is particularly critical of this movement labelling it as 'the new somatics'. He refers to the desire to semiotically read the signage of the body as risking 'dispelling subjectivity itself as no more than a humanist myth' (1998, p. 160). Despite the audience being aware of the consciousness of the bodies on stage, western audiences are taught, through textual analysis, to read theatre as if watching bodies as representational objects (a theme which is further explored in Chapter 8). Many young people used to performing have already trained their bodies to be a pleasing object for audiences' sensations. They have learnt to speak clearly, to groom themselves in a manner that takes account of their being viewed, and they have often disciplined their actions to present only what they want seen. Moreover, the actor is often partially emotionally protected from this encounter with the objective nature of their bodies, through the safety of the idea of character existing separately from the actor. "It's not me! It's my character!", has become a humorous catch cry satirising actors who invest everything in a concept of character to evade the realisation of their own physical presence on stage.

In the Malmgren technique the body is representing the performer's actions at a previous point in her life. There is no psychic protection from the construction of a character; it is clear that there is only the actor, herself, in performance. This immediately brings the Cartesian mind/body split into question. For the performer, the scene presented is rich in the imagery of remembered sensations, kinaesthetic experiences, and interconnected thoughts and feelings. The 'reality' of these enacted memories is never under question. The onus is on the Malmgren trainer to perceive, to comprehend and to honour the efforts of the trainee in being connected with these memories in action. However what is received of these memories is under question. What an audience receives is only what is expressed. A Malmgren trainer may be empathetically aware that there is more going on for the performer that is not being somatically transmitted but the emphasis in the Malmgren Studio is firmly placed on what is viewable. There is probably no stronger message to students that the western concept of representation that so dominates the western perception of performance is at odds with experiential knowledge. The performer becomes aware of how much or how little of her 'self' is being expressed through action; the performer becomes aware that the body that is viewed as her 'self' may not be who she understands her 'self' to be.

> I must concede though that there is a gap of varying degrees, and at different times, between the way one perceives oneself and the common outside perception. It is here that I must say I find it impossible to differentiate between an understanding of myself and an understanding of myself 'as an actor'... The Yat classroom has been where the gap is gently exposed. Watching someone else's is generally endearing; becoming aware of your own is generally embarrassing, baffling or saddening. Ideally it could be laughable - and it was at first - but often we feel too unsafe, like the floor beneath us is crumbling, our sense of ourselves is dissolving (Alex).

Alex is coming to grips with processes of expression. What she sees in others' scenarios is endearing to her, yet she herself, wishes that she could fully 'control' her actions so that none of this very human material could emerge. The desire to create 'mind-over-body' is powerfully strong in most of us who have been brought up watching the body as an object through television, film and video. Alex speaks of the sense of herself dissolving as she exposes herself through Malmgren scenarios. The Malmgren training is facilitating some new constellation as to her understandings of her 'self'.

Shannon Rose Riley (2004, p. 452) weaves the research of neurologist Antonio Damasio into her exposition of the integrated nature of mind and body, of imagery and expression for the performer. The simultaneity of these seemingly separated aspects of performance is now revealed through neurology as interactive and process orientated, as information flows, with 'a polyphony of receptors throughout the organism and environment'. The performer through the Malmgren training is brought into an experiential understanding of mind/body being a process and of imagery/expression being a simultaneous flow. The journey towards these comprehensions can be surprising or even disorientating, however the outcome is always a movement towards a more integrated articulation of expressive action.

Carmel:	Some of the most confronting stuff you ever do is in scenarios, because it's stuff from your real life. You are sharing with this group of people things and usually quite intense things, and more than ... When you're sharing a character you're sharing a story that's written and you're lending yourself to that role. You're not revealing yourself to people that are going to get to know you quite intimately.
Janys:	Anyone got any comments on that?
Douglas:	Oh Yeah. That year was incredible in terms of understanding. It's a privilege really to be in the room with twenty-two people. And everyone is **really** out there and being as honest as they can about their lives at that stage. And the things that I found most interesting, and I don't think I've been able to capture a way of doing it with my writing as yet, is how unpredictable and how quirky people are. You know, like, that's very difficult to get a sense of that in writing or to convey that sense in a script. I don't know many writers that actually can do that.

Not only is the performer alive to the nuances of the 'recalled images' from her performance of previous actions but she is also alive to the 'perceptual images' occurring in the moment, in the process of performing for the audience (Riley 2004,

p. 451). The audience of a peer group in the Malmgren Studio is a powerful transformative tool inherent in the training. Students working singly in the Malmgren technique are brought into an awareness of the presence of the audience. They are acutely alive to the new information flowing from the response of their peers to their performance. Carmel and Douglas, students at the Adelaide Centre for the Arts Acting course, in the above interview extract, share with the researcher how exposed as performers they feel through the Malmgren technique, which is taught intensively in the first year of the Adelaide course. Douglas, who not only is training as an actor but who also writes plays, speaks of the complexity of action revealed through the technique. His understanding is that this complexity or fullness of expression is provoked within the Malmgren Studio.

> The way in which David [Kendall] sets up the room, he creates this U shape, with the chairs around the outside. And there's something about that, which just brings all the energy in. And so every one on the side is facing towards the centre. (gesticulating) Then you've got people out here. He sits up the front here. And the people here are viewing the performer who comes into the middle. You can utilise all this playing space all the way up to the wall, but at times all he needs to do when directing you in a Laban scenario is to go OK, I want you to just, I want you to be here and just stay here. And the way in which that effects your energy, because you're utilising everyone else's energy. Yeah. I mean *Mobile*, it was like the whole room is resonating with nervous energy (Gillian).

Gillian, a student at the Adelaide Centre for the Arts Acting course here discusses the particular configuration of the audience to the performer adopted by David Kendall in his teaching of the Malmgren technique. Not all Malmgren Studios operate using this U-shaped stage. However it is common for the Malmgren trainer to sit in front of the performer, and for the audience to somewhat enclose the performer's presentation, allowing the performer to be intimately aware of her audience. Gillian indicates her awareness of the intersubjective space of interaction between audience and performers when she speaks of the whole room resonating with a particular energy. The example she mentions refers to a set of scenarios working with the *Inner Attitude* of *Mobile*, where perfomers are highly responsive to their surroundings.

Phillip Zarrilli, an Asian martial arts specialist, performance theorist, and director postulates a phenomenological model to understand and theorise about the embodied experience of actors in performance. Quoting the linguistic philosopher Mark Johnson Zarrilli firstly argues that it is difficult 'to express the full meaning of our experience' (Johnson, cited in Zarrilli 2004, p. 653). In the following part of his paper, Zarrilli elucidates a process whereby through proprioception, the awareness of the body's position, muscular placements and tension, the angles of the joints and the body's balance, new motor tasks can be undertaken, as in acting. He discusses how aspects of the lived body disappear in performance, for instance when actors are concentrating on their response to an 'other', whilst transformative new processes of bodily experience appear, for instance in the learning of a text or score of actions. In relation to the performer's body as viewed by the audience Zarrilli (2004, p. 664) argues,

> In performance, the actor enacts a specific performance score that set of action/tasks that constitute the aesthetic outer body offered for the abstracted gaze of the spectator often read and experienced as character in a conventional drama. The actor's body, therefore, is dually present for the objective gaze and/or experience of an audience, and as a site of experience for the actor per se. The actor's body is a site through which representation as well as experience are generated for both self and other. The actor undergoes an experience that is one's own, and is therefore constitutive of one's being-in-the-world, and simultaneously constitutes a world for the other.

This is the process that the Malmgren Studio makes highly visible and conscious.

5.3.5 Step 5: the beginnings of transformation through sensation

As Zarrilli (2004) suggests in his phenomenological investigations of performers' experiences of 'body', the phenomenal or lived body cannot be conceived as simply an object but rather is a multiple set of perceptual orientations.

Zarrilli proposes that a performer can build an awareness of the psycho-physical tasks that constitute the performer as an objectified character for the audience, whilst also becoming subtly aware of more deeply visceral aspects of experience, such as breath, emotional contact, precise proprioceptual placements of the body. The interconnection with more subtle aspects of bodily experience Zarrilli calls the 'aesthetic inner bodymind' (2004, p. 663). He indicates that this is what is developed in performance techniques over time and practice.

Malmgren's technique enables the trainee actor to experience those precise actions or performance scores when there is a tendency for awareness to become separated from bodily awareness. This is often the case in heightened emotional responses to circumstances. It may also occur when the actor's awareness is drawn towards complex thought. Leder (1990) writes of the ways in which consciousness may be embodied or disembodied. Experiences of this nature in the Malmgren Studio enable an actor to locate the direction for further development of acting skills, where as Zarrilli suggests an awareness of visceral interconnections needs to exist whilst being viewed. In the example below Andy, an excellent student of acting, from the University of Wollongong, discusses a scene in a complex text that he considers he performed poorly.

Andy is a student actor who has performed lead roles throughout his three years of study at the University of Wollongong's Faculty of Creative Arts Performance course. One of his third year productions has been Shakespeare's *Julius Caesar*, where Andy has recently played the demanding role of Brutus. Andy has received praise and a lot of positive feedback for his performance, however here he is lamenting that, in a certain specific scene, his ability to fill the role as fully as he could imagine was beyond his skills as yet.

Andy:	My final scenes just before I kill myself, I just couldn't get to how I wanted it to be. I wanted to be more *Bound* - so that - I didn't want to hunt for the emotion. I wanted the emotion to come through the action and it just would never come.
Alex:	So that you didn't even have to move or say anything but you're radiating something to the audience

> Andy: Yeah. And even though I knew in my heart that it had to be like that, it just – Well I deny myself that in real life. I've always walked away from it – That's where the Yat work – I mean that's one thing the Yat work has done for me – made me recognise the parts of my life that I probably do deny myself and to open myself up.

Andy realises, through Malmgren's technique, that when experiencing intense *Bound Flow* he cannot stay in action. Using Zarrilli's (2004, p. 663) terms, Andy is unable to stay in contact with an 'inner aesthetic body/mind'. He can play the action externally: Andy never lost his lines or faltered in the scene where Brutus is considering suicide. Yet at the same time Andy was unable to stay in contact with the overwhelming feelings associated with considering his character's failures. Andy relates this to the closing down of certain behavioural responses in his own life. What was missing on stage is what he denies himself in other circumstances. He recognises the need to open these aspects of his being both on stage and off. Rather than being discouraged about his performance, his realisation allows him to view the problem as a specific challenge. Alex too imagines the possibilities of being totally, viscerally in tune with a demanding stage moment. Again, this imaginative possibility becomes a challenge through the Malmgren technique.

Suzi, in the example below, has travelled to Australia from Japan to study acting at the Adelaide Centre for the Arts. In working through the Malmgren technique she has learnt to express actions in the tempo of *Strong* and *Quick*. She has also understands that a text may be interpreted as a set of performable actions with definite *rhythms* and *impact*. Her metaphor of treating the script as a musical score aligns this technique of training for performance with other movement based performance techniques developed in Japan as hybrids of traditional forms and Western modern dance, such as *butoh* and the method of Tadashi Suzuki where the use of the term 'performance score' is common in describing a set of performed actions or tasks (Suzuki 1986).

> As a performer I realised that I don't have *Strong Weight* ... because I was living in Japan until I was eighteen and I found lots of Japanese women tend to have *Light*

> *Weight* more than *Strong Weight.* I've found Australian women pretty *Strong.* I learnt piano for ten years. Before I couldn't play *Strong Weight* music, but I feel like I've learnt how to play that. Now when I analyse a script I use more *Punching/Slashing* working actions. Yes. I feel more like analysing a score than analysing a script (Suzi).

The two previous examples are of student actors becoming aware of and moving towards transformational possibilities for themselves through the Malmgren technique. The following example is contrasted to this process, with transformation in sensation occurring by the student's effort at attending to the Malmgren process. In the example below, Roger is as yet unaware of the ways in which he is changing as a performer. Yat Malmgren however has commented in a class on how he sees Roger changing. Roger related this incident of Yat's attention.

> Roger: Yat said, he said - It was the end of one lesson and I was asking him about something, I was packing up, getting some stuff from my bag and he said, "Roger. You're becoming much more *Warm*, 'Cool Man'."
> Janys: Cool-Man?
> Roger: Yes. I was like, "Sorry!?" "Yes", he said. "You're becoming much more warm." And then as we were leaving the room he said, "You're becoming much more *Strong* and *Sustained.*" I can't do the accent.
> Janys: You're doing well.
> Roger: He was saying - "It's a constant battle between his *Awake* and his *Adream*, but you're becoming much more *Warm.* You are. I can see you are changing."

Yat Malmgren here praises the change in Roger, who he has teased calling him "Cool man". The need to awaken sensations in performance, so that thoughts and images can transform into visceral impulses is a part of the actor's journey in training. Malmgren has pinpointed Roger's need to step beyond his headspace. In attending to the technique both in classes as well as in Roger's performance of Nikolai in *Enemies*, Roger is beginning to transform his own performative capabilities. He is becoming a more dynamic, a more visceral performer.

The sound is resonating, echoing loudly in this crumbling old room. The paint peels from the walls, the ceiling is stained with damp, the linoleum is worn and scratched. I can hardly hear the actors' words, the balcony swallowing their sound, but I sense their anxiety, as well as their determination to reach for their goals.

Next to me is Reuven Adiv, a seventy-year-old Israeli Method acting teacher. He's from New York, the Strasberg Studio, but he's been here at Drama Centre since I was here. He's always been passionately rigorous about his methods. Always the same processes, the same measured tones, the endless agony of his prolonged rehearsals. Now it is the day before the performance, the last run in this decaying old church, before these students face a barrage of penetrating scrutiny from Yat Malmgren and Christopher Fettes. There are no lights, no special effects, only old props, old furniture, gathered costumes and the task of this mammoth play with all its intricacies to grapple with.

It is Gorky's *The Enemies*; class pitched against class, the willingness to destroy others to protect one's interests, the sensitive mangled in the process, the young disillusioned, the cruel triumphing. The room swims with energies, Gorky's ideas swirling with the students' own longings.

I watch the students who I have interviewed, hoping for their success. Donald, pale and delicate, with what seems a dancer's body, stumbles in through the frosted door, ideas tugging at his body in so many directions that he is at once both comic and complex. Slowly through scene after scene his uncertainties, his angles of propulsion and repulsion, piece together a man willing to betray his own class to win privileges. He doesn't play at being despicable or wheedling instead he is a body that despises its own needs, a body pulled apart by its own longings.

I see suddenly why Yat has called young Roger 'Mr. Cool man', so able to be distant even when being physically present. He is at once compelling and yet dangerous, remarkably self-assured for someone so young.

Bella appears as the play stretches in action over hours, but she loses energy even as she moves. She is an idea of romance, something she has read no doubt, plus her spoken fear of playing an *Adream* character. Her natural vibrancy, the exotic dynamic of her usual presence dissipates and her feet seem hardly to touch the ground. If this is the heroine of the text, she seems to have forgotten that she is both Russian and resistant to the conventions of her class. I am peering through the text it seems to another layer, the actors losing or gaining energies as they either believe or lose faith that their performances can have meaning for the audience.

Danny, who has been in the background in a number of scenes at last emerges in a night setting. There is no night, there is no river, there are no guns. He is a peasant with not one grain of imaginary dirt attached to him. Sometimes Danny seems asleep on stage and I fear for him and what his teachers will make of it.

The sound with its echo plunges me too into a dream. The proximity of Reuven's body trying to will his students into differentiated performances, the pain of the students longing to lose themselves in the life of the play and yet ever conscious of their tasks, my own body in this place, Drama Centre, unaware and struggling to define some direction that seems so outside of myself.

Researcher's Journal 5.1 December 2000. Performance of *Enemies* by Maksim Gorky at Drama Centre London. Afternoon Thursday 7 December.

5.3.6 Step 6: the self-reflexive actor: *Externalised Drives* and *Action Attitudes*

The aim of the Malmgren technique is to allow the performer, through an in depth consideration of action, to construct or interpret textually created characters. In the latter years of Yat Malmgren's teaching, Malmgren concentrated his classes on the students' interpretation of set texts, each text illustrating a variation of an *Inner Attitude*. These texts were on the whole chosen from the classical western canon, from Shakespeare to Ibsen. Malmgren, in my two-day interview in 2001 indicated that the investigation of the remembered and reconstructed scenarios from past events were all for actors to interpret texts more comprehensively. The use of students' lives in the Studio teaching sharply brought into being not only the intensity of characters' desires/wants, the richness of their circumstantial imagery but also a strong sense of the 'other', that person or persons to whom the actions were directed. Text cannot be understood unless it is translated by the performer into situated action, where all the character's circumstances are taken into account.

In my discussions with Yat Malmgren, I unearthed the tenets he used to awaken, in Laban's term, the *Effort* that all of these connections represent for the actor. Malmgren firstly differentiated himself from Laban, who had concentrated on dance and was not as interested in character as Malmgren.

> This is because I wanted to be an actor. And I cannot think an actor not having an inner problem or the character [not having an inner problem]. And I work all the time from a character in the situation, what of course dancers don't (Malmgren 2000).

Malmgren indicated that in dance the text is totally revealed to the audience, whereas in the creation of characters there is information that is concealed from the audience at any given time. Malmgren then went on to describe for me the startling way, after many years of teaching that he had finally understood how the *Inner Attitudes* communicated with the perceived world of the character, including other people. In a unique step Malmgren postulated a figure of eight symbol, a chiasmus or '*cross*', representing any *Inner Attitude's* interconnection with others' actions through the *Externalised Drives*. The Malmgren '*crosses*' are images of bioenergetic loops. Elizabeth Grosz (1994), close to twenty years later describes this flow of body/mind in her model of the Mobius strip. Refusing to dichotomise mind and body Grosz (1994, p. 13) postulates a reconfiguring of corporeality, where bodies display a continuous 'openness of organic processes to cultural intervention, transformation, or even production'. In her model bodies display 'categories of interiority' (p. viii), such as agency and consciousness, but these are expressed corporeally, much as Malmgren had already demonstrated through his practices. Malmgren had first visualised his concept of the 'cross' of his *Externalised Drives* in a dream of two rivers meeting. In the late 1960s in the development of Malmgren's acting technique, the term *Externalised Drives* only existed in minimal references in Rudolf Laban's writings.

Here is Malmgren's (2000) description of this moment of realisation in the development of his technique.

> Malmgren: I can only remember when this seems so confusing.
>
> Janys: I want you to tell us.
>
> Malmgren: Well it was like a vision. I always remember that morning and that place And everything and I suddenly thought - the sort of the Xs - of the *four Externalised Drives,* and I little by little started to see something in it. And I got very frightened because it was so complex, that I thought I understood it but I didn't know in anyway how to be able to express it by words and I got quite horrified. It felt as if, am I going to get, go mad because it became, it hit my head or my brain in such a confusion as if something had split.
>
> Janys: Mmm
>
> Malmgren: And then I tried to then find the bits and pieces in memory of what I had realised, you know. And little by little - It didn't come in a day, or in a week, or in a month, but all the time working on it, working, working on it, until I then realised how they communicated, the outer with the inner and the inner with the outer. So the changes then that that created, the what we call it now, the *four Action Attitudes* within the *Inner Attitude* that could ... Laban wouldn't have heard about it, but after all it was there because of some, some understanding.
>
> Janys: Mmm, so you, you - Is this when you created the crosses?
>
> Malmgren: Yes.
>
> Janys: Yes, and the notion of the *Action Attitudes*.

Malmgren with this dramatic scenario captures his dawning understanding of the complexity of character action and how characters with differing perceptual modes interact with one another and their worlds. Malmgren slowly formulated these concepts, by which any *Inner Attitude* interacts in the world, into the use of *Externalised Drives* in his technique. The *Externalised Drives* grew in importance for Malmgren's, until in the last few years of his teaching these were the fundamental means through which students' were encouraged to examine text.

Examining *Externalised Drives,* students are asked to identify the tactics that they use in action in any scenarios or text to achieve objectives. In a Malmgren

Studio there is a recognition that a character brings some aspect of her body/mind into play with another, either through *Weight, Space, Time* or *Flow*. Rather than examining tactics through the use of transitive verbs (Benedetti, 1986, p.221), which may be understood as operating psychologically, Malmgren's technique highlights that some physical activity takes place to affect another. This physical change may be as small as lifting an eyebrow or twisting a foot, the Malmgren technique hunts for these physical particularities.

Douglas, one of the older students at Adelaide's Centre for the Arts Acting course, explains his own understanding of this basic tenet of Malmgren's of being in expressive action. He speaks passionately of realising the audience's encounter with the actor's body, a theme discussed in the previous section of this chapter. He stresses that it is only through bodily action that any transformation occurs and that it is only through this expressed action that anything is communicated to the audience.

> One thing that I've really sorted out in my mind, over the last two years and having gone from Laban and through second year working with Peter Duncan [At the Centre for the Arts, Acting course], who not necessarily works with Laban, but he definitely talks that language. But he said, "Yeah. You are **doing** something" And that is in a particular way. If you want to say - you can say in an *Adream* way, but you're not anybody else. You're just this **you** doing something in an *Adream* way. And the audience will read your *working actions* and your activities and make their own assumptions. They won't say, "Oh That person's doing *Adream*" because *Adream* is only for your own benefit, to help you get somewhere. The audience doesn't care if you're *Adream* or *Mobile* as long as it has communicated something **to** them (Douglas).

This process of affecting others in Malmgren's technique is plotted or scored by investigating *Action Attitudes* and *Externalised Drives*. Table 5.3 (p. 147) establishes that each *Inner Attitude* consists of two *Motion Factors*. Table 5.4 (p.167) indicates how a third *Motion Factor* can be used in action as an adjunct to an *Inner Attitude*, creating the possibility of four different *Action Attitudes*. These bring differing aspects of a body into action with other characters in order to achieve objectives.

Motion Factors	INNER ATTITUDES					
	Stable	Mobile	Near	Remote	Awake	Adream
Weight		Near Adream		Stable Adream	Stable Near	
Space		Awake Remote	Stable Awake			Stable Remote
Time	Near Awake			Awake Mobile		Near Mobile
Flow	Adream Remote		Adream Mobile		Remote Mobile	

Table 5.4 Malmgren's *Inner Attitudes* and their *Action Attitudes*[11]

In Table 5.4 the *Inner Attitudes* are set across the page. The left-hand column sets the added *Motion Factor*. *Motion Factors* can only be added where they are not a part of the *Inner Attitude* already. The table shows the resulting *Action Attitudes* created by the addition of another *Motion Factor*. For instance, in the top row of the table, *Weight* can be added to the *Inner Attitudes* of *Mobile, Remote* or *Awake*, because these three *Inner Attitudes* are lacking in *Weight*. With the addition of *Weight*, a *Mobile* character can present actions that appear to be *Near* or *Adream;* a *Remote* character can present actions that appear to be *Stable* or *Adream* and an *Awake* character can present actions that appear to be *Stable* or *Near*. These actions chart the journey of the character in text, the thought processes, whilst the underlying motivations are still directed by the *Inner Attitude*. This identifying of *Action Attitudes* indicates how characters move interactively with others to achieve wants.

Externalised Drives are created from the combination of *three Motion Factors* as set out in Chapter 2 (pp. 54-56). Table 5.5 identifies Malmgren's *four Externalised Drives* of *Doing (Exerting and Reacting), Passion (Constructing and Destroying), Spell (Dominating and Surrendering) and Vision (Ideas and Problems).* Each *Externalised Drive* is a combination of the indicated *three Motion Factors*. Malmgren in his previous description of his realisation about action saw the

---

[11] The information in these tables is available in Yat Malmgren's Character Analysis lecture notes (1979-2002) from Drama Centre London.

Externalised Drives as moving through characters and propelling characters into action. So in the latter stages of his teaching, Malmgren emphasised the concept of three of the *Motion Factors* leading to action.

EXTERNALISED DRIVE	MOTION FACTOR	MOTION FACTOR	MOTION FACTOR
DOING	Weight	Space	Time
PASSION	Weight	Time	Flow
SPELL	Weight	Space	Flow
VISION	Space	Time	Flow

Table 5.5 Malmgren's *Externalised Drives* and their *Motion Factors*[12]

Malmgren's principal concern in all his work was for expressive action on stage. He wanted forms of action or behaviour to be filled with meaning. Through the *Externalised Drives* he believed that students could relate to the kinaesthetic sensation of being driven into action with others. He often stressed that others were the obstacles to our wants. He complained over the years that students didn't know how to play actions, that most actors were self-indulgent and didn't have objectives. Malmgren felt that even the identification of *Inner Attitudes* was fraught with the possibility of playing a self-indulgent state on stage instead of producing action. His complex system of the *Externalised Drives* interacting in the form of a '*cross*' emphasised that two *Externalised Drives* create *Inner Attitudes* whilst two other *Externalised Drives* propel the character in action. This became the means through which Malmgren urged his students to consider action, their own action in the world and the action of the characters that they played.

In the following dialogue, Douglas, from Adelaide's Centre for the Arts, Acting course, speaks of the freedom he finds in discovering the use of the *Action Attitudes*. Douglas specifically relates the use of the technique beyond the experience of it in the Studio to the use of Malmgren's technique for interpreting text.

Douglas: Once we got to *Adream* and *Remote* then your ideas started to solidify about

> Laban and you could actually develop a character and explore it. You weren't stuck to just one section of an *Inner Attitude*.
>
> Janys: One variation of the work.
>
> Douglas: Not just a *Strong* and *Bound* or -
>
> Janys: Yes
>
> Douglas: - or *Strong* and *Free*. You could go through a whole range and it even dealt with *Near* (as an outer) or *Mobile* (as an outer). That's when I found the work **really** just exploded. The possibilities of playing one piece of text, they just opened up enormously.

Bella, at Drama Centre, in the next example, also comments on her understanding of the use of Malmgren's *Externalised Drives*. Interestingly, despite being from two different actor training institutions and from two different countries, both Bella and Douglas, from the previous example, came to acting training after previously heading towards studying medicine. Bella left her desires for medical training after her A-levels. The move to acting had greatly disappointed her parents. Douglas had left his medical training after several years of study, to join the Centre for the Arts. Perhaps both these students of Malmgren's technique bring their analytical abilities to these transcribed dialogues in assessing the use of Malmgren's *Externalised Drives*.

> It's more constructive using *Externalised Drives* because it does define it [the text] but paradoxically, at the same time, it moves you away from - "He's *Near*. She's *Adream*" It lets you see the journey. It defines the journey of the character. It's all about their thought processes and their emotional processes and it makes it more real, I think (Bella).

Perhaps the clearest indication of how this process of identifying specific *Action Attitudes* and *Externalised Drives* operates in Malmgren's technique can be identified through Roger's efforts in his acting in Maxim Gorky's *Enemies* at Drama Centre, London. In the example below Roger applies his understandings of Malmgren's system and language to analyse the character of Nikolai. Roger has been working on this production for his second year showing. His in-depth consideration of character takes into account *Action Attitudes* and *Externalised Drives*.

> I think Nikolai [In *Enemies*] is a *Space-stressed Near*. He has got very materialistic wants. He dominates the whole time. On his outer he dominates a lot. He is constantly dealing with *Ideas* and *Problems*. So I thought, well, that means he's *Doing* with *Passion*, which means he's *Near*. Also the fact that his objective in the play is that he'd really love to become Attorney General. He'd like to be recommended by the state to this high position and to use whatever means necessary, whether it's bribing people or whatever he can, to get there. And it's also to hold on to whatever he's already got, not to let the workers take over, which would mean he'd lose his job, perhaps, he'd lose his money, his standing in society. Ah - He's quite a hungry creature (Roger).

Roger has interpreted his character of Nikolai, the assistant Prosecutor in *Enemies*, as a *Near* character, a *Sensing* and *Intuiting* type. He has interpreted the three major *Motion Factors* that Nikolai operates via as *Weight*, *Time* and *Space*, making Nikolai, in Malmgren's terms, a *Space-stressed Near*. Roger speaks of Nikolai as being propelled into action through the *Externalised Drive* of *Vision (Problems and Idea)*. *Enemies*, written in 1906, and set on an rural estate, where a factory strike ends in a death of a land owner, was banned in Russia, due to its author's Bolshevik sympathies. Nikolai, the assistant Prosecutor although drawn as intelligent and thoughtful is condemned by Gorky as being part of an ambitious, bureaucratic class that brutally mete out so called justice against the peasants, whilst actually seeking their own advancement.

> He's [Nikolai's] calculating. He's prepared to kill people, he's prepared to bribe people, He's prepared to take whatever means necessary to, to save his own skin but also to advance his own career and to achieve his own personal gains which he is, as revealed in the third act in the scene with Tatiana, is that he'd like to be the Prosecutor, the Public Prosecutor. He doesn't want to be assistant Prosecutor, he doesn't want to be in the shadows, he would like to be the Public Prosecutor or maybe in ten years time, the Attorney General (Roger).

Roger has recognised the materialistic ambitions of the character that he plays. The two previous transcriptions of Roger's thoughts on his character were drawn from the focus group at Drama Centre for this research. However between that discussion and Roger's individual interview, the second year students at Drama Centre presented the whole play *Enemies*, as their term's work, to the staff and school, including the directors, Yat Malmgren and Christopher Fettes. I was privileged to be present at this performance. Between both interviews, Yat Malmgren has returned to Roger to give him a unique critique of his performance as Nikolai. Despite Roger's efforts, Malmgren has been relentless in pointing out what Roger has missed in his performance. Roger has dealt with the character's use of *Vision* in action; Nikolai uses *Ideas* and *Problems* in argument to advance his own status. Malmgren, however criticises the performance for lacking cruelty. Roger has not been able to capture the ruthlessness of the man. After having put so much effort into his performance, it is difficult for Roger to come to grips with Malmgren's criticism. However in the dialogue below Roger painstakingly endeavours to understand more about his own performance.

Roger: I mean, I think I got too confused as an inner with what he [Nikolai] actually wanted materially. Yeah, yeah because I think inside there might lie a *Mobility*, tremendous *Mobility*. Because if what you see as an outer is a very *Stable*, or is a very cold if you like, unfeeling sort of calculating person, then inside there's got to be a hell of a lot of *Mobility* and I think maybe I missed that because I got confused. I should have, I should have looked at the crosses more carefully. I think, seriously, I think I should have looked at the crosses more carefully. I mean I think I realise that he [Nikolai] works towards, towards *Vision* in *Ideas* and *Problems* as an outer. Because well, because Yat did say, he did say, I just remembered he said, you know, there was, there was, there was nothing inside, there was nothing inside. He said um yeah, and he says you know when I work I work inner to outer. So I think maybe what he was implying then was that I, maybe he was implying that I was working very much from an outer point of view.

> Janys: You misjudged it.
> Roger: I misjudged it in, in confusing his outer action with his inner.
> Janys: Yes, I think that's right.
> Roger: So, so, but at least I know why.
> Janys: Exactly.
> Roger: I mean I think I'd be a little bit more upset if I didn't know why.

Roger is upset. Malmgren's praise or criticism means a great deal to each Drama Centre student. Roger's emotions are revealed in his broken patterns of speech. However he has a structure through which to grapple with his understanding of this fictional being, Nikolai, to whom he has devoted so much of his energy over this term of training. The cruelty of Nikolai, in the suppression of the socialist fervour of Gorky's revolutionary Russia, is a long way away from this student who has moved to London from an outer lying British town to study. However Malmgren's *'crosses'*, his concepts of character and action, expressed as *Inner Attitudes* and *Action Attitudes* and *Externalised Drives*, are able to lead this young man forward. Roger has devoted himself in the performance to the cold justice that Gorky reveals the assistant Prosecutor meeting out to the peasants. Malmgren wanted Roger to reveal more of the character's nasty pleasure in his task. Instead of Roger being left only with a sense of failure, Roger is able to re-examine Malmgren's diagrams for *Near* characters and to rethink what he may have missed.

5.4 Conclusions

This chapter sets out a six-step process embedded in the systematic structure of Malmgren's technique of actor training. Emergent from the research, the six-step description offered by the author follows the format of introducing trainee actors to concepts of *Motion Factors* and their *Elements, Inner Attitudes, Externalised Drives* and *Action Attitudes,* Each structure adds a transformative process to the actor's development through specific considerations of the melding of viewed and experienced sensate impulses, although these considerations may not necessarily follow as a linear process. In the Malmgren technique, character action is envisaged as occurring through heightened sensory communication. Somatic impulses lead to performed action and produce sensory feedback from others. Malmgren's *'crosses'* are an image of two-way transactions between the body/mind and its environment. Whilst it is realised that the steps described may not form a temporal or even uni-directional pathway for an actor in training, they do indicate the possibilities for a widening encounter of the actor's understanding of expressive action in relation to her lived world.

The six steps offered by the author are derived firstly from her own experiential journey, but as well from the data, with the participants' narratives throwing light on the processes under description. Whilst three of the steps are linked decisively with structures embedded in the Malmgren technique, the other three, Expectations, The Awareness of Being Viewed and Transformation through Sensation, reflect processes that could be located in numerous performance practice trainings. These headings could provide the basis for further research into the commonalities of performance trainings where dimensions of learning such as prior knowledge, the impact of audience reception and muscular trainings will always play a part.

The transformational imperative in this chapter sets it aside from functioning only as a description of the Malmgren technique. In using the term transformative in regards to Malmgren's technique, the chapter begs the question of what it is about the actor that has been transformed. The ability to perform actions cannot be considered except in relation to the performer's body and its intimate interconnection with the actor's conception of her conscious self. The training involving the six steps may be considered a journey of redefinition of self, as extending the boundaries of expressive action entails changing the boundaries of habitual actions. The processes of extending the boundaries of choices of expressive action offer the performer insights into functioning in the actor's lived world.

In the following chapters an investigation into embodiment in relation to the Malmgren acting training will be taken up using a phenomenological data analysis. The Malmgren training will be placed in the larger perspective of offering new insights into embodiment in performance and the role that actor training plays in aligning the actor's agency with the material aspects of the actor.

CHAPTER 6

A PHENOMENOLOGICAL ANALYSIS OF MALMGREN'S ACTOR TRAINING TECHNIQUE

If you move without an inner stimulation then you do what one would call an outer, technically. Such movements mean absolutely nothing.

Malmgren November 2000.

6.1 Introduction

The following two chapters investigate the broad parametres of experience encountered by those studying Yat Malmgren's actor training technique. The investigation is conducted through a phenomenological frame, predicated on Heideggarian hermeneutic phenomenological research methodologies. Merleau-Ponty's (1962) re-reading of Husserl's theories of phenomenology will inform the understanding emerging from the data. This research frame can be understood in terms of the embodied experience of the meaning of the technique to actors in training. Consider first the over-riding metaphor of this thesis, Malmgren's image of intentional or motivated behaviour as similar to a pebble dropping into a pond creating concentric ripples. Each ripple can be seen as representing a broader or deepening consideration of intentional action. Each ripple contains ripples within it, so that, in Malmgren's example, as an actor questions the intentions of her behaviour, deeper and deeper understandings of that action emerge. In the same way, this wider phenomenological consideration of the context and meaning of Yat Malmgren's actor training contains all the previously established contexts. Chapters 6 and 7 presume the intentionality of the encounter with Malmgren's technique as an actor training technique for those performers skilling themselves to act in realistic drama. However, this larger picture, or in Malmgren's metaphor, this wider third ripple of understanding, connects the performer with an experience of her own embodiment and the meanings that emerge through that encounter.

Heritage from Laban

Actor Training for Theatrical Realism

Study of Embodiment

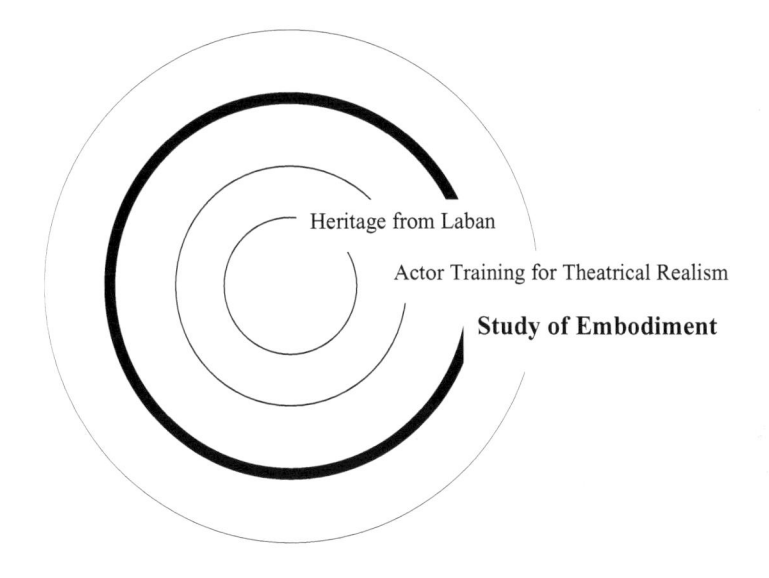

Figure 6.1 The third ripple – Contextualisation of Yat Malmgren's actor training: a study of embodiment.

Analysis of the qualitative data reveals the specific engagement of participants with their bodily experiences of Yat Malmgren's acting technique. In my interviews with participants, their reflections on the impact of the Malmgren technique contain both memories interconnected with their acting training as well as projections towards hoped for outcomes of their training. The participants jointly construct new meanings and understandings of acting as an embodied process through the focus group discussions. These became integrated in the hermeneutic cycle of understanding, interpreting and critiquing.

6.2 The widening ripples of the transformative process

In the six-step transformative process presented in the previous chapter, a trainee actor, through the Malmgren technique, shifts from regarding herself in performance as a discrete 'identity' to understanding herself in performance as an embodied, interactive process of possibilities. Through the phenomenological investigation in this chapter and the next, I align six interview themes, arising from the research interviews, with the six transformative steps set in Chapter 5 (See Table 5.1, p. 139). I view the emerging themes as part of the ontology of the conscious meaning of a performing body in training, using Merleau-Ponty's (1962, pp. 138-139; 1964, p. 42) notions of the lived body, a body, discussed in Chapters 3 and 4, containing the ambiguous interplay of being both subject and object. The six emergent interview themes are understood as the embodied encounter of acting students with the Malmgren acting technique, an encounter which engenders a conscious negotiation with the actor-in-training's 'flesh' (Merleau-Ponty 1968, p. 138). This term designates the potentialities of embodied inter-relations with the world, 'so that we may say that the things pass into us, as well as we into the things' (Merleau-Ponty 1968, p. 123). Merleau-Ponty's term 'flesh' does not refer to matter or to consciousness but rather to 'a sort of incarnate principle that brings a style of being wherever there is a fragment of being' (Merleau-Ponty 1968, p. 139). In other words 'flesh' shows itself as more than material, and forms itself through a chiasmatic relation, which 'implies an imposing and co-present hiddenness' (Hadreas 1986, p. 148).

Whilst links to the process set out in Chapter 5 are present, these next two chapters differ in regarding the Malmgren method of actor training as a means of reflecting on deeper considerations of performance training and embodiment using a phenomenological framework. These chapters explore an ontological process whereby a performer through training may become conscious of, or may become more able to integrate the material elements of the body into symbolic expression. Chapter 6 firstly links the major emergent themes to the six-step actor training process established in Chapter 5. The chapter then introduces a set of sub-themes in the data, using Benner's (1994) methods of phenomenological analysis. The sub-themes are recognised as 'meaningful patterns, stances or concerns... rather than more elemental units such as words or phrases' (Benner 1994, p. 115). In this study I have named the sub-themes to reflect processes of acting, particularly those in Malmgren's acting technique. Chapter 7 moves on to investigating the six major themes or patterns emerging from the sub-themes. These themes and their phenomenological implications are discussed through considering the themes as a six-step process.

The following table (Table 6.1) indicates the connection between the transformative steps and the emergent themes, which will be discussed in this chapter and the next.

Transformative Actor-Training Processes in the Malmgren Technique (Shown in Chapter 5, p. 139)	Emergent Interview Themes/ Phenomenological Understandings in the Malmgren Technique (Shown in Chapter 7, p. 201)
1. Expectations	1. The Actor's *Lebenswelt*: The lifeworld of the actor in training
2. *Motion Factors* and their *Elements*	2. The Phenomenal Body: New understandings of the actor's body
3. Considering *Inner Attitudes*	3. The *Chiasm*: The inextricable link between actor & audience
4. The Awareness of Being Viewed	4. Experiencing The Gap: Whose is the body that is viewed?
5. The Beginnings of Transformation Through Sensation	5. Refusal and 'It': New possibilities of expressive action
6. The Self-Reflexive Actor: *Externalised Drives* and *Action Attitudes*	6. The Transformed Body: The ongoing process of 'becoming'

Table 6.1 Inter-relation between actor training processes and emergent themes

The previous chapter, as indicated by the left-hand side of the table, considers the data from the perspective of a particular actor training process. Using Malmgren's terminology, the six-steps outline the process in Malmgren's training through which trainee actors encounter their bodies to enable specific and unique communication interconnected with an audience. Chapters 6 and 7 consider the actor's growing awareness of embodiment. The right hand side of the table outlines the six themes of embodied 'self' discovery as trainee actors begin questioning how they manifest themselves in the material world. This process leads to self-identification or transformation of embodied expression. The notion of communicating with an audience in this wider context is understood as communicating with others whilst being viewed. In this wider frame the six steps lead to a questioning of action in relation to agency, and processes whereby embodied action is reflective of agency for any participant. This larger framework and the resultant themes have required not only an immersion in the data, but an interpretive leap of empathetic understanding by the researcher. Crotty (1996, p. 3) explains this as 'gathering people's subjective meanings, the sense they make of things'. Each of the themes in Table 6.1 has been named and gathered from the recognition of 27 differing subthemes as exemplified below.

6.3 Gathering the subthemes

The data for this research has been taken from the phenomenological study of participants undergoing training in Malmgren's acting technique at the three chosen actor-training institutions, where the major question being put to each group has been, "In what ways has Malmgren's training shaped your understanding of yourself as an actor?" It needs to be reiterated that this question is not the research question but rather a phenomenological research means of drawing out narrative responses from the participants about their experiences in their Malmgren Studios. The question put to second and third year full-time students of the Malmgren technique, in three-year actor-training courses, elicited a plethora of responses. Overall, 17 individual interviews were transcribed as well as three focus group discussions, with 7 participants in the group at the University of Wollongong, 4 participants in the group at Drama Centre London, and 6 participants in the group at the Centre for the Arts, Adelaide.

The transcriptions of interviews and focus groups have been analysed using the phenomenological techniques as described in Chapter 4. The gathered meaning units or subthemes, named by the researcher, are grounded in more than the transcribed words of the participants. Looked at linguistically these subthemes may not share similar words from the transcription, but as Gadamer (1975, p. 289) suggests they have a 'shared horizon'. Gadamer has defined the phenomenological concept of the 'horizon' as referring to prior influences shaping the meaning or significance of experiences so that understandings between people move beyond formal structures. Rosen (1997) provides a contemporary discussion of Gadamer's doctrine of *Horizontverschmelzung,* indicating how not only socio-historical presuppositions influence an experience, but how also commonalities grounded in human senses colour the meaning of experiences; 'a particular sensual experience... conveys an interpretation' (Rosen, p. 214). The subthemes then have been gathered from considering the horizontalisation of meaning units, where all participant statements from the text are regarded as having equal value (Creswell 1998, p. 147).

As Benner suggests (1994, p. 116), as a researcher, I have come to this project with 'preunderstandings'. Certain forms of language, certain constructions or gatherings of words have attracted my attention more than others. The participants share some notable characteristics. Although the students were eager to speak for hours about their experiences in their actor training, they were not highly skilled at articulating the processes that they had been through. The participants are students who through their very selection into acting schools are adept at sensory rather than verbal communication. It is this skill that generally singles auditionees out for selection. Leahy (1996) highlights movement, gesture, vocal qualities and confidence as being the qualities that enable auditionees at Australian acting training institutions to successfully gain entrance. The participants' responses to the research question can be seen as efforts to express deeply felt encounters. Although lacking precise words to express their understandings the participants, nevertheless, frequently search hard for expressions that can adequately represent their felt sensations. This is not unlike the efforts of many contemporary actors in attempting to express the nuts and bolts of what enables them to act.[1]

The 27 subthemes identified consist of experiential issues that many actors would recognise as belonging to an actor's 'lifeworld' (*lebenswelt*). This is the given and experienced world that actors find themselves in, in this case predicated by the participants' choices to study acting specifically through the Malmgren technique. By gathering selected meaning units into subthemes the researcher too has already exercised a process of interpretation for as Gadamer (1984, p. 58) has stated,

> ... interpretation is not an isolated activity of human beings but the basic structure of our experience of life. We are always taking something *as* something. That is the primordial givenness of our world orientation, and we

---

[1] The twentieth century actors' descriptions of acting in, Cole T & Chinoy HK (eds) 1995, *Actors on Acting: The Theories, Techniques, and Practices of the World's Great Actors, Told in their own Words*, 4th edn, Three Rivers Press, New York, are typical in their hesitancy, lack of clarity and uncertainty as to what produces an excellent performance.

cannot reduce it to anything simpler or more immediate.

As indicated later in this chapter, each student of acting brings generalised ideas about acting from contemporary western culture to each course. Through the pedagogy of the actor-training institution attended, and the specific discourses embedded in each course, a shared world of language and experience begins to emerge for the students. This is a consequence of shared objectives. Paul Ricoeur (1981, p. 62) credits Gadamer with the understanding that two consciousnesses, situated differently, as in this case, in different countries or different Australian cities, can communicate by the fusion or sharing of their horizons. Ricoeur understood language as always situated, but the sharing of commonalities through language becomes possible when understandings of experiences are recognised between two or more as not being alien, or being like one's own experiences. Merleau-Ponty (1962, p. 338) had already pre-empted this notion in quite complex descriptions of how other's perspectives can impact and enlarge one's own, though never presuming that one ever steps beyond one's own perspective. An important aspect of phenomenology is, that it never presumes that there can be complete universality of knowledge or understanding. We are always individuals with incomplete access to each other's consciousness. This study presumes that words may only represent one way of gaining access to another's consciousness. Silences or pauses are another vital way of understanding others. Bodies witnessing and experiencing other bodies may be another real way of gaining access to other's consciousness. Tait (2000, p. 62), for instance speaks of 'somatic knowledge', where she credits 'the immediacy of speechless exchanges between bodies' as one reason for the circus' popularity. This emphasis on the sensate meanings of experiencing performing bodies, appears not only in Tait's earlier writing about circus bodies (1998) but also in Wilshire's (1991) text, *Role Playing and Identity: The Limits of Theatre as Metaphor*. Understandings can be gathered through a spectator viewing a performing body via the previous experiences of the viewer.

On the following page, the 27 listed subthemes are categorised by the researcher. The subtheme labels use terms appearing in the meaning units and/or are recognisable in an actor-training context. They aim to assist in understanding the perspectives of the participants as well as indicating the direction of the research.

1. Feeling Judged	15. The courage to demand of oneself
2. Clear intentions as the way forward	16. Vulnerability – Putting oneself on the line
3. Malmgren's technique as a classification of behaviour	17. Imitations of actions
4. Awareness of an audience	18. Competitiveness
5. Truthfulness	19. Reopening aspects of oneself
6. Learning by observation	20. Sharing the studio experience
7. Required specificity of actions	21. The stage as an obstacle to expression
8. Being accepted	22. Inhabiting one's body
9. The use of *Inner Attitudes*	23 Meeting the audience.
10. Ways in to Malmgren's technique	24. Fantasy versus pragmatics in an acting school
11. Questioning one's own and others' *Inner Attitudes*	25. Specific growing awareness of expression
12. Spontaneous physical reactions	26. The gap between the actor's and the audience's image
13. Relating Malmgren's technique to characters in text	27. 'It' – Confusion of identities
14. Self in relation to others	

Table 6.2 Subthemes pertaining to the process of Malmgren's acting technique

6.4 The context of the subthemes

The subthemes as data allow an appreciation of issues that form shared horizons of young people studying to become actors. They represent what the participants can see of the training: the technique and the participants' position within it. It is important to note that these are not the author's constructions, nor do they represent my way of teaching, but rather, these were the emerging issues contained in the participants' responses. In identifying the significance of the subthemes, phenomenologically, it is necessary to regard this data as emerging from a contextual background. The background remains invisible or unexpressed until revealed by the hermeneutical researcher. Hermeneutical or phenomenological understandings reach for the deeper meanings. As Webb and Pollard (2006, p. 35) state it, 'the text (is) the objectification of the participants' subjectivities.' The significance of this phenomenological study can be viewed in terms of the parts in relation to the whole, the specific 'objects' (or in this case subthemes), in relation to the deeper or subjective meaning of the encounter with the specific acting technique for the participants. Ricoeur (1981, p. 112) explains the next interpretive step of understanding the whole text as an 'explication of the being-in-the-world displayed by the text', rather than the researcher uncovering any 'psychological intentions which are hidden beneath the text'. To understand the context of the subthemes, it is necessary to see 'what the text talks about' (Geanellos 2000, p. 114).

6.4.1 Subtheme exemplars

Subtheme exemplars (Benner 1994, p. 117) are verbatim examples of subtheme meaning units and are drawn from both focus group transcriptions and individual interview transcriptions. The exemplars below are offered as a means of allowing the reader to experience directly the words of the participants rather than firstly meet the researcher's interpretations. Several participants contribute to each exemplar, with pseudonyms provided to distinguish their differing contributions. The exemplars provide a range of understandings of the subtheme for the reader, whilst still emphasising the voices of the participants. The pseudonym of the participant speaking has been placed after each example. (For participant profiles also using pseudonyms, refer to pages 114-125 in Chapter 4)

1) Feeling judged

The material that is brought to class seems to be indicative of something, in itself. The choice made, on some level – "This is what I will show" – Why that? (Alex).

When I've got to perform my own [script] I get highly self conscious – and I feel like I'm being judged just on me (Gina).

2) Clear intentions as a way forward

When I'm not sure of what I'm doing on stage, it's because my wants are not clear and I haven't put in place a strong enough action (Andy).

That does become like the ultimate truth, the true intention behind the action. The sincerity of the intention becomes overriding important (James).

3) Malmgren's technique as a classification of behaviour

The training provides a way of codifying and classifying behaviour within a shared context. Once these categories have been established, the challenge is to find aspects of one's own life that may fit. The categories become clearer as we watch others perform (Alex).

What Yat is trying to do is to make what you might be doing subconsciously, what you might just be taking for granted, what you might be actually doing, trying to make it logical, so you can understand it (Roger).

4) Awareness of an audience

By re-experiencing or re-creating circumstances in your mind and then playing them to an audience, you begin to, to see yourself through the energy that the audience gives off. That really did give them a view of themselves, a perspective of themselves that was outside themselves (James).

When you're in the amateur world you're doing something because you're enjoying it and it's for you whereas I think what [the school] starts to make you understand is that you're giving and it's all about affecting the audience, not just having a good time yourself but you've got to give yourself to the audience (Danny).

5) Truthfulness

The training has shown me how easy it is to slip into something other than truth – how hard 'truth' often is to attain (Alex).

If you're not changed, if you don't feel that there's a journey that's happened or there's a progression that's left you somewhere different than when you started, then it hasn't worked. Then you haven't been true to yourself, you haven't been honest (Bella).

I guess Laban does feel so true to your life, to the way people interact, the way people speak and move. And it just feels like it's fundamentally true. It's like – You want to be as precise as you can (Gillian).

6) Learning by observation

To do it through my own body is one way to approach the work and to understand it by watching other people do it is another way (Andy).

You can see it and you can empathise with them and know what they're going through and think in a parallel way (Alex).

7) Required specificity of actions

It's difference that excites an audience and expressing that choice in a clear way. And I think that's why Laban is really great. You do get stuck in habits and you know when something's getting generalised, or that it's habitual and that's when you can be precise (Gillian).

I think it definitely makes you say, "Christ! I've got to tune these things up." I hadn't even really considered whether I was *Free* or *Bound.* Simply in muscularity, whether I'm *Bound* or *Free*. It does make a lot of difference. (Danny).

I find it very difficult to play more than a few activities. I've written them down but I can't play them on the spot. I think it needs years. One has to work on these kind of tools (Donald).

8) Being accepted

So the director of this play that I had written said, "I think it's right for you. I think it's the right place for you to go." So I thought, all right and I auditioned here. And I auditioned for RADA and then I came here and the minute I came here, I just wanted to come here. Even if RADA accepted me I wouldn't go there. Who'd want to go to them anyway. But – yeah – So I came here and here I am (Bella).

'Prospero's Isle', the article in the prospectus was completely different to anything else that you see in other drama schools' prospectus'. It meant that the school was based around a methodology and it had an ideology. It knew what it was trying to do to students. It wasn't trying to create pretty faces. It was actually about the acting, which was a joy to behold! It is a very inspiring piece. You can always go back to it and realise ... it tells you why you're here (Danny).

9) The use of Inner Attitudes

I remember Yat saying, "Don't play an *Inner Attitude!*" You have to react. It's all about reacting (Donald).

Yat always says, " You think *Near* is a lump. And you forget all you've got to bring to it to make it three-dimensional, to make it some sort of character." You've got to bring three. You've got to bring *Thinking* or you've got to bring *Feeling* to *Sensing* or *Intuiting* (Roger).

10) Ways in to Malmgren's technique

You start watching yourself and then, there's a process of becoming almost a bit self-conscious about what you're doing. As soon as we started learning the *working actions*, you've almost got two things going on in your life. You're interacting with people, but you're also thinking, "That was a *Slash*. That was a *Wring*. Are they doing that in a *Near* way or *Adream* way? Was there *Flow* in that or no *Flow?*" I found that I began to bring the terminology and the framework into my everyday life (Douglas).

You're focused on it [the work] straight away. Not from playing an action and noticing people playing an action on me but more from the working actions. You might hear something and you might think, "Oh! That's like *Pressing Weight*." It could be because you're learning this new body of terms and you try and find examples of it (Lliam).

11) Questioning one's own and others' *Inner Attitudes*

You remember that lesson, and everyone was like, "Well! What am I? What do you think that I am?" (Danny).

It's so interesting to sit and think, "Oh What is everybody" You have this kind of itching to just use it all the time (Bella).

There's a lot of talking around, "Oh. He's *Near*! He's *Mobile!*" and things like that, but for me, it's more an awareness rather than putting people into boxes (Donald).

12) Spontaneous physical reactions

I sat back down. As I sat in my chair about three seconds later I just started weeping and I couldn't stop. It seemed like it just happened, like it just came from somewhere and it **needed** to come out. And later on I tried to figure out why I started weeping in class (Rick).

There's a period when your body is overacting because you can't pin anything down in your mind and you can't put it into words (Alex).

I remember you mentioned once about *Mobility* attaching itself to *Sensing* types to gain a sense of *Stability*. And that reduced me to tears at one point, the idea that I was constantly in need of some thing other than myself was very confronting and still is (James).

13) Relating Malmgren's technique to characters in text

In our last play we had a lot of different characters and I found the *working actions* really, really important in terms of making the audience understand that you were playing different characters. I found it really enabled me to go in to be different, attack the text in different ways and to make clear choices with my character (Douglas).

The important thing is that you're not playing the easy option, not pulling out the usual bag of tricks to do stuff. And trying to look for what I knew in my gut was required – that's come from a part of truth within the character. And it's having the guts I s'pose to just – play it for how you honestly feel it's supposed to be played (Andy).

14) Self in relation to others

Over two years of studying the Yat work, I feel that it has awakened my consciousness of self and my place in the world. At the start of the training, the way in which I perceived I was impacting on the world and what other people were receiving were so vastly different (Megan).

I suppose my initial response to the work was, even though you're going through it step-by-step, it was so overwhelming, because it just opened so many doors into viewing the world. As you work through the different *Inner Attitudes* you begin to understand, not only yourself a little bit better but other people (Douglas).

Yat Malmgren's training has helped me to find who we are as people and how other people function through everyday life (Rick).

15) The courage to demand of oneself

I thought it [the Malmgren technique] was important for me because I've always been terrified of improvisation and I don't feel comfortable without the script and being put to the test. So this class helped me overcome a lot of that fear and **I liked being scared**. I like overcoming fear. I think it's important for success in things (Andy).

The thing that I really appreciate about what Yat teaches – He stresses it all the time- is that we shouldn't be afraid of what we like and dislike. Not being afraid of your reactions to things, or to people, or to ideas, or to whatever. You should be involved in everything (Bella).

16) Vulnerability - Putting oneself on the line

You make yourself vulnerable. Many other people are in the class at any one time and you have to trust them. And sometimes that's hard to do and other times it's not but it depends on who's in the class and also who's in your scenario as well (Rick).

For me, the classes have always been a safe place, and exposing myself in performance has taught me experientially that if the performer is prepared to give freely from herself, then there is no sense of exploitation of the actor. If I make an empowered decision to allow myself to be vulnerable I am in control. If on the other hand I feel unsafe or that I don't want to give something of myself, and it is demanded, I begin to feel exploited and my defences start to block my creativity and free flow. I think it is so important for an actor to want to give, and that is the key to an empowered performance (Megan).

17) Imitations of actions

I found one of the aspects that I didn't like about [the method] is I felt that people were either imitating what they'd seen or [they] caught on to a few key words and used that. I almost felt that they were faking what they were doing to pass in that week in that certain scenario whatever that was. And I felt for me that that diminished the usefulness of the work (Gina).

I believe that some people come to the work and say, "Well, I have an understanding of what a particular type is and I can see this person being like that when they do this and so I'm going to write a scenario based around those circumstances and place myself within it." So it's an imitation. And so what they're risking is nothing of themselves (James).

18) Competitiveness

The environment itself for me was the offputting thing, because I didn't like the competitiveness (Gina).

It was the first time I was getting on stage and doing stuff and suddenly we had to get up and really do something, to try and put something into practice. And also I felt a tremendous pressure to try to, not to please, but to at least show that I could actually do something! I found it really, really difficult (Roger).

Literally in an acting institution it is competitive and people are fighting to, to dominate, and then they get the roles. So that's natural, and I actually think competition is quite healthy (Andy).

19) Reopening aspects of oneself

We've examined the four [*Mental Factors*], *Intuiting, Thinking, Sensing* and *Feeling* and then we've discovered that OK maybe one of those things isn't something that we rely on a great deal. So then I started to look. "Why aren't I operational in these ways? Why am I rejecting that? What is it that I am rejecting so that I can start accepting it again?" It's not as easy as just saying, "Oh. I'm closing myself down in those ways, I should open them back up." And so you start edging it back towards you and you sort of start to get a sense of what you've been missing out on. You start applying yourself back into those places (James).

It's difficult but you do learn. You learn what bit you have to work on. Everyone has one *Mental Factor* that's a little bit out of synch with the rest (Bella).

20) Sharing the studio experience

We **christened** this room! (Carmel). (Everyone laughing) We put *Flow* in the room! (Lliam). (Lots of animation)
Janys: You put the *Flow* in this room? And now it resonates with that? (Laughter)
The walls have changed colour! (Douglas). [The walls are green – the colour of *Mobile*]

We always wanted to pull this practical joke on you Janys. I was going to say, "Show us a *Punch*" and we were all going to go (purses lips as if *Punching* with lips) I was going to get the whole class to do it (Megan). (lots of noise/laughter)

21) The stage as an obstacle to expression

I think that there is often a feeling response to **being** on stage. I know that happens to me a lot, that it's hard to stay centred or something because just the act of being on stage can knock you out of that (Megan).

In the last year, when we did exercises, I was shaking on stage, I was so nervous but today I was trying to concentrate on what I was doing and there were moments when if I snapped out of it I'd suddenly be conscious of the audience and suddenly be nervous but I just had to focus back in and become really involved in the situation (Bella).

22) Inhabiting one's body

It's a weird sensation. If you sit yourself down and watch everybody else and not do it yourself you become very passive. You need to experience the Yat work in order to grow from it. I don't think you can sit down and watch the class and go, "Yes. This is how I do things". I think for me it was a physical thing first (Rick).

Personally what I found most difficult is that I do a lot of stuff up here. (taps head). And it's not about that. If you could play the film that's inside your head, Yat would love you, but it doesn't work that way. Finding the organic sensual part of the training is for me personally a hell of a lot more difficult than understanding the work, or doing any of that. It has to be putting up there (taps his head) into there (indicates forward action)(Danny).

23) Meeting the audience

I think the theatre is about an audience and so therefore what we say and what our bodies do cannot be contradicting. So it's good to have an objective audience there who's saying, "Well! You might think you're doing this but in fact you're not!" So to have the audience giving you feedback is really important in your growth as a performer (Andy).

The audience will read your *working actions* and your activities and make their own assumptions. They won't say, "Oh That person's doing *Adream*" because *Adream* is only for your own benefit, to help you get somewhere. The audience doesn't care if you're *Adream* or *Mobile* as long as it has communicated something **to** them. Laban gives you an insight into your habits and a way out of that, so that you can try something different in a rehearsal room and hence offer something different to an audience or someone else on stage (Douglas).

24) Fantasy versus pragmatics in an acting school

You start with all these ideas of what the environment of an acting school is going to be like – and then you are initially responding to your ideas and not to what actually exists (James).

There's literally so much going on that it is really difficult. You've got such long hours. Your focus isn't just on the rehearsal exercise, you've got voice projects, you've got improvisation and then you've still got to turn up every morning and do ballet and movement and all of this other stuff and also just a battle to stay healthy because it's not a healthy environment at all you know There's 90 people sitting breathing in the same air for twelve hours a day. If you take on personal issues as well I can image it would be phenomenally difficult. I think if you if you do allow those things to affect you too much ... You've got to know what you're there for (Danny).

25) Specific growing awareness of expression

I suppose the Yat work has enabled me to become a more conscious actor. I'm not suggesting that I have reached a plateau of understanding about myself, but that I can perform or propel myself into action without shocking myself: I can put my intending in place and achieve something close to what I anticipated (Megan).

When we were exploring *Stability,* I felt for the first time that I was able to present myself onstage in a way that was comfortable – to the point of shocking myself! (James).

26) The gap between the actor's and audience's image

I guess one thing that doing Yat has taught me, that maybe my perception of myself is not quite what everyone else gets (Gina).

I think it does get easier to accept standing in front of a group of people thinking you're presenting something and everyone in the group saying, "But that was Bound!" - or something you thought it wasn't (Gary).

27) 'It' - Confusion of Identities

So over the course of the last two years I was able to question how and why I do certain things, act and react in certain ways and to certain situations. This has been tough and has caused me much fear, in class and outside of class. This is what is difficult; my constant questioning always brings doubt into my mind as to whether I am a competent actor and human being (Rick).

We described what we went through, at separate times, as 'It'. This 'It', I suppose is an intensified period of uncertainty, where you are becoming aware that the world sees a different you, one that you did not choose, one that you may not like. You feel completely out of touch with yourself and cry intensely and spontaneously at something you can't grasp. This for me, is often accompanied by adrenaline, a completely blank mind and the need to be with someone I can trust. Actually, my mind may be working at a hundred miles an hour, but only with self-focussed paranoid thoughts and I am unable to control them. It feels blank because if someone asks why I am upset I can't find the actual chain of events and I can't calm myself. Although, you may not come to the end of this period with a clear and certain vision, you do feel better somehow, and things about yourself drop into place with greater ease as time goes by (Alex).

6.5 A shared background

The words of the participants ring with a passion and openness that indicate that studying acting means far more to the participants as students than becoming adept at a set of skills. 'Sense of self' is intricately bound up in the processes undertaken. This attribute clearly fluctuates over the journey through the participants' actor training. Acting or learning this technique of acting seems to have prompted a deeper enquiry into who the participants are as people, the nature of their being. This of course harks back to the popular culture depiction of 'Method' acting; actors in the 'Method', as taught by Strasberg and his followers, are expected to dig deeply into their own psyche and invest themselves totally in their acting processes. Most acting students would, at the least, be aware of Hollywood's 'Method' actors and the psychological investments of which they speak. Stanislavski (1973, p. 129), in speaking of the actor's role offers the following advice.

Your decision to take up a stage career implies first of all your willingness to open your heart to the fullest possible perception of life. An actor who devotes his talent merely to the reproduction of the facts that he has observed in life, cannot, however talented he may be, cast so strong a spell on the imagination of the spectators as to force them to shed tears and remember long afterwards not only *what* they had seen, but also *how* they had seen and heard. This can only be done by the actor who has mastered his desire for self-admiration, achieved the highest possible degree of self-possession, and trained himself to show the utmost possible goodwill to his fellow-men: it is only such an actor who can detect the organic as well as the accidental traits in human passions, and can split them up into those which are less important, that is to say, those that apply only to the character he is representing at the moment, and into those permanent ones that are inherent in the very nature of the feelings. But he can achieve this fusion of himself and the character he is representing only if he learns to love him and if he distinguishes what is only accidental and unimportant in him from what constitutes the very substance of the man on which the entire through-action of the part can be built.

The tradition of viewing the acquisition of acting skills in the light of a heroic quest is still inherent in many trainee actors' minds. In the quote above, Stanislavski links ethical development with an actor's ability to perform characters on stage. Stanislavski contends that actors must fuse with the characters that they play and that the attention to the minutiae of human behaviour assists in this fusion. Stanislavski's language reflects the passion that he purports to be necessary to study acting. In similar ways the participants studying the Malmgren technique reflect this kind of passion. They scrutinise their own abilities and characteristics and in particular they indicate how sensitive they are to the reception of their acting by their teachers and by audiences. Stanislavski's heightened language, in speaking of 'your willingness to open your heart' and of 'the very substance of the man', suggests that there are deep and concrete truths about human nature. Despite postmodern questionings of essentialisms, this attitude to acting clearly underpins the expectations of students of acting in the twenty first century. The subthemes reveal elements of an heroic quest, where a desire for a Stanislavskian mode of integrity appears in the participants' emphasis on notions of 'truthfulness', 'acceptance', 'courage' and 'vulnerability'. This twentieth century background to the tradition of acting often colours the way in which the Malmgren technique is encountered. Malmgren's technique in its structure, the categorisation of actions and characters into the *six Inner Attitudes* perhaps encourages students erroneously to search for some notion of an essential nature of themselves and the characters that they represent in their training.

Jerzy Grotowski (1973, p. 37), a later, equally well-respected theoretician of the art of theatre performance comments on the processes of acting with an almost spiritual set of expressions.

> But the decisive factor in this process is the actor's technique of psychic penetration. He must learn to use his role as if it were a surgeon's scalpel, to dissect himself. It is not a question of portraying himself under certain given circumstances, or of "living" a part; nor does it entail the distant sort of acting common to epic theatre and based on cold calculation. The important thing is to use the role as a trampoline, an instrument with which to study what is hidden behind our everyday mask – the innermost core of our personality – in order to sacrifice it, expose it.

Both Grotowski and Stanislavski set the stage for acting students in the twenty-first century to consider acting in terms of an investigation of character, with the outcome being the revealing of a 'hidden' aspect of being. This shared horizon of understanding, that is, of the actor as heroic artist, may also be considered as the starting point for the actor's journey through the Malmgren technique. It is a staring point that will be quickly challenged.

6.6 A surprising experience

Despite the essentialism suggested by the shared notions of acting that students bring to their studies, the Malmgren technique plunges them experientially into processes of performativity that are in direct contrast with what they have previously understood. It is clear from the subthemes that the participants experience intense feelings of vulnerability, of uncertainty as to how they are received, leading to at times a fragmentation of their sense of selves. These experiences run in direct contrast to the heady Stanislavskian notion of the individual, heroic actor. This study takes account of these processes and the awareness, from the subthemes, that the journey through Malmgren's technique is an uncertain one. If the experience of the Malmgren technique is not that of Stanislavski's heroic journey or Grotowski's spiritual quest, it is also much more than a set of handy tools or acting skills to be used on stage. In Malmgren's technique the quest is for expressive embodiment.

As broached in Chapter 3, one of the dominant contemporary perspectives regarding performing bodies is that of the culturally constructed 'self' or identity. Performativity, within this model is viewed as the means of constructing distinct characteristics, which allow for the formation of cultural identification, or the recognition of cultural differences. This is a linguistic or symbolic model, and rests firmly on the reception of performance, relating performativity to everyday performance as well as performances on stages, or with specified audiences. As Judith Butler (2005, p. 14) has said, 'the body is always given to us, and to others, *in some way*.' Here she refers to the fact that as cultural creatures we are already immersed in distinct modes of reading bodies. To take it further she is arguing that we cannot ever escape the discourses that construct our viewings of bodies although we can subvert these discourses. Butler is speaking in particular of everyday performances or behaviours that construct gender, but her work has had a direct impact on ideas about performance and in particular about the construction of bodies through performance.

Interestingly, it is the constructed nature of each performing body, 'the body as signifier', that is immediately visible through the Malmgren technique and which is intuitively responded to by the audience. Ethnicity, gender, class, attitudes towards or divergent from dominant discourses, all are at once apparent. In Malmgren's technique, each performer brings her own language, her own narrative, her own imaginative longings to each exercise. The Malmgren trainer identifies patterns or rhythms of action that actors are required to perform, the context of these remain the choice of the performer. Many of the dominant discourses that construct performers may not be immediately apparent to the performer. The sense of self that any performer has constructed may be at odds with the ways that performer is viewed. Obvious examples are characteristics of gender, height, weight, sex, colouring, the use of distinct colloquialisms or accents. Discourses surrounding these characteristics may surprise the performer.

The vulnerability of each performer, as witnessed through the subthemes is understandable if as suggested in Chapter 3 the performer's body is understood as a site where identity and subjectivity are not necessarily congruent. As suggested in Chapter 3, the performer's body may be considered as a process where subject positions are fractured or are momentary. This may be compounded as any performer identifies with or rejects the ways in which she is perceived by the studio audience. The actor's sense of self can shift and waver as her identity and her agency merge or separate.

Butler has been criticised for eliding the materiality of the body from her arguments about culture and language defining the ways in which bodies act and receive each other. Nussbaum (1999) in particular criticised Butler for not taking account of the substance of the body, and therefore not assisting the material conditions of 'real' women. Butler has also been questioned about the role that organic nature plays in the understanding of what is acted and what is received. In "There is a Person Here'; An Interview with Judith Butler' (2005, p. 16), Butler refers to Merleau-Ponty's image of the *'chiasmus'* where binaries of organic and inorganic are exceeded by his concept of intertwining. Butler is not denying the reality of the materiality of the body. She is interested in the ways in which human agency constitutes a reality intertwined with the non-human. 'There are many aspects of language, including its gaps and silences, that are profoundly constitutive of what we are, and might be said to operate as part of what interpolates both the human and inhuman.' (2006, p. 16) She uses the term 'interpolates' to indicate that human consciousness infuses the non-human to comprehend this intertwining. By 'interpolate' Butler implies that consciousness contributes to whatever matter that it considers, but that matter itself may be conditioning our consciousness at the same time (hence the image of Merleau-Ponty's *chiasm*). Her call is for her readership to become more aware of their projections. Butler is interested in the way that human agency creates norms but also the ways in which it contests norms and creates 'otherness'.

This is, I believe, a useful place from which to start the analysis of the processes underway in the Malmgren training. With its emphasis on the recognition of rhythms of speech and gesture, the processes of delivery of action, patterns of speech structures and pauses, the angles of the performing body's movement, the Malmgren technique creates a space in actor training where the discourses surrounding a performer's body can be viscerally experienced and acknowledged. In removing the emphasis from content, and placing the emphasis on bodily-observed movements, agency is returned to the trainee. Agency becomes the crux of what is observed by the studio audience. This agency can be as normative or as transgressive as any trainee chooses. The Malmgren Studio becomes a forum for the construction of 'selves' through embodied action. What is expressed enters the material and symbolic realm, creating my notion of a quest for expressive embodiment for actors in training.

6.7 A phenomenological approach

In Merleau-Ponty's preface to the *Phenomenology of Perception* (1962, p. ix), he reiterates Husserl's conception of a generalised intentionality that interconnects beings with the world through perception, which he defines as

> consciousness, through which from the outset a world forms itself around me and begins to exist for me. To return to the things themselves is to return to that world which precedes knowledge, of which knowledge always speaks, and in relation to which every scientific schematization is an abstract and derivative sign-language, as is geography in relation to the country-side in which we have learnt beforehand what a forest, a prairie or a river is.

Merleau-Ponty's 'perception' is not some objective or physiologically comprehended operation but instead an already situated and interconnected interaction, a being-in-the-world emergent understanding, which reflects upon the very world that it emerges from. Like Heidegger's *dasein*, Merleau-Ponty's 'perception' is more philosophical than biological or scientific.

Intentionality in Merleau-Ponty's conception is an act in itself, for in the *Phenomenology of Perception* he positions the body as that vehicle which carries intentionality, creating meaning through acts of signification (1962, p. 320). As Merleau-Ponty makes clear, the subjects of my study, or any study, are present only through the mediation of their bodies. The so-called perceiving subjects of Malmgren's technique are neither transcendent consciousness nor purely physical bodies but are rather 'The perceiving subject or lived body' (Madison 1992, p. 88). Merleau-Ponty has remarked at numerous times within the *Phenomenology of*

Perception (1962) and then later in *The Visible and the Invisible* (1968) that as language is to thought, so the body is to the mind. Language structures and expresses thought – so Merleau-Ponty (1962, p. 194) understands that the body expresses and structures the mind through intentionality.

> We must therefore recognize as an ultimate fact this open and indefinite power of giving significance – that is, both of apprehending and conveying a meaning – by which man transcends himself towards a new form of behaviour, or towards other people, or towards his own thought, through his body and his speech.

He sees the role of the body as '...to ensure this metamorphosis. It transforms ideas into things' (1962, p. 165). He compares this to a work of art (1962, p. 151).

> A novel, picture or musical work are individuals, that is, beings in which the expression is indistinguishable from the thing expressed, their meaning, accessible only through direct contact, being radiated with no change of their temporal and spatial situation. It is in this sense that our body is comparable to a work of art. It is a focal point of living meanings, not the function of a certain number of mutually variable terms.

Viewed phenomenologically, the student actors apprehend their bodies as giving meaning, via their acting exercises, to their 'being'. In that moment of performance, and in the Malmgren exercises each actor is alone on stage. In that time and space they have the opportunity to become as united in meaning as a work of art. This message streams out from the subthemes. It is not necessarily the way that it is taught. The initial naïve readings of the subthemes are complimented by deeper hermeneutic or phenomenological understandings. In viewing the subthemes a journey of discovery emerges about the participants' bodies, where participants begin the study of acting as if with an invincible self, the old notions of the artist with hidden depths prevails. Then a pattern emerges of vulnerability and exposure, through being witnessed in action, then the fragmentation of realising that any body may be read in many ways and then the re-integration of a new sense of agency. It is the actor's sense of self, a self in process of materialising, which is put into performance in each exercise, an experience of the actor's being, that is tested and scrutinised through the Malmgren methods attention to the actor's body.

For as James McCaughey (1998, p. 9), a Melbourne director and lecturer at the Victorian College of the Arts has said in an early article about bodies in theatre,

> ... [the body] is [where] we express ourselves. It is where we choose to be like other people or accept being ourselves. It is where we seek to transcend our limitations or collapse beneath their weight; where we accept our folly or try to conceal it ... In what we do with our bodies, we make clear how much we are tied to routine or how much we transcend it, how inventive we are. Or how imaginative, energetic, slothful, confident or afraid.

11 moves to 1. 1 moves to 3. 3 moves to 8. 8 moves to 4. 4 moves to 12. 12 moves to 5. These are the first sequences of Laban's A Scale, one of Laban's space harmony scales. As any body moves it passes through points in space. The A Scale is one possible set of movements taking the body flowingly around an axis of space defined by Right Deep Forward and Left High Backwards.

I don't know that I am moving very flowingly. I am demonstrating the A Scale to my Wollongong Acting students. Privately moving through the A Scale fills me with delight. It is as if the long sweeps of movement open out possibilities and are themselves joyous. However it is not the same moving the scales in front of students. I am not a dancer. I want the students to feel what it is to move about an axis of space; I want them to experience the sensations of having a direction around which they move. But can I move flowingly enough to entice them on the journey?

I am remembering Yat leading his Space classes. He danced! Even as we muddled our feet and physically stammered our way through the scales he sailed across the floor.

5 moves to 7. 7 moves to 9. 9 moves to 2. 2 moves to 10 and so on. Heidegger said you are born to ask just one question. Jung said so too. But what if your body never assists you? What if the direction you are moving in is constantly hampered with your own stoppages and refusals? That's called Bound Flow. When I told Yat that I was teaching his movement and that I was

unsure of doing so he was \very kind, generous. "It is those who are the most wounded who can often be the best teachers."
Researcher's Journal 6.1 April 1998, Faculty of Creative Arts, University of Wollongong, *Space* class.

CHAPTER 7

SIX THEMES: MERLEAU- PONTY'S *CHIASM*

I had asked Laban which of the four Mental Factors you think is the most important. And he said Time.

Malmgren November 2000.

7.1 Introduction

In the previous chapter I presented 27 subthemes arising from the research data, feelings and thoughts about acting, the Malmgren technique and most importantly about the participants' understandings of themselves. Referring to constructionist theories of identity formation, I described how Butler (2005) aligns her symbolic or linguistic model of gender formation with Merleau-Ponty's concept of intertwinement or the *chiasm*. For the purposes of this study, I identified the body of the participant as that site where an intertwinement of meaning about performance is formed both for an audience and more importantly, in relation to this study, for the participants in their journeys through actor training. This phenomenological conception of the performing body is not the objective body of scientific research but rather Merleau-Ponty's body, a pre-objective body already in 'communion' with its perceived world (Merleau-Ponty 1962, p. 213). From immersion in the subthemes, I argued that the participants were involved in processes of transformation in relation to their sense of their embodied selves. This chapter continues this investigation of the participants' growing awareness of embodiment, growing identification with their embodied expression, and growing ability to communicate with both audience and other actors whilst being viewed. This chapter is predicated on the investigation via the six emergent interview themes introduced in Chapter 6. This chapter in conjunction with Chapter 6 may be regarded as part of the third ripple of contextualisation of the Malmgren technique of actor training; the hermeneutic meaning of the technique as a transformational understanding of the actors' embodiment.

7.2 Six emergent themes

Drawing on the phenomenological perspectives outlined in the previous chapter, I have clustered the subthemes under six principal emergent themes. Whilst the subthemes are working concepts that make the overall data more accessible, the principal themes arising from the data reveal a set of experiential processes initiated via the Malmgren technique of actor training. These processes can be compared across several sites of actor training and performance. Each one of the themes stands independently, as arising through actor training, and in particular Malmgren's actor training technique. As outlined in Chapter 4 a phenomenological analysis of data reveals a general structure to describe the phenomenon under investigation (von Eckartsberg 1998). Viewed in order, the six emergent themes, arising from the interviews, represent the general structure of the transformational process instigated by the Malmgren technique. The transformational process identified brings into question the actor's sense of self as reflected through an actor's body, the meaning of that self in relation to an audience and the implications of that meaning in a wider world.

In the table on the next page, the subthemes that reveal the major emergent themes are listed (with bracketed numbers referring to the list of subthemes in Table 6.2, p. 181 of Chapter 6 and the listed subtheme exemplars on pages 183–190).

Interview Themes/ Phenomenological Understandings in the Malmgren Technique	Subthemes in the Malmgren Technique revealed through the data (See Chapter 6)
1.The Actor's *Lebenswelt*: The lifeworld of the actor in training	Fantasy versus pragmatics in an acting school (24) Being accepted (8) Sharing the studio experience (20) Competitiveness (18)
2.The Phenomenal Body: New understandings of the actor's body	Inhabiting one's body (22) Ways in to Malmgren's acting technique (10) Required specificity of actions (7) Malmgren's technique as a classification of behaviour (3) Relating Malmgren's technique to characters in text (13)
3.The *Chiasm*: The inextricable link between actor & audience	The use of *Inner Attitudes* (9) Questioning one's own & others' *Inner Attitudes* (11) Learning by observation (6) Imitations of actions (17)
4.Experiencing the Gap: Whose is the body that is viewed?	The gap between the actor's and audience's image (26) Feeling judged (1) The stage as an obstacle to expression (21) Awareness of an audience (4) Truthfulness (5)
5. Refusal and 'It': New possibilities of expressive action	'It' – Confusion of identities (27) Vulnerability – Putting oneself on the line (16) Spontaneous physical reactions (12) The courage to demand of oneself (15) Reopening aspects of oneself (19)
6. The Transformed Body: The ongoing process of 'becoming'	Clear intentions as a way forward (2) Meeting the audience (23) Self in relation to others (14) Specific growing awareness of expression (25)

Table 7.1 Emergent themes arising from subthemes

7.2.1 General structure of the phenomenon

In calling the general structure of the six emergent themes a process of transformation, I am referring to the phenomenological transformation, located by Merleau-Ponty, in his search for a pre-linguistic perception, when he stresses,

> I say that my eyes see, that my hand touches, that my foot is aching, but these naïve expressions do not put into words my true experience. Already they provide me with an interpretation of that experience...(Merleau-Ponty 1962, pp. 212-213).

The transformation of consciousness that Merleau-Ponty speaks of is the realisation that every subject/body is inevitably also an interpretive body. The six themes outline a process where actors in training through Malmgren's technique become aware that the performing body is the medium through which any pre-linguistic or imaginative world can be expressed. They also become aware that the body is the obstacle to that expression. The process allows them to encounter the reality that they are objects in the interpretive world of others and themselves, just as others are to them. They learn that the material elements of their own bodies may restrict the ways in which others interpret their performative bodies. Moreover they understand that these dimensions of consciousness belong to each of the embodied beings they encounter.

The following sections of the chapter will look closely at the six themes, the subthemes that have informed each theme, and the wider phenomenological implications resulting from the themes.

7.3 The actor's *lebenswelt*: the lifeworld of the actor in training

1. The Actor's *Lebenswelt*: The lifeworld of the actor in training	Fantasy versus pragmatics in an acting school (24) Being accepted (8) Sharing the studio experience (20) Competitiveness (18)

Table 7.2 Subthemes constituting the first emergent theme

It is through the performance of a person's body that, as Merleau-Ponty (1962, p. 303) has stated, 'I am at grips with a world.' The lived-world or 'lebenswelt' of Husserl's (1970) phenomenology is as much an affective experience as a sensed one, as much an experience of memory and hopes for the future as an experience of the present, as much an experience of the mythical as the factual, of the instinctual as of the rational. In this sense, the 'lebenswelt' of the participants consists of all that they reveal through their participation in the research project. However for the purpose of clarifying the first major theme regarding Malmgren's technique, 'The actor's lebenswelt: the lifeworld of the actor in training', I have identified the four constituent subthemes in Table 7.2 on the previous page. These reveal something of the lived world of acting students in general and differentiate tertiary acting students from tertiary students of other disciplines.

The lived-world of one set of people may be invisible to another set even if present in the same circumstances. As Ference Marton (1992, p. 254), a phenomenologist interested in the psychology of learning, has written,

> One important thing about the differences in our understanding of the world around us is that they are, in the most cases, virtually invisible. We are not aware of the fact that we see the world in different ways because we are not even aware of the fact that we see the world in a particular way. We tacitly believe that we simply see the world as it is and we also believe – without any further reflection – that our fellow mortals do just the same.

The student who chooses to invest herself in a full-time acting course inhabits one such 'invisible' world. The choice is at odds with many of the reasons that students enter tertiary study, such as to gain a particular outcome in a career or a particular income through their education. The student actor chooses to study acting despite the clearly known and often stated facts that there is little work for actors and that chance can often override talent in determining how work is gained. Clearly the student actor values something other than a conventional career path.

In each of the four subthemes listed as part of this theme in 'The actor's *lebenswelt*' (see Table 7.2), the participants reveal their imaginings about acting schools in general, about their particular school and about their relationships with other students. These subthemes of the *lebenswelt* of the performer appear to exist as much in fantasy as in the sensed reality of the tertiary institution. For in Merleau-Ponty's (1962, pp. 165-166) conception, the body is ambiguous because it both releases agency into the lived world through intentional action, whilst it also secludes agency from the human world, as when the body is lost in memory or fantasy. Merleau-Ponty (1962, p. 168) describes this as metaphysical, 'the coming to light of something beyond nature'. Merleau-Ponty uses the term to refer to sexuality and all the accompanying fantasies about erotic relationships to illuminate this process. However I am here using the term metaphysical in relation to actors' fantasies, which I have observed to have the same kind of power as sexual fantasies. In an acting school, the actor's consciousness is constantly constructing stories about acting and acting schools. These may or may not lead to intentional actions but they do interconnect with possible intentional actions.

Participants reveal some of their lifeworld of studying at an acting school where Yat Malmgren's method is taught through the two subthemes, 'Fantasy versus pragmatics in an acting school' and 'Being accepted'. These subthemes could be labelled as positive indeterminate aspects of an object (in this case an acting school) (Merleau-Ponty 1962, p. 331; Hadreas 1986, p. 48). A positive indeterminate aspect of a phenomenon cannot be presently perceived but is nevertheless held as existing. I call these indeterminate but believed in aspects of the participants experience of their acting schools, the 'legendary' ideas about acting that keep young acting students afloat, the myths and dreams that keep motivating these students in their studies.

In the example below, Carmel from Adelaide's Centre for the Arts speaks of the qualities she valued in her acting school prior to auditioning to join the program. Through choosing to speak of these expectations of her acting school whilst being in her final year of study, Carmel re-evaluates certain aspects of her training.

> I've had **many** friends graduate from here [Centre for the Arts, Adelaide] and I've always been aware of it and always expressed an interest in it. For a while I thought I was too old to go back to school. When I was in my early twenties, I was like, "Oh! I can't go back to school, I'm too old!" Then I had a bit of a wake up call and I realised I'm not too old. I was really interested in the Laban[1] work. I looked at the other schools around Australia and I'm from Adelaide, so that was appealing to me, but I really was drawn to the work, to the Laban work. I've read a lot of books about Drama Centre and the Actors Studio and all that stuff and I thought it seemed, more the avenue to go down. With the way I work, in my reading of people in life and the way I like to communicate, Laban seemed to be able to spell that out for me in a way that I already intuitively understood, but it could also fill it out for me (Carmel).

Carmel hints at the legendary dimensions to her idealised acting school. She wants the Adelaide Centre for the Arts acting course to resemble what she has read of Drama Centre, London or Strasberg's Actors Studio in New York. Through reading of Malmgren's technique in famous actors' biographies (See Yule 1994;

---

[1] Malmgren's technique is termed simply 'Laban' at Adelaide's Centre for Performing Arts.

Callow 1995), Carmel intuitively believes that it may provide her with the possibilities of success that she imagines and at the very least a richer understanding of the way people behave and communicate. This is part of the meaning or *lebenswelt* of her attending this school. Past stories of actors being scrutinised in 'Method' trainings spring to mind and may well be providing Carmel with a deeper meaning as to her own experiences.

The indeterminate but wished for aspects of the Malmgren training form its context. Carmel intuitively places the Malmgren training among western Stanislavski-like trainings that presume a clear and consistent concept of character. A desire to study character-based acting is understandable in the light of Carmel's prior acting experience within the Australian film industry where realistic depictions of character dominate the screen. The training seems to promise an investigation of character that is at once personal and that will impact on the student's effectiveness in acting. The exact investigation offered will appear through the analysis of later themes. The legendary aspects of acting schools offering this type of technique hint at the possibility of acting success based on the histories of successful actors who have undertaken similar methods.

In the second two subthemes, 'Sharing the Studio experience' and 'Competitiveness' (See Table 7.2), the participants reflect upon their active engagement in their classes and in particular their Malmgren technique class. These two subthemes reveal the inter-relational processes of being immersed in an acting school that teaches Malmgren's work. The subtheme of 'Sharing the studio experience' reveals the intimacy with which the participants relate to one another. The manner in which acting students share jokes about their schools, the training premises, their staff and the ways in which they share in descriptions of one another's presentations or performances, all reveal a depth of sharing of selves that is different to that which generally occurs in courses delivered as a lecture/tutorial mode. The participants' *lebenswelt* for a large part relies on the workshop inter-relations of the students and the staff within the program. Seton (2004, p. 67) refers to the 'intercorporeal' nature of experiences in actor training, recognising that what happens between bodies in actor trainings can be contextualised both phenomenologically as well as socially. Rather than viewing actors' bodies as individual and discrete entities recognised for either a depth or lack of talent, Seton suggests that the intercorporeal nature of any actor training is an accountable means of evaluating it. The sense that the participants are bound up with each other, in each other's achievements in the studio course emerges in each of the focus group discussions, as well as in the individual interviews at all sites. Here much of the discussion relates to what others have presented as much as what the participant herself may have experienced. Merleau-Ponty (1962, p. 168) describes this diffused experience of reality as an, 'opening out upon 'another'', a heightened intersubjectivity, where parts of the participants' are invested in each other. This is an important means whereby students value an acting course.

Burgoyne, Poulin and Rearden (1999), in researching the effects of acting on student actors in Missouri, observe the 'boundary blurring' of actors and their performed characters. The Stanislavski system or as they call it the 'inside-out' approach to acting, increases role or self 'blurring', however the 'outside-in' approach, a more physically based approach to character creation, still results in 'boundary blurring'. Whilst these authors were wary of these 'blurrings', my understanding from the subthemes gathered in the interviews is that these inter-relationships create charged experiences of meaning. Seton (2004, p. 69) questions the ways in which these experiences are managed in actor training. His comparison of actor training with counselling methods promotes a conscious awareness of the interpersonal skills necessary for actors in training. This factor of the training institution's care of students appears pertinent as to the outcomes of 'Sharing the studio experience'.

In the subtheme of 'Competitiveness', Carmel elucidates the kind of physical commitment that an acting school demands of any performer.

> I'm just readjusting because this only started this week, being here for 12 hours a day and so this is only the third day in and I'm feeling really worn out and the thought, that when I get home I've got to do homework and stuff and then get to sleep, wake up and be back here ... I have a strong personal life outside of school, which is also why I had trouble in first year to, to change. I had a really established life and had to say no to people all the time because I had to write my scenarios and stuff, and I kind of expected it to be easier. I thought drama school was going to be really easy, but Laban took a lot of thinking and I realised that I had to commit to it otherwise there was no point doing it. I hardly see anyone outside of school now, and I just go down to my

> beach house on the weekend and do the work and just see my partner. I just thrive on this work and I think anything outside of that is secondary in my life now, I just love to be committed to it and then the good times that I have are from being successful, more of a celebration instead of life being a celebration (Carmel).

Carmel is willing to make sacrifices in her personal life for her acting. She strives to achieve the goals set out by her course. In each Malmgren class she is watched and evaluated. Categorising this example under the subtheme of Competitiveness comes from Carmel's desire for success in her Malmgren technique. Competition is often the initial way students comprehend or value what is being asked of them in the new environment of an acting school. In every class, faced with an audience, Carmel wants to accomplish the set *Inner Attitude/Externalised Drives* exercises. However, similarly to acquiring any physical skill, not every student is able to master Malmgren's *Inner Attitude* exercises immediately. As with playing a set of scales, or dancing a set choreography it is clear to all in the Studio when an exercise is achieved or not achieved. Carmel acknowledges that writing and performing the required scenarios is taxing.

The skill required to achieve Malmgren's exercises is similar to Stanislavski's concept of 'public solitude' (Carnicke 1998, p. 178). Actors in training must contact imaginary circumstances, intentions and images of others whilst being observed publicly. There is a complexity in synthesising all of the necessary elements in this 'highly systematic process' (O'Connor 2001, p. 52). This kind of self-actualising desire, the setting of goals and the achievement of them, may not assist in motivating every acting student. In contrast to Carmel, Gina has a negative response to the competitive pressure exerted in the Malmgren training.

> It seemed to almost become like there were tricks of the trade that people used to present work, because it became quite competitive for a while there ... or for everyone to keep up. I found one of the aspects that I didn't like about it is I felt that people were either imitating what they'd seen or caught on to a few key words and used that and I almost felt that they were faking what they were doing to pass that certain scenario, whatever that was. And I felt for me that that diminished the usefulness of the work. It felt like that cheapened it all. And it frustrated me because it was a class

> project I felt we all came in to watch each other and to support each other. And if people were bullshitting then I didn't want to watch them. And it was just so that they could reach a level higher than the rest of us then that to me is – lying (Gina).

Gina, in the example above, criticises other participants in her class for not representing themselves 'truthfully'. Questioned as to why the others in her class disturbed her efforts Gina replies that the competitive nature of the class is 'offputting' (see exemplar Subtheme 18, in Chapter 6, p. 187). Gina challenges the relatedness of other students' Malmgren exercises and finds them lacking in an aspect of acting that she values highly, 'truthfulness'. Whilst students attempt to physically and vocally express the structures of the *working actions* of the particular *Inner Attitude* being presented, or the *directions in space* required for the exercise it may be difficult for some students to stay consciously interlinked with a sense of 'self'. Seton (2004, p. 34) argues that affectivity expressed as vulnerability in actor training is 'the willingness to affect and be affected by' another, and is a key constituent of the cultural capital of the actor. However in the early development of individual actors in the Malmgren technique it is necessary to develop particular sensate skills. Casey (1998, p. 211) refers to 'corporeal schemata', where reshaping of bodily skills presents a particular 'form or pattern' as a 'basic way of doing something'. In this sense 'truthfulness' in performance, is not necessarily the only basis for examining Malmgren exercises. An exercise may be accomplished by a student having gained a functional knowledge of the *elements* of an *Inner Attitude*, establishing these as a means of considering acting. Vulnerability may be expressed through the desire to present work in the Studio setting, whilst acquiring these new skills.

Andy suggests (see exemplar Subtheme 18, in Chapter 6, p. 187) that competition is a part of the professional actor's world. Turning up to auditions, being prepared, structuring audition monologues or other materials and all of this whilst meeting sets of other physical demands is a necessary skill for a professional actor. The Malmgren training incorporates an element of 'competitiveness', demanding a presentational mode from students, in every class, reflecting conditions that will be met by actors in their profession. However the Malmgren technique is about acquiring a physically based language that differentiates performed behaviour. If approached through a perception of competing it is possible that witnessing the actions, abilities or presumed motivations of others may undermine a desire or will to perform.

The *lebenswelt* of the acting student consists of a complex mix of both highly physicalised and emotional demands. Indeterminate but sustaining beliefs about acting schools and the successful futures they can construct for students in their chosen careers contribute to the lifeworld of acting students. The stories surrounding different Malmgren acting schools inevitably contribute to the choice a student makes about training in a highly competitive field where career paths are not clear-cut or guaranteed. The physicality of Malmgren's training is at once both a personal and intersubjective set of experiences, where the reception of each actor's daily performances hold meaning for that person as well as for each of the others in the ensemble of actor trainees. Seton (2004, p. 52) locates the problem of 'misrecognition' in actor training where actors are regarded as autonomous agents and are judged on the basis of having 'talent'. However, the Malmgren technique emphasises the acquisition of a physically based language, accessible to all acting students who apply 'the work'. Furthermore, questioning dominant perceptions of what is being exchanged between actors and audiences alters the modes in which performed embodied action is undertaken. When every performed exercise is understood as a means of communication between the actor and an audience the emphasis shifts from an exercise demonstrating 'talent' to being a question of what any performer has to express.

7.4 The phenomenal body: new understandings of the actor's body

2. The Phenomenal Body: New understandings of the actor's body	Inhabiting one's body (22) Ways in to Malmgren's technique (10) Required specificity of actions (7) Malmgren's technique as a classification of behaviour (3) Relating Malmgren's technique to characters in text (13)

Table 7.3 Subthemes constituting the second emergent theme

The next set of subthemes listed together form a major theme surrounding experiences of the participants in recognising their performative bodies. 'The phenomenal body' is one that can be sensed, observed, and that 'asserts itself as a rootedness ... in its physical field' (Garner 1994 p. 99). In Malmgren's actor training the sensate experience of the performer's body is paramount. However in every day existence we are often unaware of the corporeality of our bodies. Each of the subthemes in this major theme relates to the specific ways in which the Malmgren technique draws the consciousness of the trainee actor to the physical nature of performance and in particular the performer's own body in performance. This theme looks at the fluctuating awareness of the participants' sensate body encountered in Yat Malmgren's training. The expression of the performer's body as a series of *working actions* is the starting point for Malmgren's technique. In this, Malmgren's technique is similar to other acting techniques, which begin with a physical score, such as Barba's training (Risum 2001) or Grotowski's (Wolford 2001). By comparison, a Stanislavski-based actor training technique may start with psychologically placed goals (Cohen 1992), or targets (Merlin 2001).

The first of the subthemes of this theme is, 'Inhabiting one's body'. This brings together data from the research participants that reference a dawning recognition, through the Malmgren work, of their carnal and grounded reality. As well, the participants describe a growing comprehension that it is through their body that they are recognised in performance by others including spectators. This research indicates that some actors in training are less aware of their embodiment than others. Leder in *The Absent Body* (1990, p. 1) argues that experience is often not centred on bodily awareness. For some it may come as a shock that any audience meets the body of the performer before any verbal communication takes place.

In Chapter 5, I discussed the case of Megan, a student at the University of Wollongong who grew up on a southern NSW commune. In interviews Megan recalls being emotionally shaken in her presentations in the Malmgren acting classes conducted in the Faculty of Creative Arts. For Megan 'the land was more me than my body'.

The awakenings of my consciousness of my body, as an entity separate from my [previous] environment, is a journey on which the Yat work has been a catalyst and a guiding structure (Megan).

Megan has become identified with a place and a group. She refers to her upbringing within the commune as 'a cult and I didn't have any independent or individual arena'. Megan often finds herself unable to be physically aware of what she is presenting in a studio class to the class audience. In her scenarios she strongly identifies with the subject matter of her scenes, usually to do with her land and the people who lived there, whilst her physical action in the class recedes from her own awareness. In the focus group discussion Megan reveals that, 'I know that I've tried to do what I thought were free-flowing scenarios and they were so clearly bound-flowing and everyone else in the room could see that, but I couldn't see that and often there are things that everyone can see'. Without the ability to clearly differentiate sensations of differing muscular movements Megan is often surprised by the analysis of her performed actions. It is a new experience for her to consider her embodiment, other than that of her past, which is interlinked with her communal land. Her awareness of herself, until her actor training, has been directed away from an awareness of herself as a body and towards the group identity. Megan has not been aware that her previous experiences there were grounded in her corporeality. This awareness had 'recede[d] from direct experience' (Leder 1990, p. 1).

The next four subthemes of 'Ways in to Malmgren's technique', 'Required specificity of actions', 'Malmgren's technique as a classification of behaviour', and 'Relating Malmgren's technique to characters in text', refer to the specific manner in which Yat Malmgren's technique requires actors to consider bodies in performance, particularly their own bodies. These four subthemes together highlight a means of witnessing the material and distinctive ways that bodies move and sound.

Malmgren's technique begins by questioning the physical forms by which any body opens into action in its lived–world: the technique begins by drawing attention to each student's 'Surface Body', a term that Zarrilli (2004, p. 655) uses to refer to that aspect of embodiment through which bodies receive and transmit sensory inputs and act in the world. Students begin to watch others and themselves, applying the terminology developed in the technique. Here, Douglas is speaking of the attention he began to place on the ways in which bodies move as a consequence of his Malmgren technique training.

> It opened so many doors to viewing the world. To begin with, through the *working actions*, we were working out that even in watching animals, sometimes, they *slash* and *punch*. The whole physical world is broken up into those *working actions*. So for me, it started off with, "Wow! We've got all this stuff. What am I doing? *Flicking* or ... ?" (Douglas).

Douglas becomes aware of a physical aspect of expression. He sees that bodies in the world have muscular actions. The attention of the students is awakened to a physical world, a world of sensation through which they view and listen and are viewed and listened to.

This requirement of the Malmgren technique, of matching particular terms to movements and vocal expressions, is not so very different to the learning of any dance or singing technique. Actors who are adept at movement or who have had previous movement training more easily produce the required movement shapes in Malmgren's technique. However, often these body shapes and gestures are produced without a deeper, or as Zarrilli (2004, p. 661) terms it, 'Aesthetic Inner Bodymind' connection. Zarrilli, in using these terms, is referring to a subtle awareness produced through time in embodied learning techniques such as yoga, the martial arts and acting, where attention can stay centred on and become refined as to the workings of the body.

It is common, for example, for trainee actors in the first stages of their Malmgren training, to be unable to perform the required scenarios whilst also being aware of their attention, integration of breath, and their visceral motivations. The first *Inner Attitude* usually studied in the Malmgren technique is that of *Nearness* (see Chapter 2, Table 2.3, p. 30). Actions in *Nearness* can often be habitual, functional or without thoughtful or emotionally connected motivations. To begin with the student of Malmgren's technique is simply asked to identify certain movement patterns and to find these in everyday or 'Surface Body' (Zarrilli 2004, p. 655) actions.

When working with the 'Required specificity of action' acting students begin to question why it is that certain specific action sequences are more difficult for them to achieve than others in the class. Twentieth century movement therapists such as Moshe Feldenkrais (1972, p. 3), Ida Rolf (1977, p. 23), Gabrielle Roth (1989, p. 30) and Anna Halprin (1995, p. 14) stress that self-image and movement are interlinked. In the Malmgren technique the actors come up against limitations, not through exploring characters but through exploring images of themselves. Barbara Sellers-Young (1998, p. 177), a proponent and teacher of *Nihon Buyo*, a classical Japanese dance form, has devised techniques to incorporate the Japanese concept of *ki*-energy into the training of actors in order to release imagination through the performer's body. She is only one of many western acting trainers who now encourage the use of movement techniques drawn from a range of Asian cultures in acting training. She links images of the way actors understand or perceive their bodies and selves as influencing what they can achieve in performance. Phillip Zarrilli (1995) also emphasises the enhanced connection of body and mind achieved by actors trained in traditional forms such as Keralan dance-drama *kathakali*, or martial arts *kalarippayattu* as well as in *t'ai chi ch'uan*. The Malmgren technique does not explore '*ki*-energy' as it is called in Japan, or '*qui*' as it is called in Chinese practices. Rather Malmgren trained actors gain awareness of the subtlety of shifting movement patterns in creating differing motivational perspectives or images. It is through attention to specific movements, *tempo-rhythms* (see Chapter 2, p. 53) associated with the *Inner Attitudes,* that connections arise with specific internal landscapes or meanings. Each of Malmgren's *tempo-rhythms* (and there are 96 – 16 in each *Inner Attitude*) holds a differing visceral meaning for the performer. Although Malmgren's actor training technique is distinct both historically and structurally from the above mentioned physical performance approaches, the Malmgren technique shares a commonality with its holistic mind/body approach.

Below Bella speaks of relating an internal or aesthetic quality to the manner in which she vocally produces her lines in performance. She uses the Malmgren technique and its terminology to communicate the exact modes or *tempos* in which she wishes to play scenes in *Enemies* by Gorky (1972). Bella speaks of the sensation of producing the words in particularly recognised *tempo-rhythms*.

I do like to work on the *tempo*. Something that Yat goes on about all the time, and I think really makes a difference, is *flexibility* of lines. I think it is more important to me than any other *tempo*. I like not to chop things up [words/sentences], to kind of keep the *flow* of things. Also I think it is the fact that it is a feminine quality, you know, it does add a certain sexual femininity to it. You've got to be, a bit of *direct*, it is so

> *contending.* But I do like to steer away from that. I think *tempos,* I mean the *working actions,* I like working for them because you have the physical sensation of something. And if you get that into the voice it does bring so much more energy and such a kind of internalised quality to it (Bella).

Bella enjoys producing *flexible working actions* on stage (*Slashing, Wringing, Flicking, Floating*), linking these with her own sensations of the sexuality of a character. She finds that physicalising the *working actions* allows her a connection with deeper meanings about her character's motivations or internal images. The *working actions* operate like a dance that connects rhythm and breath to deeper drives. This identification of particular movements in Malmgren's technique, the *working actions*, begins with recognition of discernible parts of the actor's body.

Sellers-Young (1998, p. 2) is critical of western dance trainings where students through watching a dance teacher and themselves in a mirror, copy certain movement sequences. This objectification of the functioning of distinct body parts, she believes leads to the fragmentation of bodily energy as well as a fragmentation of sense of self. Malmgren's technique, whilst requiring differentiation of bodily parts, sets this possibly fragmented experience within the container of the actor's previously lived actions. The scenarios presented, where particular movements are required, are often drawn from the actor's prior experiences, melding each performative gesture within a more flowing concept of self presentation. Performed habitual actions, whether an actor always works with tightened musculature or always acts in a *quick* or a *sustained* rhythm are often linked to actors' self-perceptions. Habitual bodily gestures or stances are readily pinpointed in the Malmgren technique. Students are propelled into a process of questioning of their habitual actions as the Malmgren technique links these with personality types as set out in Malmgren's Character Analysis notes (Malmgren, 1998). The attention of the actors in training is brought to their 'Surface Body' (Zarrilli 2004, p. 655) and interlinked with a questioning of motivation.

The link between movement, gesture patterns and imaginative landscapes leads to the next subtheme in this section, 'Malmgren's technique as a classification of behaviour'. As actors in training begin experimenting with embodying their understandings of the Malmgren terminology of *working actions* and as they witness others in the studio changing between specific *working action tempos*, they begin to consider the Malmgren technique as a means of exploring characters for the stage. In observing others' specific gestural and movement patterns, it becomes clear that an audience is able to understand character from movement and voice, and that the actor herself may be comprehended by an audience in this manner. Actions start being read as narratives about a character or the performing body.

In the example below, Danny from Malmgren's Drama Centre, London decides that his task as an actor is to create clear on-stage actions enabling an audience to comprehend that his character in the presentation[2] of Gorky's *Enemies* (1972) has an *Inner Attitude* of *Nearness*. In speaking of his technique we see a young man reorienting his comprehension of character from the representation that he wants for the audience's benefit to what an embodiment of character might mean for him. The sensations of this reorientation are new and confusing. Danny below offers an example of the fourth subtheme, 'Relating Malmgren's technique to characters in text '.

> I always knew, during the rehearsal process, that I was working for *Nearness*. So I had to involve 'warm' *[Strong and Sustained tempos]*, 'cool' *[Light and quick tempos]*, 'materialistic' *[Strong and quick tempos]* and 'human' *[Light and sustained tempos]*. I had to keep those characteristics prevalent and it was interesting to see where they slotted into the text. I tended to be more kind of going, "Hey! This is wrong." as opposed to "Look! I'm working for this to be right." You just get the feeling – that's not how that line is meant to be said in the scheme of things (Danny).

Danny is using the first tools of the Malmgren technique, finding specific *tempos* of action to delineate character for performance. In doing so he begins to experience an intuitive interconnection with a world that he cannot yet express, a pre-cognitive expression linking his ideas about a fictional character with his bodily expressions.

Overall this theme of 'The Phenomenal Body: New understandings of the actor's body' charts the beginnings of actors bringing attention to the corporeality of bodies in the experience of their Malmgren training. This encounter with the ways in

---

[2] *Enemies* by Maksim Gorky was presented by Group 38 at Drama Centre, London as a second year showing of a rehearsal exercise, directed by R Adiv, on 7 December 2000.

which bodies, most importantly their own, open into action in the sensed world becomes a sub-set in the overall experience of their training. Whilst this awareness may fluctuate or never be present in everyday life, in the Malmgren training it is a necessity. In the Malmgren technique, the attention is directed towards the *shapes* and *tempos* of actions, gestures and vocalisations. Whilst simply simulating these specific forms is an adequate start in the exploration of Malmgren's terminology, finding the connections to the images or viscerally placed motivations that produce specific *shapes* and *tempos* produces questions for trainee actors about their somatic expression.

7.5 The *chiasm*: the inextricable link between actor and audience

3. The *Chiasm*: The inextricable link between actor & audience	The use of *Inner Attitudes* (9) Questioning one's own and other's *Inner Attitudes* (11) Learning by observation (6) Imitations of actions (17)

Table 7.4 Subthemes constituting the third emergent theme

The next emergent theme houses Merleau-Ponty's (1968, pp. 152-153) image of the *chiasm*, the overarching symbol of this chapter. In *The Visible and Invisible*, which was published posthumously in Paris in 1964, Merleau-Ponty, in his chapter on the *chiasm* establishes an intertwining of the body with itself, a body that can both see as well as be seen, a body that can touch as well as being tangible. In this intertwining of perceiving body and tangible being there is a 'non-difference' (1968, p. 255) and yet the two are never congruent or over-lapping. Merleau-Ponty suggests that this wavering awareness between considering a body as a sensing object and a subject or agency produces the space for interrogation of *being*.

> it is because of it that the body is not an empirical fact,
> that it has ontological signification... (Merleau-Ponty
> 1968, p. 308).

This major theme of 'The *Chiasm*: The inextricable link between actor and audience', suggests that Yat Malmgren's formulations of *Inner Attitudes* operate phenomenologically to interrogate the actor's embodied being both in performance and in life. The concept of *Inner Attitude* plays a vital role in this phenomenological encounter or theme and stands at the heart of a chiasmatic relationship between audience and actor as well as actor and herself, for the performer using Yat Malmgren's technique of actor training.

In the subtheme of 'The uses of *Inner Attitudes*', actors in training question Malmgren's concept of character personality types, who perceive the world in particular ways and interact with others and objects on the basis of their perceptual type. Malmgren never used the term perception. The *Inner Attitudes* in the Malmgren technique are discovered always in relation to the actor's actions, character, movements and through accentuating the need for awakening the *Sensing, Intuiting, Thinking* and *Feeling functions* in the trainee actor. James comments on the exploration of character types in the Malmgren technique below.

> The most difficult thing about this technique for many people around me to get hold of was the idea of, "What was a particular type?", because that was always left for them to discover, which to me was more empowering. But for some people around me it became an issue of "How can we learn from ourselves in this way?" (James)

The investigation of *Inner Attitudes* or character types through action has been empowering for James as it questions the very nature of his perception. Madison (1992, p. 84) argues that perception has been understood as an activity, which, 'goes on inside a cognising subject'. He elucidates how Merleau-Ponty's phenomenology instead posits that the body/being and the world are in relation, where one is not separated from the other. As Madison would ask, 'What is the world before it is theorised?' (1992, p. 87). Madison argues that perception is a concept not an experience (1992, p. 83). In Malmgren's typology of *Inner Attitudes*, each type of character opens into a particular sort of world-in-action, as if that world already exists. For the *Sensing* type the reality of an empirical world is ever present. For the *Thinking* type this may not be the case, the world may be met conceptually. For a *Feeling* type every movement may be a movement towards or away from liking or disliking what is met. An *Intuiting* type may formulate the world on the basis of past experiences. It is not a matter of a character perceiving in a particular way, it is rather that any character is already immersed in a world. Yat Malmgren (2000) has used the metaphor of a child in the maternal uterus, as an image of an *Inner Attitude*, saying that when the individual goes into action it is like the shock of being born, because a unique world is born with that action.

The second subtheme, 'Questioning one's own and others' *Inner Attitudes* ', brings to the foreground the process by which trainee actors begin to recognise the individual ways in which they move into action in their worlds. Malmgren's training rests on the recognition of *Inner Attitudes* as character types, and the performance of the set tempos that belong to each of the *six Inner Attitudes*. Malmgren never encouraged the conflation of the use of *Inner Attitudes* for performance to the use of categorising performers themselves, however, this conflation is in part engendered by the process whereby performers use scenes from their own lives to comprehend the character types. Comprehending *Inner Attitudes* through scenes taken from actor trainees' lives has led Gina (below) to question the way she is seen by others.

> When I couldn't get [perform] *Stable* [in the Studio], everyone was saying, "But you're so *Stable!*" And I was saying, "But I'm not! I'm not!" And everyone said, "Oh You are, you are!" And they gave me all these different examples. They said, "This time! This time!" And I was going, "But that's not me!" because even though – I mean obviously there are times when I'm very *Stable*, but then there are times when I'm everything else (Gina).

The performer, Gina, inhabits the ambiguous space of being both the perceiving object for the audience and subject of perception for herself with more awareness than most. Performing specific *tempos*, belonging to *Inner Attitudes*, accentuates the differing access that trainee actors have to moving in specific ways and to performing particular actions. This differentiation creates questions about the *Inner Attitudes* in relation to the actor's sense of identity. In the example above Gina is aware that she is more than a *Stable* character, the *Thinking* and *Sensing* type that her audience of fellow students have seen. Their recognition may stem from Gina's abilities to perform actions with particular sequences of *working actions (tempos)*. Gina fluctuates between seeing through their eyes that she has indeed performed actions in the past in this manner, but she feels that she is more than simply this. In the Studio, when watched by her peers she is unable to perform *Stable* scenarios. The energy in this dialogue may be clear to the reader through her repetition of what she and others have said. In this animated repetition Gina questions the manner in which she inhabits her world, even whilst the interview is occurring. She recognises that she can produce the *Stable* actions, that she hadn't produced in her 'Yat' class, and that she has an objection to being viewed in this manner. Through this dialogue, questioning the meaning of Malmgren's *Inner Attitudes* in relation to herself and her performances Gina is left with questions about performed characters and the being of characters on stage.

Gina's questioning is part of a developing consciousness about action that is viewed. Here she is shown in a flux of negotiation with her own materiality, the materiality of her body's actions. *Stable* is not as Gina knows herself but as she considers it she realises that there are times when it is so. Even if this is the case Gina believes she is more than just that. Gina is involved in a dialectical relation with the concept of performed *Stability*. This negotiation or chiasmic outcome Merleau-Ponty terms the *flesh* (1968, p. 139), a possibility that is constantly open to becoming through interaction.

> The thickness of flesh between the seer and the thing is constitutive for the thing of its visibility as for the seer of his corporeity; it is not an obstacle between them, it is their means of communication ... It is thus, and not as the bearer of a knowing subject, that our body commands the visible for us (Merleau-Ponty 1968, p. 135).

Flynn (1973, p. 123) emphasises that this intimate viewing of ourselves, by ourselves, should never be mistaken for identification. Rather it is a process 'of happening, it is forever unachieved.' Gina is involved in a process of interrogation. The third subtheme, of 'Learning through observation' follows, for if we can see ourselves through others, which is the initiating point of Gina's interrogation, then there is the possibility of bodies understanding new processes of being through observation. This subtheme reflects the reversibility that Merleau-Ponty (1968, p. 147) refers to.

Jimmy's *Mobile* always stays with me. It was one of the most moving things I have ever seen and I'd never seen Jimmy do anything like that. I don't know if it was coming from some deep dark point of truth or what it was but I have always wanted to 'hit'

> something like that. It gave me a whole schemata. I struggled with *Mobile* so much (Andy).

Andy is overawed by a character devised and performed by Jimmy for all of the acting students in Wollongong's Faculty of Creative Arts in a program called Performance Week. Jimmy's character in this performance was presented as an example of a *Mobile* character. Jimmy played a murderer, who is revealing his deed to another man. When Andy speaks of this performance as coming from 'some deep dark point of truth' Andy doesn't imagine that Jimmy has lived through this experience, nor that Andy has met murderers who have lived through the experience. Instead Andy has understood something new about a man in these circumstances, something communicated viscerally that Andy perhaps hadn't encountered previously. In remarking that this viewing of Jimmy's presentation has given him a whole schemata, Andy reveals that he has comprehended something new about *Mobility* by viewing Jimmy, which has then aroused in him new goals for his own performances.

It would appear that Merleau-Ponty's embodied phenomenology reveals the transformative power and mystery of the meeting of bodies in performance. The link between audience and performer in a chiasmatic, intersubjective space carries the possibility of bodies constituting new understandings through their meeting and of stepping beyond the constructivist vision of reading the body only as representation. As Peta Tait (1997, p. 214) identifies:

> The body is an object in the text ... as well as representing subject positions. The spectator views the actions and movements of other bodies ... with the understanding acquired through experiences of her own body.

As a trainee actor watches others in the Malmgren technique, they may understand others as representing subject positions for various discourses, but they also observe the way other actors move, facial gestures, timbre and rhythms of voices, and through affective memory and affective imagination, they understand things about both themselves and others. The possibility also exists for any audience member to understand or grasp that nothing much is being communicated or is being transmitted through a performer's body. Any lack of expressive action becomes equally clear to an audience by the means of body meeting body in a chiasmatic connection.

Below James speaks about 'Imitations of actions', the fourth subtheme in this major theme of 'The *Chiasm*: The inextricable link between actor and audience'.

> When people weren't being honest to their own experiences, that exchange, where you begin to see yourself through the energy that the audience gives off didn't occur, because the person went into the scenario knowing it was a construction. It's an imitation. Whereas when the scenario comes from you as a person and you feel you're being honest and investing in that and risking that, the reflection you get back from the audience causes an emotional response (James).

James reflects on the immediacy of the intertwinement between actor and audience, of a process where an audience response has an immediate and differing effect on an actor depending on how 'invested' the actor is in the performative actions. In the Malmgren technique this is apparent to the performer, because either the scenario is drawn from the actor's life or it is a construction, as James points out. James' use of the terms 'honest' and 'honestly' will be considered under the subtheme of 'Truthfulness' of the next major theme. However for the purposes of this theme, and the subtheme of 'Imitation of Actions' the import of this notion for the participants lies in a felt difference between performed actions in which actors invested some part of their identity and actions in which this personal investment was not the case. The subtheme throws light on the affective communication linking actor and audience in ways that move beyond representation. Gina, below speaks about her own problems of imitating.

> If all you are striving for is to imitate something else then I don't think it is worth anything. But within the Yat work I think we were doing it [imitating] because we were inexperienced and unsure of ourselves and when we saw a scenario done well, we would use them as a template. We didn't necessarily do exactly the same exercise. I'd try to think of a scenario in my life that was similar to that. It's an attitude I don't like in myself, but I think it was clearly because I didn't want to fall behind (Gina).

Gina, who later feels that Yat Malmgren's method is devalued because of the possibilities of imitating actions that are not connected to her own sense of self (see exemplar Subtheme 17, in Chapter 6, p. 187), here examines why she has chosen to act in this way. Her desire to compete in the Malmgren studio class has turned her acting choices into functional choices to keep up with the presentations of others. Her processes of learning have been stultified as she states that imitating, rather than investing herself in her actions 'is not worth anything'. The sequences of action, the pattern of working actions and gestures can be copied as can setting scenes in similar contexts to others, the 'Surface Body' in other words can be a copy of another's. The interconnection to the more reflective forms of embodiment that Zarrilli (2004, pp. 661-665) identifies, 'The Aesthetic Inner Bodymind' and 'The Aesthetic Outer Body', link an actor's felt meaning with recognition of being an object for the audience's 'gaze'. Without these modes of embodiment the meaning of the performed actions is diminished for Gina. As James has suggested, the biofeedback of energy investment by the performer and then energy response from the audience reconnecting with the performer, this circuit of viscerally placed energy and meaning is negated through merely functional actions.

In this major theme, of the 'The *Chiasm*: The inextricable link between actor and audience', I have described the ways in which performing bodies in the Yat Malmgren training relate to their own engagement in reflection of their being-in-the-world. This act of considering at the same time as being an embodied subjectivity arises in direct consequence of performing Malmgren's *Inner Attitude* exercises for an audience. It is an intercorporeal experience creating a link between the 'self' and the 'other-than 'self'. Casey (1998, p. 213), a phenomenologist and philosopher who writes primarily about place, calls this 'the intermediacy of the body' and 'the inter-place of the lived body' seeing this space as the junction between biology and culture in any learned movement technique. The phenomenology of Merleau-Ponty in his last publication *The Visible and the Invisible* (1968) suggests new insights into the ways in which alterity is recognised through this chiasmatic body/being. The first sense of 'otherness' results from the disturbance of the meeting of our bodies as objects in the world. In this major theme, I have indicated how the *Inner Attitude* exercises foreground the recognition of this intercorporeality. I have suggested that the Malmgren technique presents an awareness of an affective link between audience and actor, as well as between actor and actor, through this intercorporeality. This occurs when performances move beyond the functional to an intersubjective exchange where the actor makes herself vulnerable through an investment of her sense of self in the performance. The unique position of the actor in relation to this intertwinement of the meeting of the known and unknown aspects of an embodied subjectivity, body/being, will be taken up further in Chapter 8.

> We are milling around on the hot concourse outside the West Chapel in the Golders Green Crematorium. I am seriously jetlagged. I am not used to London in June. Wollongong was mildly grey and wet but this weather now in London is glaringly hot. Bodies in suits, other glamorous bodies, well dressed, well heeled, they are all here for Yat, past students, present students, past staff, bodies crowded from the gates to the nearby chapel. I can't see how we can all possibly fit in. I stand back a bit from my friends, Group 18, they want to meet and greet but I am not quite up to it. I flew in only yesterday from Sydney and none of this seems quite real yet. My feet don't seem to be connecting with the ground but rather I feel I am swaying aboard a boat on waves. Everyone is chattering, spotting friends, some from years ago, spotting celebrities. The current Drama Centre students stand out. They look so very young. The mob from Group 18 and Group 17 and some from Group 19 are clustered close to the chapel door. I am flattered when famous graduates greet me. I peer sometimes at faces trying to recognize the student that I once knew, but mostly I am struggling to comprehend the finality of this. Yat is dead.

Researcher's Journal 7.1 June 18th 2002, Funeral of Yat Malmgren.

7.6 Experiencing the gap: whose is the body that is viewed?

4. Experiencing the Gap: Whose is the body that is viewed?	The gap between the actor's and audience's image (26) Feeling judged (1) The stage as an obstacle to expression (21) Awareness of an audience (4) Truthfulness (5)

Table 7.5 Subthemes constituting the fourth emergent theme

In this next theme, 'Experiencing the Gap: Whose is the body that is viewed?', the subthemes constituting this theme reveal the participants' preoccupations with the ways in which they are viewed in performance in their Malmgren training in relation to their sense of selves. The term 'the gap' arose in the focus group with the Wollongong acting students. It was discussed further in their individual interviews. It had captured some meaning for them of their training experience, a questioning gulf between who they imagined they were and who they were being reflected as in performance. In interviews at the Adelaide Centre for the Arts and at London's Drama Centre, this sense of trainee actors being reflected by teachers and audiences in new and unforseen ways emerged as a significant theme in the research.

The previous theme in establishing the link between the performer and her self-viewed action as well as the link to the audience, presented the ambiguity of the chiasmatic interconnection. The two positions of the body being both viewer and viewed through Merleau-Ponty's philosophy are never congruent. Even prior to his final work *The Visible and the Invisible* (1968) explicating the concept of the *chiasm*, Merleau-Ponty had ascertained the indeterminacy of the subject-object position. In his *Phenomenology of Perception* (1962, p. 208) he emphasises this. 'I can never say 'I' absolutely.' In terms of performance this could be translated as the notion that the audience has as much to say about my presentation as any 'I' that is inhabiting the performance. The audience has an access to the performed body through viewing another body/being.

In the subtheme of 'The gap between the actor and the audience's image', participants begin an ongoing negotiation between how they are received in performance and how they intend to present in performance in response to the Malmgren technique. In comparison to other techniques, which may also involve reflections from acting teachers, directors or audiences, and which may also involve processes of negotiation as to what is being presented by a trainee, the Malmgren technique pinpoints primarily physical expression. The reflection moves away from representational negotiations towards corporeal considerations. Using one case of Carmel's experience from Adelaide's Centre for the Arts in one particular scenario, I hope by concentrating on the minutiae of this instance to reveal something more fundamental.

> In one particular scenario, I think it was from *Mobile*, I was supposed to be *Punching*, and it was the most angry I've been with someone in my life, and hurt. And when I did it I had this twisting in my foot. I really wanted to hit the guy [an imagined character in the scene] but because I quite loved him and he was a good friend, DK [David Kendall] pointed out to me that I had this twisting in my foot and I was resisting and it wasn't really a *Punching* scenario. At the time I was just so worked up and I was going, "Yeah it was! It was!" I provoked a bit of response out of DK because I was a bit stubborn and thought, "I know! You weren't even there!" But he was more interested in talking about my physical actions that I was supposed to be doing. I was thinking past that going, "No! The feeling inside me was *Punching!*" (Carmel).

Carmel questions the nature of her performing body when she thinks that her memory of an event has a more elemental substance than her teacher's viewing of her performance. She reveals that she was thinking, 'You weren't even there!' The circumstances that she remembers and replicates have a solidity for her. Likewise David Kendall is able to pinpoint the twisting motion in her foot as a delineating *shadow move* in the scene. As Malmgren (1979) has defined, *shadow moves* are movements of any part of the body made without conscious volition. Carmel's twisting foot *shadow move* is an unconscious movement on Carmel's behalf, reflecting a *flexible* rather than *direct* element of movement. The elements of movement in *Punching* are *Strong*, *Direct* and *Quick*. Kendall doesn't discuss whether Carmel is angry but reflects that the *working actions* presented are not *Punching* ones. The twisting in Carmel's foot places the *tempo-rhythm* in *Wringing*. Later Carmel further considers this encounter with her performed-self.

> I recognised DK was right. I had to sit down and analyse what I was fighting against this guy for. He was making a personal attack about me. His motivation was coming from a love for me from within, but he was trying to hide it by trying to put me down and make himself look better. Then he made a personal attack on my boyfriend. My action should have been something different. To make it *Punching* it should have been to protect my boyfriend, like your child when you are about to protect your child from a predator or something. I had mixed up what my goal was. So I went away and that was one of the most beneficial scenarios for me (Carmel).

Through a process of interrogation with herself Carmel understands why her foot moved in the way that it did, why she did not present the *Mobile* scenario that she intended to, and a clarification of the feelings she had towards the imaginary man in the scene. Madison (1992, p. 89) in critiquing Merleau-Ponty considers the relationship between a 'body/being' and the inhabited world as being a relationship 'to what it is not'. Through phenomenology the subject and object may be regarded as:

> an *internal*, two-way or *circular* relation in which,…, each term of the relation exists only through its *dialectical* relation to the other (Madison 1992, p. 88).

In Carmel's case the object of consideration is her own foot. It appears to be autonomous to her as her intention in the scene was to produce a *Punching/Slashing* movement. *Punching* and *Slashing* are the two *working actions* in the *Mobile* variation of *Quick/Bound*. Carmel enters the interrogatory space that Madison (1992, p. 88) refers to with a willingness and consciousness, which the Malmgren technique has ignited for her. The scenario being spoken of was performed more than six months prior to the research interview and clearly the experience still resonates with emotional energy. It is unclear how long the interrogatory process lasted for Carmel about this one scenario, or when it was resolved but the period of moving from one position – 'I know! You weren't even there!' to the second position, 'I recognised that DK was right', to the final position of being able to say, 'To make it *Punching* it should have been …' is the movement across the gap that this theme elucidates. Carmel moves from placing herself as the subject (disembodied), then as the object (embodied), then being objective about her subjectivity (embodied/subjectivity).

The gap referred to in the naming of the theme is the wavering awareness between the consciousness of being an agent and the consciousness of being a viewed body or object in one's own field of perception. The dialectic that Madison speaks of is the ability to interrogate both positions. Casey (1998, p. 210) in examining the means by which human bodies acquire movement skills, rejects the notion that a bodily practice can be a totally specific cultural practice. In the processes of learning bodily skills, Casey sets out that whilst the skill may be culturally instigated at the same time it is reshaped when taken up by an individual. It is the awareness of this point of negotiation that this theme highlights.

In the subtheme, 'Feeling judged', the judgement that the participants spoke of in relation to the Malmgren technique has to do with performing scenarios based on the trainees' lives. The Malmgren technique does not stipulate the content of any scenario. However, as Alex states in the exemplar for 'Feeling judged' (See exemplar Subtheme 1 in Chapter 6, p. 183), the scenes that students choose to perform in the studio begin to reveal something about that person for the studio audience. The temporality of the studio initiates a disclosure of the being-in-the world of each performer to the others in the studio and to herself. Merleau-Ponty (1962, p. 433) in speaking about temporality argues,

> two temporalities are not mutually exclusive...because each one knows itself only by projecting itself into the present where they can interweave.

We can begin to know the past history of other trainees as they project that history through their performances in the present. The participants experience a dawning awareness of the unfolding nature of themselves in action through time. The three-year structure of the participants' courses at each of the research sites contributes to this formulation, where students progress within a cohort across a three-year training. The actors in training are known in their courses for what they have achieved across the period of that course. In these Malmgren trainings the choices of scenarios can subvert or enmesh the trainee actors in perceived identity roles.

> I think it's specific - it's not specific to Yat, but when you have classes where you have to get up to present something from your own life, probably in that way it is mainly Yat, but when you're just letting yourself open to the rest of the world and, even through there's people you trust in the class, you're always going to have conflict with someone in the class as well, and it makes you think "Okay, I'm showing this to somebody else - I've got to trust them and I've also got to -". I don't know, you have to think about what you're doing before you get up there and ... it's all a matter of calculation, in some respects (Rick).

Rick is very aware of the persona that he may be creating through his Malmgren technique classes. Whilst not using the word judged he implies that his considerations upon what he presents in his Malmgren classes are limited by possible reception by others. He is calculating what he can perform. His image of himself is not fully revealed because of perceived judgement by others. He knows himself to be more than what he performs. Conversely, his sense of self is never fully revealed in his performed actions. Through his fear of judgement he lives in the gap of knowing himself as something more than his performances. The 'gap', as revealed by the participants, is not a cerebral state, but rather a visceral experience, where confusion, anxiety and self-questioning are present.

Madison (1981, p. 25) proposes the phenomenological negotiation of the type that Rick is involved with.

> Even though the body can turn back on itself, take itself for its own proper object and in this way accomplish a kind of reflection, it never succeeds in *coinciding* with itself. This circularity never results in an *identity*.

Madison (1992, p. 92) terms this separation, or non–coinciding a 'diacritical' relationship, which because it is a relationship of meaning or significance, moves the body in its world towards 'expressivity'. It is through the experience of this 'gap' that meaningful movements emerge. These movements themselves hold within them the interpretation of 'the inter-referentiality' of the bodily subject and perceived things (Madison 1992, p. 92).

The third subtheme in this major theme, of 'Experiencing the Gap: Whose is the body that is viewed?' is 'The stage as an obstacle to expression '. Feelings of fear about the possibility of revealing a gap may be subliminal to the consciousness of a trainee actor. However, a performer may experience anxiety on stage or prior to performance, a performer may shake uncontrollably in performance or experience nausea prior to performing or on stage. The difference between performing actions in every-day life in comparison to performance on stage is located in the Malmgren training through the process of repeating actions from life. The obstacles to the expression of these actions become a point of interrogation for the trainee actor. Participants spoke of realising why they were shaking or fearful. The training provides the possibility of reflecting on the difference between being fully absorbed in their embodied actions or being aware of the gap between their intentions and the audience's reception of their performance.

James in the group interview of Wollongong acting students speaks of his body being terrified when performing. James is an older trainee who before being accepted into the Wollongong Performance course had auditioned repeatedly for the Victorian College of the Arts Acting course. In several of his annual auditions he had reached the short list of auditionees considered for entrance to the course only to be unsuccessful. James is deeply invested in the notion of becoming a professional actor. In the response below he locates the reason for his panic in a Faculty of Creative Arts production of Peter Barnes' translation (1989) of Frank Wedekind's *Lulu*[3]. James realises the obstacle to his on-stage expression and begins to find the means to integrate his agency with his viewed body.

> Playing Marquis Casti-Piani in (Wedekind's) *Lulu*, I panicked through the whole process. I wanted so badly to create something that was so important and so affecting for the other performers, and so disturbing for the audience, and because I had all those expectations in place, what I wasn't doing was just allowing it to sit with me. I was going through the motions of performing ... but I wasn't actually doing it inside my body. So, I think that it's really important for me to find that distance, not distance from the material, but distance from my own responses to what I'm engaged in – so that my passion cannot get in the way as much. Because what that was creating for me was a sense of fear – because I knew I wasn't achieving what I had set out to do, and so what I was giving off was something that I felt out of control of and that was completely wrong for the character. And I think what I came to is that it was my passion that was getting in the way, passion about wanting to be a great performer (James).

James in this interview relates an interrogation with himself that he has lived through during a theatrical season of a major production in his course He recognises his body in these circumstances as 'experiencing the gap'. The body that the audience viewed was not congruent with James' performative intentions. He realised his obstacle has been his blinding passion about an idea of himself. The physical actions he has scripted for his character and performance were not

---

[3] Peter Barnes' translation of Wedekind's *Erdgeist* as well as *Brusche der Pandora* was published as *Lulu: A Sex Tragedy* in 1989. The Faculty of Creative Arts, University of Wollongong staged this particular version of the Lulu stories at the Illawarra Performing Arts Centre, Wollongong as a graduate production, directed by J Kevin on 10-20 May 2000.

interconnected with James' breathing, his attention, or his intending. He wasn't 'actually doing it inside [his] body.' His awareness of an audience watching these actions sent his body into a state of panic. Even whilst performing James became aware that he had absented himself from the performance. James' interview continues to reveal that on the final evening of the season of *Lulu*, James was able to use his Malmgren technique to recognise his panicked body and take steps to begin to align the modes of his embodiment (Zarrilli 2004, p. 664).

The awareness of an audience is what allows a performer to negotiate this 'inter-place' (Casey 1998, p. 213) of being object and subject in an effort to develop an integrated body/mind experience. The next subtheme 'Awareness of an audience' in this major theme relates the effect that the audience's presence has on participants in questioning their corporeal presence. In this position of heightened awareness, the participants at times spoke about notions of truthfulness. The subtheme 'Truthfulness' is placed in this major theme of 'Experiencing the Gap' as it appears the participants are using the terms 'honest', 'honestly', 'truth' and 'truthfulness' to indicate how at ease or how uncomfortable they feel with their chosen physical expressions in relation to the their ideas about their characters and performance. This 'misrecognition' as Seton (2004, p. 52) calls it, where actors consider their actions as emanating from their 'autonomous agency' is recast in this analysis as a disjuncture between their subjective position and their viewed or objectified position. The arising interrogation, which occurs firstly as a felt experience, is the substance of this theme.

Bella in the following example has found herself performing her role of Tatiana in Gorky's *Enemies* (1972) but at the same time critical of her own performance. Whilst in front of an audience Bella has become separated from her body, which moves into a functional mode devoid of the deeper modes of her embodiment, such as Zarrilli's (2004, p. 661) description of the 'Aesthetic Inner Bodymind'.

> I just felt that I wasn't being truthful and that is the most important thing to me in acting. I was just too conscious of what I was doing, I wasn't involved in it. I wasn't experiencing it. I was in the play, but it was a play with results rather than going through the process (Bella).

In each of the subthemes constituting this major theme of 'Experiencing the Gap: Whose is the body that is viewed?' actors in the Malmgren training become aware of imbalances between their image or feelings about their body in action and the materiality of their body in action. The presence of an audience sparks this negotiation into existence, which the Malmgren technique encourages through precise analyses of *Inner Attitudes* and *Externalised Drives*. Each subtheme highlights the minutiae of means that the participants take in this subtle communication with themselves about their viewed selves in the awareness that for each the viewed body is not merely an object. This dialectical interrogation is imbued with felt meaning for the participants, as it brings into question deeper understandings of who they wish to represent on stage, what ideologies, and the purpose of acting for each participant. The training promotes an awareness of this 'inter-place'. For some this negotiation may be experienced as a set of uncomfortable or anxiety-creating experiences in which actors in training move, seeking more congruent expressions of themselves in performance. The Malmgren training offers the possibility of articulating these interrogations through the technique's concentration on expressive action, that which can be seen or heard. These processes hold the possibilities for future more synthesised or expressive performative action.

7.7 Refusal and 'it': new possibilities of expressive action

5. Refusal and 'It': New possibilities of expressive action	'It' - Confusion of identities (27) Vulnerability - Putting oneself on the line (16) Spontaneous physical reactions (12) The courage to demand of oneself (15) Reopening aspects of oneself (19)

Table 7.6 Subthemes constituting the fifth emergent theme

The negotiations for the actor in training between a viewed sense of being and a felt sense of being, revealed through the previous major theme, may be witnessed in numerous performance trainings (Blau 1982; Riley 2004; Sellers-Young 1998; Zarrilli 1997). The next major theme, 'Refusal and 'It': New possibilities of expressive action', is particularly pertinent to Malmgren's model of actor training. This major theme is one of a process of acknowledged reconstitution of self, or of the new sense of self, emerging from studying Malmgren's technique. The theme covers experiences of the participants witnessing new modes of feeling and functioning produced by the training.

The term 'It' arose in the group interview with Wollongong actors in training. Alex in the exemplar for the first subtheme, "'It' – Confusion of identities', demonstrates this experience clearly, emphasising both the anxiety and also the relentless self-probing occurring in a period of time in the Malmgren training. This period of uncertainty about how the participant is representing herself, how she is viewed in comparison to her felt image of herself varies. Below James speaks of this.

> I stayed up nights just thinking about all sorts of things in relation to the Yat work and myself and putting things into different perspectives and just thinking, like, constantly, to the point of not sleeping ... You're taking these things to heart, taking them into yourself and applying them to yourself, and looking at yourself, from within that term and the meaning of that term. ... Often what I found for myself in the classes ... I found it difficult not to enter some sort of emotional state ... responding to ideas about myself that I hadn't thought before or hadn't come to terms with at that time. (James).

James is not the only participant to speak with the heightened emotions displayed in the example above. Bella, Rick, Danny, Megan, Alex, Roger, Donald, Lliam, all spoke of at times overwhelming feelings produced by their training about their sense of identity.

Phenomenologically the meaning of such an experience may be revealed through considering Merleau-Ponty's (1962, p. 82) notions of the habitual body, where a practical or impersonal consciousness of a body is maintained on a daily basis. Events, which may have affected the phenomenal field of a body/mind, may cause sedimentation in the body/mind, a lack of adaptation to the present. In this case the events in the past remain, almost as a commitment to the past by the body/mind. Present actions may retain traces of the past, because the past is structuring all movements forward. Merleau-Ponty is not speaking of phenomena affecting the psyche. His whole argument rests on the basis that mind and body cannot be separated; the person moves in the world taking the past with her. Actors in the Malmgren training may become aware of these traces providing new and felt ways of considering their viewed bodies.

Physical constraints specific to individual bodies may bear a meaning on their viewing as Casey (1998, p. 215) highlights. He specifies that the shapes and motions of specific bodily performed actions can have cultural meanings that are localised. This localisation, I argue, can be as specific as being pertinent to different theatrical styles. Directors may 'misrecognise' (Seton 2004, p. 52) so called 'talent' when it comes in the shape of a certain height or weight or gender. Casey (1998, p. 215) calls this kind of localised meaning 'taste', 'where bodily determination as useful and skilful is submerged in matters of preference and value.' The growing awareness of theatrical cultural norms, shaping the ways in which bodies are viewed contributes to the questioning of the differential between audience reception and felt expression of the actor.

Merleau-Ponty (1962, pp. 76-82) as a means of reflecting on the way past experiences structure present movement gives the example of the phantom-limb where a patient continues to experience a limb which is missing. There has been a refusal of the body/mind to take in the experience of the loss of the limb. This repression may be carried forward into other temporal possibilities as habitual modes of engaging in the world. In the case of the performer however the habitual mode is challenged through the reflections described in the previous major themes that are a part of the actor's process in the Malmgren technique.

Merleau-Ponty (1962, pp. 160-161) gives another example, which may help to clarify these processes. He gives the example of the teenage girl who is forbidden by her mother to see the man she loves. The girl 'loses her voice'. Merleau–Ponty views this as a rejection of intersubjective relationships with others. The body/mind of the girl retreats from inter-relating with others because of the past loss.

Whilst each of these examples may be viewed as extreme in relation to the situation of the trainee actor, Casey (1998, p. 217) refers to "'ghosts' of an embodiment unknown to itself" to highlight the way in which bodily symptoms may be masking social determinants. The actor who displays, what may be thought by many directors as, hysterical or uncontrollable behaviour may be in a new process of negotiation with herself about socially restrictive norms that have been unconsciously shaping her movement.

In the example below of the second subtheme 'Vulnerability – Putting oneself on the line', Megan who has been through a lot of tumultuous feelings in presenting scenarios in her Malmgren training, discusses with great awareness what has held her performances back alongside her willingness to be vulnerable.

> I really didn't want to do that [scenario] and I really didn't want to show the class that [scenario] because it didn't fit in with the identity that I'd chosen to construct. But now I mean to be able to show these things and recently I've been able to. I was even conscious that I didn't want to show people weakness because I didn't want people to think that was me (Megan).

Megan is able to use the word identity. She understands that she had constructed an identity in the past that was now at odds with what she was being asked to perform. Megan has not wanted to cry in front of the rest of the class, because being 'weak' is not how she has wanted to be seen. She is now able to reveal more of herself (see exemplar Subtheme 16 in Chapter 6, p. 187). In fact Megan has cried after many performances in her Malmgren training, a spontaneous response to the circumstances of presenting her scenarios. This crying has provoked comment among other class members but it has not been a performative aspect over which Megan has had control. She has not wanted to cry but at the same time she has been unable to stop herself from crying. Her body/mind has been adjusting to the present. Like the young woman who loses her voice in *Phenomenology of Perception*, Megan's behaviour has been stemming from a relationship to the past, of which she has only been partially aware but which is embodied and still carried with her. Megan has been willing to stay vulnerable throughout the process, despite her feelings of confusion and despite her tears. The movement through these processes has allowed a new awareness of her embodiment to emerge.

The third subtheme in this major theme follows on from this, 'Spontaneous physical reactions'. In the example below Bella speaks of being in a rehearsal for Gorky's *Enemies,* which occurred on the evening previous to the interview. In that rehearsal Bella suddenly, and without any previous intention, threw a chair in her scene, playing Tatiana, in Act 2. Reuven Adiv, her director had stopped the scene and reprimanded her for unprofessional behaviour.

> The thing is that people don't like *free flow*. They don't like it. I do let my emotions overpower me and I don't actually do anything about it. I've always done things like that. But the thing is I like the fact that Yat has OK'd it. I'm allowed to be hysterical in my constant state of *Mobility* (Bella).

Bella's chair-throwing incident is still a point of contention. The other three participants in the interview, where Bella discusses this behaviour with bravado, laugh and remonstrate and are quite vocal as Bella insists that Yat approves of what Bella calls her hysteria. Whilst there is an element of joking to Bella's claims, there is also a sense that she recognises that she is involved in a process. Her director Reuven Adiv had not approved of her rehearsal behaviour and witnessing this incident, as I did, it was clear that Bella moved beyond the limits of professionalism in a rehearsal. The throwing of the chair in the rehearsal was a spontaneous outburst of anger. Yet Bella brings this up in a discussion of '*free flow*', a term implying an inter-connectedness with the past. Bella has, in the interview, expressed her dissatisfaction with her abilities to play the role of Tatiana, a leading role in *Enemies*. Bella knows that she can empathise with the role, but she can't find an integrated way of creating actions in the role. She can feel like Tatiana, but she doesn't know how to act like Tatiana. Bella has been watching herself whilst on stage. She has been feeling separated from her performance. She immediately relates the chair-throwing incident to Yat. She understands intuitively that the Malmgren technique is in some way promulgating this kind of outburst.

Bella in this experience displays a habitual mode of operation, an engagement in the present that has a dimension of memory or the past structuring it. Both in her group interview as well as the individual interview Bella is deeply engaged in deciphering the meaning of her performance as Tatiana in relation to her Malmgren technique and her sense of self. This refusal, the outbursts of unintegrated behaviours in the studio, is stimulating new appraisals of Bella's sense of self.

In the next subtheme, 'Courage to demand of oneself', Bella shows the kind of determination it takes to continue developing as an actor, given the confusion that she is experiencing.

> I just have this constant anxiety. You know, today, every time something goes wrong, I do so give in to it. Maybe I'm just doing the wrong thing. If I should be doing this I should just be able to do it. I should be an actress if that's what I'm meant to be and if I'm not then what's the point in wasting my time. I mean so many times I've thought, right, I'm going to leave. I'm going off and I can't take this anymore. It's so gruelling. It's a constant kind of battle with yourself. You constantly have to be fighting for something. It's such a complicated thing. It's not a material thing that you can see and go back to it. You just don't know exactly what it is that you're going for. You have this vague concept in your head. It's so difficult to get there anyway. I've got no patience. I just want to do it now. I want to do everything perfectly. That's not realistic but I still want to do it (Bella).

Again Bella is caught in a swirl of conflicting emotions with only her intentions of maintaining her training holding her in the process initiated through the Malmgren technique. Her despondency is palpable and yet she is continuing in the course at Drama Centre. The Malmgren process stresses awakening the *Sensing, Thinking, Feeling* and *Intuiting* abilities of each performer in order to extend the range of performed actions. This awakening, by working through the full range of *Inner Attitude tempos*, reflects which *tempos* are performable by the trainee actors and which more difficult. This witnessing in itself may become demanding, the constant comparisons and obstacles of which any performance training consists. Bella is depressed by her own inabilities in performing the role of Tatiana in Gorky's *Enemies* in the way that she wants to. As the training brings obstacles in performing to the attention of the trainee actor the intention to keep consciously developing and performing despite the reflective effort required may rest on courage or tenacity.

The last subtheme, in this major emergent theme of 'Refusal and 'It': New possibilities of expressive action', is the subtheme of 'Reopening aspects of oneself'. The process of the Malmgren training allows the recognition that certain modes of being-in-the-world have been closed off or left behind. The ensuing action has been narrowed. Bennan (1967, p. 74) argues that,

> The stable meanings [the habitual body] are the sedimentation of acts accomplished awake, containing the remains of our acts of consciousness, which cling as

memory and which consciousness bears with itself in its movement of existence.

In becoming aware of the difficulties in specific expressive actions by trainee actors, attention can be directed towards a process of regaining what has been abandoned. This process requires an acknowledgement of past affective memories. The process may not be fully conscious and is as much an embodied freeing of action as a conscious act of liberation. Alex below begins to examine her actions in her Malmgren training. She is grappling with new thoughts even as the interview proceeds.

> At the time I remember thinking, "Oh my God! Maybe **that's** what was happening to me in the classroom." Maybe I was super-sensitive about the audience and that's why I would stop after two words into my script, into my Yat piece, 'cause I would always stop and feel better. Then, "Oh! Sorry, sorry, sorry! Can I start again?" I don't remember it as being sensitive to the audience and feeling some disinterest from them. I just remember it as forgetting my want, forgetting my lines but maybe it was. Maybe it was! (Alex).

It is dawning on Alex that an audience's perceived disinterest in her has blocked Alex's abilities to perform. Phenomenologically her body/being has refused to participate in the face of the audience's separation. This refusal is so great that Alex is considering whether she should continue with her aims to be an actor. The realisation is the beginning of new options, new ways of being for Alex. Below she talks further,

> I think before the course I would try to be impressive or clever, whereas what people respond to is just something more human and vulnerable and real (Alex).

In seeking an audience response Alex is led in new directions in her performances. This may form the basis of a new configuration of her self-identity, where she can operate more easily in the face of an audience.

'Refusal and 'It': New possibilities of expressive action' brings to light the ways in which bodies in the Malmgren training intuitively express the emergence of more integrated modes of action in their lived worlds. Often these movements in the Malmgren training may emerge as felt and irrational actions or 'symptoms'. These can provide insights into sedimented modes of behaviour, which may have been socially constructed through specific socially delimiting conditions and structures. The pressure on performers to account for their viewed selves in relation to the image they may have already of themselves is a physical and psychological integration beyond that which is required in other less reflective trainings. Under these pressures physical manifestations of shifting notions of self may interrogate sedimented or habitual self-images. The Malmgren actor training provides a system where these encounters can be considered as well as providing a safe arena for new vulnerable constitutions of self to be enacted.

7.8 The transformed body: the ongoing process of 'becoming'.

6. The Transformed Body: The ongoing process of 'becoming'	Clear intentions as a way forward (2) Meeting the audience (23) Self in relation to others (14) Specific growing awareness of expression (25)

Table 7.7 Subthemes constituting the sixth interview theme

The final major theme revealed by the participants, through their interviews is a growing awareness of themselves as embodied beings involved in a meeting with others through performed actions. The participants reflect on the Malmgren training as a journey which has resulted in an enlarged sense of their being-in-the-world, through a growth of awareness of the participants' embodiment. Although these phenomenological terms are not the ones used by the participants, the awareness of being viewed yet inhabited bodies and what this means to the participants actions in the world is the substance of this theme.

In 'Clear intentions as a way forward', the participants discussed the ways in which they dealt with an audience viewing their on-stage or performed actions. At Adelaide's Centre for Performing Arts, students in particular spoke of stepping away from the specificity of the Malmgren technique to work more generally with processes of using transitive verbs in order to delineate performed actions. The desire to be fully involved in any performed action was vitally important for all the trainee actors. However, in particular at Drama Centre, the question of the specificity of the action was uppermost. The means of delineating character was more pressing for students at Drama Centre.

All the trainees were aware of intentionality. They had goals for themselves and for their characters. Below Donald speaks of becoming realistic about his goals or intentions.

> When I was twenty-one, I was very eager to get to these goals. Now I realise it needs lots of years. When you see these stars on television or these fantastic actors doing Hamlet or whatever, they've been doing that for ten years maybe. So, when I do these rehearsal exercises, I always try to work for something of the work, [ie the Malmgren training] and hopefully to do that play in two years again. But I've got a history. I knew what we were working for [in *Enemies*] and how it felt at that time and I'm extended. So I don't think whatever we do for a rehearsal exercise, it's not a finished product. It's more like a progressing into Yat's work (Donald).

Donald is a slightly older trainee actor than most of the participants, and an international student at Drama Centre. He sees himself involved in an ongoing process in his acting and in the development of his 'Yat work', as the Malmgren training is often called. He has set some clear intentions in order to reach his goals. In terms of his present 'rehearsal exercise', the performance of Gorky's *Enemies*, Donald knows what he is working for in the text. This means that he has analysed his character, Pologhy, using Malmgren's terminology. Donald is also clear about what the character wants and is doing in each scene. Donald states that he has created a history to understand Pologhy and has researched the text and its historical context to establish the character's history or biography. In fact Donald has visited Novgorod in Russia, Gorky's birthplace, and has watched a three-part documentary on the life of Maxim Gorky. By stating that he knows how it 'felt' Donald clarifies his empathy with the Pologhy's intentions or desires. Donald states that he is 'extended' by which I gather that he is trying to fully inhabit the actions that he is playing onstage. Later Donald speaks of his growing confidence in the choice of his character's played actions because he has been building an understanding of how Pologhy sees the events of the play unfolding and what Pologhy wants for himself throughout these events.

Clarity of intention may not always be possible for actors in training, as is indicated in a number of the major themes above, however, in this last major theme, intentionality is revealed as a prime contributor to integration of performance at all levels of the training.

The second theme in 'The Transformed Body: The ongoing process of 'becoming'' is 'Self in relation to others'. The concentration in the Malmgren training as to the precise physical and vocal expressions of any actor's body places intense scrutiny on the trainee actor's sense of self. Most of what the participants spoke of was their personal journeys through their training and their awareness of themselves throughout the training. The emergence of a growing awareness of an embodied self is what constitutes this subtheme. Not all participants spoke of this awareness, but most did at times, even whilst at other times the same participants were still unclear and full of self-probings.

Below Andy, from the University of Wollongong, speaks with clarity about an embodied sense of self.

> I think you have to know yourself. How can you play another character if you don't know yourself; if you don't know how your body moves, if you don't know how you sound like, if you don't know who you are, how can you play someone else? Otherwise the characters you're playing will be confused ... I do think you need to know who you are but you can never fully know, and you never will, and it's always a process that keeps going. Like actor training, like everything, it never stops. It's something that keeps evolving (Andy).

Through the training, which Andy sees as ongoing, Andy understands himself and his engagement in performance as an embodied and evolving process. Again the emphasis on a developmental model of 'becoming' both as an actor and person is clear, stemming from the Malmgren training.

Andy acknowledges that he is situated as a performing body. The audience is implicated in Andy's self knowing. Likewise with Roger, below, although Roger does not mention an audience, the audience is implicated in his new appraisals of himself, in that he is now considering what he can do as an actor. Roger has never before thought about how he was considered by others.

> This school - You learn so much about yourself. You really do through the work [Malmgren's technique] as well. It's just amazing. You think you've changed a lot. You look back on things you used to do in your life, different episodes, different points, and you really know, "No. You haven't. You've just become more aware." For me, before I came here, **I hadn't ever had to look at myself** this closely. I'd **never** had to look at myself, what I think I can do, what I think I can't do, as closely as this, because usually, I don't know, I just didn't. I was constantly just trying to get on. Maybe I just didn't take the time to do it (Roger).

The students are brought into a new alignment with others as they progress through the Malmgren technique. This position will be reflected on further on Chapter 8. However this new relationship with others also appeared in the subtheme of 'Meeting the audience'. Participants who were more at ease with their performed actions, or who had grown throughout the training to become more comfortable with their performed actions, spoke in particular ways about their relationship with audiences.

In the statement below, Douglas from Adelaide's Centre for the Performing Arts speaks about communicating with an audience. He has earlier grappled with the notion that it is only the body of the performer that is viewed. Whether the performer uses Malmgren's technique of Inner Attitudes to alter performance actions or not, the only body viewed is that of the performer herself. Douglas concludes that Malmgren's method is to be used in the light of communication.

> You can't ever lose sight of the fact that you're trying to communicate to the audience. You are in communication with someone else while you're being absolutely unselfconscious and trying to play an action or do something onstage in the full capacity of your being (Douglas).

In a somewhat similar vein, although more explicit in terms of what communication might mean, Donald from Drama Centre speaks about his relationship as an actor with the audience in a particular performance.

> At the moment I'm interested in taking them [the audience], guiding them, on a travel, going along with the play. At the moment I'm more interested in taking care of them. I'm still looking for a human relationship to the audience and guiding them with me. But I had a problem on Friday morning. I had a bicycle accident and I couldn't cycle in and I was very annoyed because of that, so in my first scene it felt a bit harsh. I felt I was pushing towards the audience and I was worried because it's very important to get the attention of the audience and to make them understand immediately rather than leaving them in a complete mist, [wondering] why is he doing this and why is he doing that, or I don't understand all this fuss or whatever (Donald).

Donald illustrates the need for a relationship based on care with the audience, guiding them through the narrative of *Enemies*. Donald is aware of the kind of communication that he wants to establish with this particular audience for this particular play. Earlier he had mentioned, 'listening very carefully' to the audience. He had said laughter can 'reassure you' whether the audience is 'on your journey or not'. Donald is aware when an incident outside of the realm of the play impacts on his relationship with his audience.

The specificity of Donald's performed actions is interlinked with his communication with an audience. Previous themes have dwelt on awareness by participants when communication has not been established with audiences, when there has not been a reciprocal relationship.

The last subtheme in this major theme, of 'The Transformed Body: the ongoing process of 'becoming'', is 'Specific growing awareness of expression'. It highlights the participants' search for greater expressive ranges in their performances. Below Danny speaks about moving character choices away from his habitual range of actions.

> I think personally I'm only just beginning to reap any benefit [from the training] but you know I think it's coming as it continues to happen it's just a process of work and you know yourself that it is intense work and it's very easy to see the development in those around you. I mean we're being provided with the tools and putting them into practice. And it just makes you think I've really got to think this character through and I've just got to go in taking risks, creating a character, moving, moving away from myself, Don't

> be, tricked in going down the easy road and keeping it close and just being persuaded because it's a bit easier that it must be like this (Danny).

Danny is aware of what actions feel comfortable in performance for him. He has watched others develop in their acting technique using the tools offered through the Malmgren training. He is aware that he needs to hunt for actions beyond his usual range of actions. He refers to mastering these possibilities as a process of work. There is a sense that this process could take time.

In this theme are emphasised, intentionality, an embodied sense of self, a specifically chosen relationship with the audience and finally the growing specificity of performed actions initiated through Malmgren's actor training technique.

7.9 Conclusions

Whilst it is clear that constructivist depictions of the performer's body as linguistic representations have substantially contributed to the understanding of performance as socially and historically situated, models of embodiment (Casey 1998; Leder 1990; Madison 1992; Merleau-Ponty 1968; Zarrilli 2004) have enabled an investigation of the complexities of the performing body and the ambiguous nature of embodied subjectivity in performance. This twenty-first century phenomenological investigation of the experiential elements of the Malmgren tradition, which govern the transmission of the acting technique, reveals that the Malmgren technique may provide a transformational embodied learning process, enabling actors in training to become more consciously aware of their embodied agency in their lived worlds.

The data and analysis of the phenomenological meaning of the Malmgren acting technique to the research participants, as set out in this chapter and the previous Chapter 6 illustrate that the technique may be regarded as a possible means of expanding trainee actors' interactions with their lived worlds. In this chapter the identification of six emergent interview themes of transformed embodiment for actors indicate firstly actors' awareness of imaginative worlds. The research points towards symptomatic, unconscious yearnings that acting students can seek to communicate. This analysis illustrates that actors through undertaking a Malmgren training may become better equipped to utilise their bodies as the locii for the expression of their imaginings. Performance through the training is recognised as one location of that expression, rather than the sole location of it.

The phenomenological methodology utilised in this Chapter 7 and the previous Chapter 6 have enabled trainee actors to reveal their own more encompassing perspectives of their use of their Malmgren training, rather than using it solely for the creation of characters for realistic performances. These chapters indicate the driving desire of the participants to find embodied expression for their felt or imagined worlds. The notion of an unconsciously expressed sensibility is reflected in both Laban and Malmgren's terminologies as *inner effort* (Laban 1948) and *Inner Attitude* (Malmgren 1988). Both suggest a pre-symbolic set of desires or longings that may unfold in action through time towards the symbolic. Malmgren's *Inner Attitudes* and *Externalised Drives*, however, locate the openness or resistance to these desires as already being apparent and expressed unconsciously through the body and this influencing every action, sound, gesture and shadow move of the body.

This phenomenological research indicates that the notion of *inner efforts* or *Inner Attitudes* perceived through action is a dominant dialogue in the trainee actors' perspectives. Merleau-Ponty (1964, pp. 12-27) writes of something similar; the desire to perceive the world 'pre-linguistically' is to recover the sensibilities of unreflective perception. Connolly and Lathrop (1997) link the philosophy of Merleau-Ponty and the movement theories of Laban through their common emphasis on bodily and movement experience. Likewise this thesis uses phenomenology as an approach to highlight the experiences of actors in training in the Malmgren technique. The research links phenomenological concepts of chiasmatic inter-twining of subject positions and subjects' bodies, where the experience of the participants in action is put under scrutiny.

Chapter 6 and 7 suggest how Malmgren's technique distinguishes itself from other acting techniques, particularly those working from purely psychologically or emotionally based approaches to actor training, while at the same time presenting itself as more than a physical skill for actors. The emphasis on bodily experience allows the Malmgren technique to be linked to emerging research on performative experience and embodiment (Legrand 2007; Riley 2004; Zarrilli 2004). The possibility exists of teaching the Malmgren technique via a phenomenological approach, where Merleau-Ponty's philosophies of embodiment can compliment the practice of the training, enabling students to distinguish between their experience of their actions and any representational placements of their actions. The technique through this means offers the possibility of studying processes of embodied communication rather than viewing the Malmgren technique as primarily describing character types.

The embodied processes revealed through each theme, as discussed above, highlight the possibility of the development of new and more expansive modes of interaction, which extend beyond the boundaries of craft-based performance skills. Whereas an actor in training may imagine that a recognisable set of tools await the actor, the Malmgren technique may begin the process of revealing to the trainee actor how limited concepts of embodied identity and interaction with others define the range of their expression as a performer. The *Inner Attitudes* of Malmgren's technique, rather than representing empirical perceptual constructs, may offer a way of differentiating processes of interaction between an embodied subject and her lived world. Offering a phenomenological perspective on this process may enhance these outcomes and increase the effectiveness of trainees' performative communication.

As Leder (1990, p. 103) suggests, the human body is able to disappear from awareness as the ontological basis for the processes of consciousness with which it identifies. The bodies in these interactive positions are 'absent' (Leder 1990). In Malmgren's *Inner Attitudes* for instance, three of the *Inner Attitudes* – *Awake*, *Mobile* and *Remote* – are interactive processes of consciousness characterised by inattention to their somatic underpinnings. In contrast *Near*, *Adream* and *Stable* are *Inner Attitudes* constituted through and by an embodied agency that is able to reflect upon that embodiment. In the latter stages of Malmgren's development of his technique, Malmgren required actors to work only through the three consciously embodied *Inner Attitudes* even whilst exploring the other three. He insisted that trainee actors concentrate on working above all through sensation. Actors in Malmgren's technique are led through experiences, questioning interactions with other students, the audience, and the trainer. Habitual movement based interactions are reflected and analysed, with the aim of enabling alien or new ways of being-in-the-world and of communicating between bodies to emerge. These may be regarded as corporeally situated processes that actors in training investigate. This possible expansion of interaction with the world may enable an ongoing inquiry into embodied action for performers.

I leave the last words to one of the research participants, Alex.

> The training takes a desire to put oneself forward – on one hand so publicly, yet at the same time within the safety of the theatre conventions of ritual. I do not mean to imply that there is an essential unchanging self that is waiting to be uncovered through this technique ... If the purpose of theatre, or perhaps method acting, is to make meaning, this process of personal clarification is in the name of communicating the text and the character to an audience; through oneself, through the self that others read ... The training has provided me with the practice of getting up and sharing myself with others. It has confronted me with how difficult that can be ... It has taught me steps towards consciously owning what I do onstage and offstage (Alex).

CHAPTER 8

PRE-LINGUISTIC REFLECTIVE COMMUNICATION

Effort is silent. Effort in itself is a moving situation which will be effected outside of ourselves.

Malmgren January 1988.

8.1 Introduction

This chapter aims to add another ripple in the metaphoric image of widening concentric ripples created by a pebble dropped into a pond, representing the horizon of meaning available to actors through Malmgren's approach to training. The chapter will investigate the ripple of meaning of Malmgren's actor training technique in relation to non-verbal communication and the wider understandings of this communication for performative bodies. This research follows on from Chapters 6 and 7, where Malmgren's technique of actor training was investigated through hermeneutic phenomenology in relation to embodiment.

This research began by investigating a principal question about Yat Malmgren's technique of actor training: **In what way does Malmgren's actor training contribute to the understanding of the performative body?** In this thesis I have created an expanding set of contextualisations through which this question is investigated. Whilst Chapter 2 set the context of the research as investigating the Malmgren technique's inheritance of terms and practices from Rudolf Laban's dance techniques, Chapters 3 and 5 revealed the processes and structures by which Malmgren's actor training technique differentiates itself from other embodied actor training methods designed for realistic theatre. In Chapters 6 and 7 hermeneutic phenomenological inquiry methods illuminate the theorisation of trainee actors' gaining an expanded and synthesised embodiment through the study and practices of Malmgren's technique. This chapter represents the final, broadest metaphoric ripple of my research. It explores insights into Malmgren's actor training in relation to non-verbal communication between performative bodies. The chapter places these insights in the context of contemporary performance practice in order to establish the Malmgren technique as relevant in contemporary Australian actor training. Each new wider ripple of contextualisation encompasses the totality of the previous ripples. The phenomenological research indicates in Chapter 7 that the Malmgren technique can enable actors to reflect on the physical expression of their symptomatic, unconscious imagined worlds, allowing possible transformations of agency to occur through their learning of the technique. The chapter established the beginnings of questioning for some, not only of their modes of personal representation, but also of their modes of theatrical representation as a means of communicating with audiences. In this chapter I argue that the possible dawning awareness of the visibility of unconscious symptoms and desires through pre-linguistic reflective communication may enable trainee actors to take new directions in *Space*, including the self-initiated development of new approaches to performance. This chapter argues that Malmgren's *Flow* is the principal means whereby bodies, through minute physical movement sequences create affective and often unconscious modes of communicating with other bodies. The growing awareness of this pre-linguistic reflective communication may alter the ways in which bodies perceive the establishment of 'otherness'.

8.2 Pre-linguistic reflective communication

Investigating the effects of the broadest ripple of contextualisation of Malmgren's actor training technique encompasses awareness of the performer's non-verbal communication between human bodies. In Malmgren's terminology performing bodies create *shadow moves* (see Chapter 2, p. 51). These sequences of small gestures move in *directions of space* and are means through which Malmgren's *Inner Attitudes* and *Externalised Drives* are partly visible for an audience. As shown in Chapter 7, through the example of Carmel and her twisting foot (pp. 224-226), the attention of a performer can be drawn through Malmgren's technique to subtle, unconscious performative movements allowing a dialogical interrogation to occur between the felt or imagined meaning and the embodied meaning of movements. It is this world of Malmgren's *shadow moves* that is explored in this chapter.

I refer to the communication between bodies as **pre-linguistic reflective communication**. I use the term pre-linguistic because this performative communication operates outside consciously symbolically structured dimensions, defined by language or intention. Others may intuitively note bodily stances indicating angles of the body in space, gestures, and sounds. These may also appear less consciously via symbolic forms in dreams, of either the communicating body or of those who respond to these non-verbal communications. However in both of these cases, for the body expressing these forms there remains a lack of awareness of the totality of the communication. Grosz, (1990b, p. 18) in writing of Lacan argues that the unconscious 'obstinately rejects being understood by conscious intention'. Conceived within Merleau-Ponty's (1968) embodiment of 'flesh', it is possible to understand that the meaning of the interaction between bodies can never be fully symbolised. Butler (1999) argues that Foucault mistakenly presumes that bodily inscriptions require a power outside of themselves to come into existence; rather she argues that inscriptions form through diffuse and active webs of social structuring. Macke (2005, p. 13), a contemporary phenomenologist, argues that any reflection of a surface body is not 'real' but rather offers a 'portal that, if entered, leads to yet another story of our lives'. These pre-linguistic communications offer unshaped possibilities rather than differentiated communications of meaning to others.

The term 'reflective' situates this communication within Lacan's (1999, p. 216) concept of mimesis, where an ego or identity is established through the differentiation between itself and otherness through a mirroring process. In terms of performance, Wilshire (1991, p. 167) suggests that mimesis operates as an unconscious means whereby performing bodies establish likeness:

> as conscious bodies they take the roles and expressivity of others in the group, and a nascent self appears because the body begins to react to itself as such a being. ... the body's response to this mimetically induced other "in" itself is itself mimetically conditioned by others...

Chapter 7, through the phenomenological research outlined how trainee actors experienced the Malmgren technique, some becoming cognisant of the material aspects of their performative actions. This chapter aims to synthesise this meaning of the Malmgren actor training technique within a broader frame, in pre-linguistic reflective communication. The sites of these investigations, as throughout the thesis, are the individual bodies of the participants engaged in the research.

Heritage from Laban

Actor Training for Theatrical Realism

Study of Embodiment

Pre-linguistic Reflective Communication

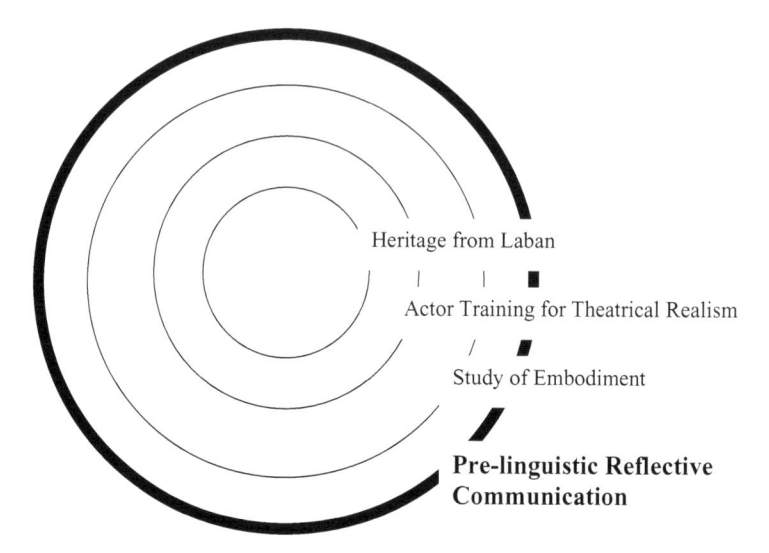

Figure 8.1 The fourth ripple – Contextualisation of Yat Malmgren's actor training: pre-linguistic reflective communication

8.2.1 Phenomenological insights about and other contemporary approaches to performative action

In Chapters 6 and 7 the phenomenological research indicated that Malmgren's concepts of the actor's body moving in space, under the influence of reflective ideas and desires, represents a body in action, which, whilst purposeful, is also meaningful in an objective sense to any audience. Through the Malmgren technique, the body as a site of action may become the means through which the actor not only meets the world but also via her engagement or intertwinement with it, structures her viewed 'self'. This structuring in the Malmgren model is referential to all action and becomes one aspect of a more expansive notion of performance; a life performance.

In the latter phases of Grotowski's 'research' on performing bodies, his interest was in 'Art as a vehicle' (Wolford 2001), where actions relating to songs or ways of moving can alter the performer. His emphasis shifted from being about the interconnection of the performer with the audience to being about the interconnection between the performer's experience and the performer's action. The 'vibratory songs' (Wolford 2001, p. 120) and repeated precise physical scores Grotowski instituted in rehearsals, he maintained created energy transformations for the performer. As well as the actor's 'score' (Grotowski 1975, p. 179), Grotowski was concerned with the 'inner action' (Richards 1995, p. 28), which had to do with actors contacting inner emotional landscapes. Similarly Malmgren's *Inner Attitude* tempos aim to interconnect actions with imaginary and emotional associations, which have meaning for the performer. Whilst Malmgren himself concentrated on the meanings that his *Inner Attitudes* generated for audiences, this thesis through Chapters 6 & 7 has indicated that actors undertaking actor training through the Malmgren technique may be as concerned with the ways in which their action is developing their embodied sense of 'selves'.

As Wilshire notes (1991, p. 232) the body is the locus of only partial consciousness at any time and the first and third party viewing, or understanding of meaning of that locus, are particularly intertwined. Through the *Inner Attitude* exercises, this structuring of the meaning of a body in action, being viewed in a studio or other performance setting, can be configured in numerous ways; multifarious embodied identities can be performed through changes in language, rhythms, gestural shapes, action and use of space. Actors in training in the Malmgren technique may become aware of the possibility of multiple or fractured identities for themselves, through which they are in communication with others whilst only being partially aware of their own transactions.

Postmodern actor training techniques such as Anne Bogart's Viewpoints (Herrington 2000) often begin by using physical improvisation to deliberately fracture staid or habitual performative actions. Whereas Malmgren's technique rests on analysis of text and aligning constructed text based characters with an *Inner Attitude* and the tempos belonging to any *Inner Attitude*, Viewpoints creates physical responses between performers often prior to any text being explored in rehearsals. Herrington (2000, p. 156) claims that the use of Viewpoints as an acting technique for the exploration of text based characters provides 'an emphasis on instinctual behaviour and physical expression'. Lampe (1998, p. 187) in describing Viewpoint's techniques as undertaken at the Saratoga International Theatre Institute pinpoints the challenge of instilling the physical movements created through Viewpoints' improvisations with 'internal life'. The actors may be capable of creating spontaneous moves through improvisations however associating these moves with text may be more directorially problematic. It seems that whether an actor begins through releasing a set of intuitive physical choices or begins through an imagined empathy that is then moved, there can still be problems of keeping both verbal action and *inner effort* interconnected in rehearsals and performances.

Chapter 5 established Malmgren's *Inner Attitude* and *Externalised Drive* exercises as aiming to develop the ability of actors to corporeally differentiate character based performances. Chapter 7 indicated through the phenomenological research that Malmgren's *Inner Attitudes* whilst being experienced as interiorities, are expressive of ideas and desires, which are partially apparent to viewers as well as to performers, through *shadow moves*, angles of the body created in space and bodily movements. In this process actors may experience a heightening of awareness of pre-linguistic reflective communications being transmitted through their own and other actors' bodies. Through a cognisance of the narratives that these gestures, stances and sounds can transmit, the actor through Malmgren's technique is offered a unique opportunity to reconsider her placement in these narratives. In addition, actors are encouraged to learn to draw on intimate understandings of the minutiae of their bodily actions in order to create subtleties within performative choices.

Contemporary dance has clear synergies with this process, both in terms of the readership by the audience and in terms of the experienced interiorities of the performer that may be only partially expressed through movement. American born, Australian choreographer, dancer and dance theorist Karen Pearlman (2001) recognises the thorough systematics that Rudolf Laban's theories offer to choreographers. Quoting Susan Leigh Foster's *Corporealities*, Pearlman (2001, p. 218) emphasises that each analytical structure of Foster's, and thus of Laban's, houses an intelligible reading of the body for the audience. She speaks of reading 'the physical mind'. In the same way Malmgren's *Inner Attitudes* and *Externalised Drives* are kinaesthetic structures, interconnected with particular experiential states, that may allow an audience to read the body/mind of the performer as well as the possibility of allowing the performer to reflect on her own body/mind.

The themes emerging from Malmgren's actor training as set out in Chapter 7, particularly that of 'Experiencing the Gap: Whose is the body being viewed?' and 'Refusal and 'It': New possibilities of expressive action', indicate that actors, training in the Malmgren technique, may experience a fragmentation of their habitual sense of 'self'. If the trainee actors become aware of the pre-linguistic reflective communication that is continuously moving and shifting between the actors and others, understandings of how they are appearing and how they are representing themselves may become distorted. Any analysis of action produces an emphasis on the particular. Some of the participants experienced the fragmented nature of their situated selves more keenly than others. Those trainees with more fixed identities or more fear about moving their understandings of themselves, may be more encumbered with a sense of fragmentation through the technique, whilst others may experience the movements away from habitual actions more fluidly. This has also been reported as being the case in other actor trainings. As noted in Chapter 7 (p. 206) where Burgone, Poulin and Rearden (1999) found that a Stanislavskian training of actors produced uncomfortable 'blurrings' between student actors and their characters, so too in Bogart's Viewpoints actors have been reported as feeling alienated from their text by creating movements to which they then need to relate (Lampe 2001, p. 187).

Where agency and the consciousness of the meaning of the performance for the audience are not congruent, the sense of a fractured identity may be more intense. As Braidotti (1994, p. 196) asserts for any female subject, viewed as a process, identity and subjectivity may be corporeally moving moments. Braidotti argues this in terms of the female subject, where a dominant patriarchal discourse separates subjectivity from assumed identity. Foucault's (1990) theories of power and bodily inscription could be used to analyse these occurrences, but this thesis has utilised phenomenological analysis to concentrate on the individual and transformative processes that have allowed actors to experience uniting actions with their identities. This may be considered in any actor's performance in a Malmgren studio setting, but perhaps more so, not only for female subjects, but any performer who does not fit into the dominant subject viewed through the popular media, that of white, male and heterosexual. Clearly the journey of Megan through the Malmgren technique's *Inner Attitude* exercises results in this participant acquiring a new set of self-perceptions through the dichotomy of her experienced understandings of her identity and her viewed understandings (See pp. 153, 187, 210, 234). At one moment an actor may be consciously identified with her action and the audience's collective meaning of it or response to it. Yet at another moment an actor may subjectively be at odds with the actions she is producing for the audience. In Megan's case these experiences in

Malmgren's acting technique lead Megan not only to understanding herself as a constructed identity (p. 234) but also to value the Malmgren technique as an 'arbitrary' and 'taxonomical' system of human behaviour (p. 149). It has not been necessary for Megan to believe in any essentialist 'truth' of the technique for the technique to have benefited her transformation of self-perception. Through the questioning of the actor's body-image (Bergson 1913) through any performance or bodily expression, the Malmgren actor training technique aims to heighten such possibilities of transformation of habitual actions.

8.2.2 Transformation through the *Inner Attitudes* and *Externalised Drives*

Most styles of actor training initiated by Stanislavski's system refer to the transformation of actors into other characters (Benedetti 1986; Gronbeck-Tedesco 1992). This performative transformation often implies more than a changed representation, rather it equals an extension of the actor's experience into new or unaccustomed aspects of herself in action. The underlying assumption of an embodied transformation of an actor into a different character is not limited to modernist actor trainings but reappears throughout performance history. From the use of masks in Greek Tragedy (Campbell 1959) to the modern use of the mask in actor training (Eldredge 1996), from the ritualised theatre of the medieval mystery cycles to modern ritual theatre (Innes 1981), transformational processes have been integral to theatrical tradition. Actor training that emphasises transformational possibilities can be analysed as producing encounters with the alien or unknowable aspects of the actor's being.

The emergent themes in Chapter 7 suggest that given the systematic nature of the Malmgren technique actors may consciously form new ways of being viewed. They are not propelled by a ritual, or masked in attempts to embody new identities. Rather it is the actor's choice intentionally to keep working through Malmgren's system. On a less conscious level, observing scenarios prepared by fellow students in a Malmgren studio setting may draw trainee actors into considerations of altered embodied ways of being. The theme of 'The *chiasm*: the inextricable link between actor and audience' in Chapter 7, reveals some of the participants encountering a feeling of discomfort when required in the Malmgren technique to produce *Inner*

Attitudes that are not part of their habitual range. Amongst the participants there were varying responses to this experience.

The subtheme of 'Imitations of Actions' indicates that some participants in training in the Malmgren technique decided to retreat from embodying non-habitual or newly experienced *Inner Attitudes*. It is clear even from this relatively small study that the Malmgren technique may not always shift an actor's range of performative actions, nor will it always expand an actor's embodied agency. However Malmgren's technique does involve learning about the subtleties of embodiment with which actors are involved. In the flux of exploring *Inner Attitudes* and *Externalised Drives*, new understandings of the meaning of action may arise for each individual. The Malmgren technique offers the possibility of performative transformations through the work on *Inner Attitudes* and *Externalised Drives*. When the opportunity of performative transformation is utilised it may lead to a conscious process of embodied individuation, set amongst the web of 'kinesthetic involvements' with an audience or other actors (Wilshire 1991, p. 78).

8.2.3 Malmgren's 'evolution' of action

In Chapters 6 and 7, particularly through the theme of 'The Transformed Body: the ongoing process of 'becoming'', many of the participants speak confidently of finding new ways to be in the world or of finding who they are through the technique. The experience of the Malmgren actor training may enable this alteration in an actor's subjective considerations of 'herself' in action. Malmgren's emphasis as to the use of this specificity of action was on the independent ability of an actor to bring the text of any play to life for an audience. However, Malmgren's modernist position was that there is a single correct interpretation of any text, one that aligns with the author's original intention. Malmgren extended the specificity of performative action that he taught to be used by his trained actors in castings. The actor, in his view, could like a chameleon, shift her embodied action for the casting, reflecting the character that was being cast. In both examples, Malmgren stressed the independence of the actor through the learning of his technique's transformative processes. Malmgren also spoke of an 'evolution' of action in terms of the *Inner Attitudes* stating,

The evolution is definitely that a child starts with *Nearness* and moves towards *Adream*. That is when it comes to *Adream* because of puberty, so *Sensing* and *Feeling*. And then it starts to bring all the time to *Adream*, but they don't develop the *Vision*. So they can never come into *Stable*. And this is the tragic thing, because when you take away *Vision* from *Adream* – what is the media – then you can't create *Stability* (Malmgren 2000).

In this statement Malmgren suggests a movement of *Inner Attitudes* across a lifetime. His emphasis on the development of *Stability* reflects his hope for the development of perspectives and actions that take others into consideration. I asked if Malmgren believed that his work provoked this 'evolution' of *Inner Attitudes* towards a greater development of *Space*, implying a greater consideration of others. He replied,

Well in a great deal it works. It works a great deal. But not with the majority (Malmgren 2000).

In this research, Malmgren's 'evolution' of action through the study of his *Inner Attitudes* and *Externalised Drives* is regarded as synonymous with the performer's desire to reach for the ever-elusive congruence of self-identity with action. Whilst this is an aim of the work both in Malmgren's perspective and my own, Malmgren clearly is less than optimistic that it can be achieved. Malmgren's regret was that often actors' desires resided in the realm of seeking celebrity status and that actors often did not transform their desires towards more altruistic visions. This research indicates that the transformation that the Malmgren technique may offer is related to the actor's embodiment and can have repercussions on the directions in which the learning of the technique is put to use. Working within realistic styles of theatre and film is only one outcome. Participants spoke openly of writing for performance, of dancing, of directing and of theatre making.

Malmgren's actor training technique is not the only actor training technique that claims possibilities of transforming performers in an evolutionary mode of becoming more expressive. Tadashi Suzuki using his physical training for performers speaks of the need to regain 'our physical faculties' for 'our essential selves' (1996, p. 156). In order to heighten expressive abilities in actors, Suzuki's training offers a restorative process for 'dismembered' physical functions. Suzuki (2000, p. 67) also speaks of the problems of linking language with action:

> when words enter into it [the performance] you get terribly divided. When you are divided, bodily sensations are weakened. ... Cut off, the body in its entirety renders service for the sake of speaking, and a gap develops.

In this conversation with *butoh* exponent Hijikata Tatsumi, Suzuki indicates the pitfalls of actors being separated from their most integrated and most communicative expressions. This desire for actors to be physically expressive whilst at the same time interlinked with the 'relational construct' (*ibid*, p. 67) of the text, Suzuki terms a 'transformation'. It seems that a number of acting techniques used for contemporary practice pursue the same kind of outcomes pursued by Malmgren's technique, that of a highly expressive and fully integrated performative being.

Feminist theorists locating the site of cultural and socio-linguistic formations of identity have investigated the body in the light of transformative possibilities of identity. Al-Saji (2001) investigates Merleau-Ponty's (1968) incomplete 1968 article, *The Visible and the Invisible,* in the light of Henri Bergson's (1944) ideas about duration. She postulates that it is not simply acts of conscious will that bring a body into a differentiated state but 'every sensation, every experience of colour and every movement of the hand, expresses my whole existence as a singular becoming' (2001, p. 110). Al-Saji here emphasises the openness of the body to temporality and any response of a body being viewed through temporality as a means of adapting or 'becoming'. This philosophy of 'becoming' has strong resonances with Malmgren's notions of transformation. Both are formed through time, with a certain degree of will, but also through an unconscious bodily set of responses that are shaping the body/being and that are in part intersubjective experiences. In learning of the complexities and subtleties of performed action within Malmgren's technique, processes of 'becoming' are enhanced but always circumscribed within the intersubjective milieu of wider cultural contexts.

Grosz (1990b, p. 2) adopting a feminist perspective on Lacan's theories of ego formation, questions the very means of the foundations of knowledge predicated on consciousness belonging to an individual subject. She argues using Lacanian philosophy, the ways in which any subject is incapable of 'fully knowing herself' (p.

13). Consciousness, in Lacan's terms 'the ego', is constructed through libidinous investments in fantasies about the subject herself and about others (p. 30). In Lacanian terms this is a moving yet boundaried identity, where the ego operates deceptively to split or differentiate the subject from others (p. 47). In terms of desire Lacan identifies all desires and productions of the ego as 'meconnaissance' (cited in Miller 1988, p. 170). This inability of any ego to know itself in full becomes Grosz' argument for searching for new ways of conceptualising subjectivity.

In Malmgren's system the desire to search for the subject's congruent *Inner Attitude* and *Externalised Drive*, where each action that the embodied subject creates is aimed at more fully articulating that embodied subject's desire, may be in many ways, an impossible yet empowering journey. Each action can lead to reflection, which can lead to further action. Moreover performance, either of 'self' or of assumed character in a Malmgren studio is created within the web of understandings of the audience. The performer creating an exercise or a performance is not necessarily congruent with the consciousness of the meaning of that performance for the audience. The body of the performer may become more apparent to that performer as a site of intersection of numerous fields of meaning including socially or biologically constructed systems of meaning. The ability to reflect on these outcomes is dependent on the flexibility of the learning environment as much as on the independent performer.

8.3 Malmgren's *Flow* and meeting of the 'other'

Peta Tait (2008) recognises that the role of the emotions in acting in theatre scholarship has been relatively under examined. She challenges the conventional Stanislavskian actor training notion that performing bodies express universally recognised emotional feelings (2008, p. 84). Instead she contends that performative bodies expressing emotions 'in realist theatre is imitative of the prevailing social languages for emotion'. Performing bodies when expressing emotions are constructing or imitating already socially defined norms of expression.

Malmgren's practices through the analysis of his *Motion Factor* of *Flow* (See Chapter 2, p. 27, and Table 2.1, p. 29) offer a highly articulated means of investigating the ways in which performing bodies communicate emotions. Pre-linguistic reflective communication in this sense considers the shifting patterns of small gestural actions in performance, which reflect the changing and felt experiences of the performers. A key aspect of embodiment in performance in Malmgren's technique and theories is that of the 'flow of action': the interconnection of one moment with another not only shapes the experience of the performer but also shapes the subtle movement patterns of gestural physicality. Both Merleau-Ponty (1962) and Bergson (1913) developed sophisticated conceptions on the role of gestural acts in the enactment of human intentionality. Temporality and the notion of a Bergsonian interval of adjustment to a lived world (Bergson 1944) may be accommodated through Malmgren's usage of Laban's term, *Flow*. *Flow* can be understood as a physical constriction or expansion, towards or away from a lived moment. As such it has been interpreted as the *Mental Factor* of *Feeling* of the performer (Malmgren 1988, See Table 2.3, p.30, for *Inner Attitudes* with *Flow*). However Malmgren's *Flow* can be interpreted more clearly as affectivity, an ever-present response of the performer to her world of perception. Martin (1990, p. 38), a phenomenologist, writes of a self that 'pours into and draws from or 'intertwines' with the world beyond', capturing the sense that the fluid interconnections with the perceived world shape the embodied subject's sense of being. This bears a strong resemblance to Malmgren's *Flow*. Csikszentmihalyi's (1990, 1996, 1997) Flow is also surprisingly similar to Malmgren's *Flow* but only in as much as it relates to Malmgren's *Free Flow,* where movements are interconnected. Csikszentmihalyi describes the ability to be totally absorbed in any activity so that time disappears. Any sense of judgement is set aside. Whilst this is the case for actions arising from Malmgren's *Inner Attitudes* involving *Free Flow* the antithesis is the case where *Bound Flow* is involved. An affective response can make every action problematic and disengaging.

Whilst it is true that emotion and feeling are integral demands in the art of performance, differing performance and acting techniques refer to or utilize concepts of emotion in radically different ways. The notion of being able 'to express emotions' through action is often seen as being part of an actor's training (Benedetti, 1970, pp. 226-236). Malmgren, however, takes a physical approach by seeing *Flow,* as Laban originally denoted, as describing the fluidity of movement in a body. *Free Flow* describes viscous movements, whilst *Bound Flow* refers to movements that retract or that are likely to stop. *Free* and *Bound Flow* are expressed through every part of the actor's body; whether arms or legs cross in any action, whether hands move across a face or whether they rest at an angle on a table, whether the upper part of a body twists around the axis of a body, all of these movements express Malmgren's *Flow* either *Free* or *Bound*. Pre-linguistic reflective communication in Malmgren's technique is the usual means through which this opening towards or retreating from the lived world is expressed.

Carrie Noland (2007, p. 1) uses Merleau-Ponty's concepts of gestures (*gestes*), tiny, sometimes hardly perceptible, physical acts, whereby 'the animate human form can execute, the movements by means of which the body explores the world' in order to analyse the artistic work of video artist Bill Viola. She indicates how Viola using performances of sequences of gestures captured on video expresses 'how socialized beings manage to convey spontaneous, unscripted meanings through sedimented forms' (*ibid*, p. 2). In the artistic works of Viola that are analysed by Noland, that of his '*The Passions*' series (1998), there are deliberately no meta-narratives, rather Viola's video works concentrate on performing ranges of emotions. What Noland suggests is that, unlike mechanical action, human action is constantly mediated through an affective 'layer of experience' (*ibid*, p. 4). Noland emphasises the action orientated and intentional ways in which bodies express affectivity. Likewise Malmgren's *Flow*, whilst sounding perhaps slightly ethereal is instead a highly grounded means of reading the affective communication moving between performing bodies and their audiences.

In Malmgren's model of human action *Flow* is conceptualised as the pre-formative function in the body, the pre-symbolic movement that shapes the actor's physical and imaginative state. As the performer is interconnecting with her perceived reality, so her language is being formed through her interweaving of her sense of being in the world, and consequently her body and actions respond with degrees of attraction or repulsion to the 'otherness' of what is met. *Flow* in Malmgren's sense is not a state but an interconnecting movement that carries with it a developing sense of subjectivity.

> I speak all the time to them about pre-birth. So that if you have the uterus and you are living in liquid, you are not breathing and so it's a shock to be born. The uterus becomes like an *Inner Attitude* in which you live, but don't play actions. So you have a shock, you come outside, and then you come into air. I always tell them

how women give birth in water and the baby swims. So they hear something – they move and then they act as an actor. And then you have to think that the liquid in which you were in the uterus is now the air outside. So that now you live in an enormous uterus and that is your *Mobility*. So *Mobility* comes before anything (Malmgren 2000).

Here Malmgren expresses his conviction that *Mobility*, which is Malmgren's *Inner Attitude* of *Feeling* and *Intuiting*, comes before and is the substratum of all action. The world is our uterus, which is our feeling and intuiting. Action is the shock that propels us into being.

This maternal metaphor of Malmgren's envisions the perceived world or 'other' of the subject being a uterus in which we swim constantly in feeling connection. This analysis notes similarities between Malmgren's image and several feminist philosophers who have constructed images of a pre-linguistic state of being in relation to processes of affect. Irigaray (1993, p. 185) plays upon an image of an evanescent, sensual pre-linguistic meeting with the world as 'other', in which the subject as position has not yet been formed. Her writing vibrates with the awakening possibilities of a new formulation of the relationship between oneself and other through 'the fecundity of the caress'. The body is a touching and touched dwelling and Irigaray (1993, p. 191) asks, 'How to preserve the memory of the flesh?' Olkowski (2000, p. 80) takes Irigaray's suggestions of 'morpho-logic' further calling for affectivity to be thought of as fluid. What one feels in the here and now can be viewed as an ever-changing stream of affectivity that interlinks life forms, stepping outside the boundaries of bodies, subjects and the determinable. Olkowski hopes for a process that no longer differentiates between inside and outside, a process that is constantly in touch, and constantly resonating.

Braidotti (1994, p. 14) also places affectivity at the root of the comprehension of action.

> Many contemporary critical thinkers bank on the affective as a force capable of freeing us from hegemonic habits of thinking. .... Affectivity in this scheme stands for the preconscious and for the prediscursive; desire is not only unconscious but it remains non thought at the very heart of our thought, because it is that which sustains the very activity of thinking. Our desires are that which evades us in the very act of propelling us forth, leaving as the only

indicator of who we are, the traces of *where* we have already been – that is to say, of what we have already ceased to be.

Malmgren's *Flow*, evolving from Rudolf Laban's consideration of the body in movement, has striking resonances with theories of embodiment emerging from postmodern feminist thought (Al-Saji 2001; Sisholm 2000; Stoller 2000). Feelings in performance can be conceptualised as the substratum of the actor's bodily experience of desire, that which interconnects one's actions from one moment to the next. The Malmgren technique postulates that this *Flow* is visible and able to be apprehended by an audience or 'other'. This is in contrast to ideas about actors' emotions being found in manipulating the physical states of actors (Bloch, Orthous and Santibanez 1996), or being found by adding emotion as an ingredient to the mix of an actor's imperatives (Hagen 1976, pp. 46-51).

This chapter argues that in a contemporary performance context Malmgren's actor training technique has substantial and unique information about processes of embodied communication to offer actors in training. Whilst the technique through its history has already demonstrated the uses for which it can be made in realistic drama, this chapter suggests that the Malmgren actor training technique can also have a useful role a contemporary actor training setting. Whilst not suggesting it be used for a rehearsal process in contemporary performance this thesis suggests that the Malmgren technique can be used as a tool for extending the range of performative actions of actors, for the development of any actor's conscious embodiment of agency and for the development of an awareness of pre-linguistic reflective language.

I am at the old Drama Centre once more. Oliver, a young journalist, had contacted me in Australia only weeks before a planned trip to London, asking to interview me about Yat Malmgren. The timing was such that I decided to meet him here. The old Methodist church at 176 Prince of Wales Road has been converted into a private art gallery now. Drama Centre has moved to Clerkenwell, a split with the past. This old building though has retained its distinctive atmosphere. It has been structurally strengthened; the gallery is no longer a safety hazard. The walls are newly painted but the floors have been left, wooden and worn, letting the past seep up from the floorboards.

> Oliver has come across Yat's name when mixing with actors and has some inkling of Yat's distinctive teachings. He wants to write an article about him. He is eager to hear all that he can of Yat's method of acting. We drift from room to room, festooned now with art works; an installation of rope and wood and small glass bottles is in Room 2, another installation with a 1960s model television and bed and cupboard is in the old costume room. I am smiling at the incongruity. We sit in the old church; an arthouse video is playing on a huge screen. I am speaking of *Inner Attitudes* but the figures on the screen are jostling and falling and the action grows too violent to speak casually. We move upstairs, up those well-worn flagstones, into Yat and Christophers' former office, skirting sculptures set on the floor. I am aware that Oliver does not know what each step means to me, the past sliding into the present with an ease that only happens in dreams. There is the door connecting their office to the gallery, hardly ever used in the past, now open as visitors mill, peering over the edges of the new railings to the space below, much as we used to when showings by the first years were forbidden to us, the students. Oliver is taking copious notes. I walk as if in a film, a ghost from the past, speaking about the present.

Researcher's Journal 8.1 November 16th. 2007, 176 Gallery, London.

8.4 Malmgren and sexual difference in performance

This chapter has argued that Malmgren's actor training technique can enhance the awareness of pre-linguistic reflective communication, which Malmgren directed towards the skill of creating specific and subtle performative actions. This research has indicated that this developing awareness may result in new and enhanced embodied agency for performers. The chapter has argued that a growing awareness of the pre-linguistic reflective communication, expressed as subtle gestural patterns of movements in *Free* and *Bound Flow*, may enable a questioning as to how performers meet their lived worlds. The next section of this chapter takes a more theoretical approach and basing itself on feminist theories of embodiment suggests ways in which pre-linguistic reflective language may shape concepts of 'otherness'. The feminist phenomenological model of agency being corporeally, historically and socially situated and being a process whereby the body is encountered as a threshold of interacting forces has allowed the proposition that new positions of culturally transformative agency are possible (Braidotti 1994, p. 238). Whilst Malmgren and many who study his technique have directed their attention to the development of realistic performances for stage and screen, Malmgren's actor training technique as argued below, may enable the development of actors' agency towards considerations of new performative styles or culturally transformative actions.

In Chapters 6 and 7 the phenomenological research investigates the actor's body as the ambiguous meeting place or *chiasm* of materiality and subjectivity. This next section of this chapter argues that this *chiasm* is the locus of an awareness of 'otherness'. For actors, a developing awareness of how they constitute 'otherness' will affect the directions in which their skills are applied. This section of the chapter explores the experiential and ambiguous site of the actor's body as that 'inter-place' (Casey 1998) where this fundamental understanding may arise.

Where feminism directs criticism of Merleau-Ponty's work and his image of the *chiasm*, it is primarily due to his assumption of a neutral lived body (Young 1989; Sullivan 1997; Butler 1989; Grosz 1994). Although Merleau-Ponty (1962, p. 154) states that sexuality is bound to bodily existence and an intrinsic element of being-in-the-world, he never provides an account of sexual difference. Luce Irigaray (1993, pp. 176-177) scrutinizes Merleau-Ponty's *chiasm* and concludes that his mode of being, the *flesh*, is monosexual. Merleau-Ponty has projected his own male, heterosexual position and occluded otherness. Instead of the reversibility of subject and object positions that Merleau-Ponty supports, 'a difference without contradiction, that divergence between the within and the without that constitutes its natal secrets' (1968, pp. 135-136), Irigaray (1992) assumes that sexual difference is present and precedes any chiasmatic intertwining of subject and object, creating meaning in the world. For her subject and object may intertwine but their positions are irreversible and asymmetrical, due to the primacy of sexuated bodies (1993, p. 157).

This criticism that the chiasmatic intertwinement (and in this thesis this specifically refers to the intertwinement between actor and herself as body, actor and another actor as body and actor and audience) involves more than a reversible position, is of vital importance in the construction of otherness or alterity in the Malmgren technique. Lacan, although not a phenomenologist, was profoundly influenced by phenomenological understandings about the body (Bonner 1999, p.

232). He limited the concept of the feminine, placing the masculine within the dimension of the ego as part of the symbolic order and the feminine as 'outside' this in the realm of 'the unsymbolizeable' (O'Connell 1999, p. 65). In this model, women only enter the symbolic or the linguistic domain via a masculine definition of it. Judith Butler (1993, p. 22) whilst using Lacan's model of ego formation by delimiting what is symbolised and so possible for the ego to desire, never views the constructions of identity, in this case gendered identity, as pertaining to a pre-existent subject. Butler (1993) relies on temporality to view identity as performed processes. Butler refers to matter as, 'a process of materialization that stabilizes over time to produce the effect of boundary, fixity, and surface we call matter' (Butler 1993, p. 9). In her view these embodied discursive practices are always determined through language. Natalie Wilson (2005) argues that language emerges from the body and that in the interconnectedness of language and materiality, the individual physical specificity of bodies has been less examined.

In terms of performance, gender forms one of its elemental, enculturated foundations. Cultural taboos in many communities allocate women and men to differing performative practices, the extremes of which are the known expulsion of women from performing *Kabuki* in Japan in the early part of the seventeenth century, and the exclusion of women from the Elizabethan stage. Lisa Jardine (1983, p. 9), in *Still Harping on Daughters: Women and Drama in the Age of Shakespeare,* suggests that the full impact of the historical absence of women in Renaissance theatre has not been dealt with. Lesley Ferris (1990, p. 19) in exploring this invisibility writes:

> as far as the illusionistic art of theatre is concerned ... women had absolutely no part in their own dramatic image-making. Theatrical production provided ... a visual and verbal performance of man's imagined women.

An imagined woman may still be the referent for an audience, even when the female body is present. Normative pressures and bodily constrictions in performance have been well researched, in an Australian context (Tait 2000; Kiernander 2000; Parr 2005). As Tait (2000, p. 65) points out, 'performing bodies habitually exist within a field of words', that is bodies as words, the prescription of socially constructed sexual identities is already situated and reinforced through audience reception.

Whilst this is the case, Merleau-Ponty's phenomenological metaphor still holds meaning in a philosophical understanding of the ontological basis for embodied being. Although Irigaray (1992) is critical of Merleau-Ponty, she reshapes his symbols of the *flesh* and the *chiasm* rather than rejecting his work outright. She may be regarded as sympathetic to the phenomenological approach (Grosz 1994, p. 105). However, for Irigaray the chiasmic intertwining of toucher and tangible, of subject and object is a sexuated meeting (Irigaray 1993, p. 184), both as a corporeal and as a linguistic interaction. Whilst Butler (1993, pp. 1-2) claims gendered subjectivity is maintained via regulatory practices, thus placing all sexual difference in the realm of the symbolic, Irigaray (1992) has a more pervasive vision of sexual difference. The intertwined entities in Irigaray's vision of the *chiasm* do not create cohesion, rather they create 'a form of plurality which announces itself as overflow and threat of boundaries, a "more than one"...' (Sisholm 2000, p. 93). The chiasmatic relation is interdependent and each aspect of it is able to dominate at the expense of the other. This is Irigaray's vision of alterity. Whilst she postulates the possibility of a radical feminine corporeal subjectivity grounded in a vision of the maternal-feminine, she asserts that otherness may be negated, devoured or blotted out. In this, Irigaray's assertion (cited in Diprose 1994, p. 36) is well known, that women have become invisible in language and philosophy, that they only exist in relation to the determinations made for them by men. Buckbinder in *Performance Anxieties: Reproducing Masculinity* (1998) uses Butler's critiques of gender formation to suggest that masculinity too is an unstable and performatively constituted identity. He argues that men are pressured through culturally constructed notions of competition. It would seem in the Merleau-Ponty chiasmatic entwinement of material and subjectivity that all bodies are open to complex and shifting identity formations, where the experience of otherness, particularly expressed as sexual difference, is vital in the placement of any subject position.

For the female performer and theatre-maker the gap between an imagined space, which would be receptive to the maternal-feminine, is an interval still dominated by the problematics of the gaze. All bodies in performance are shaped by dominant discourses about acceptability. In *The Doll's Revolution*, Rachel Fensham and Denise Varney detail efforts to establish a place for women's voices and women's bodies in Australian theatre and the backlash against those efforts in the context of postfeminism (2005, pp. 33-40). Irigaray (cited in Shisholm 2000, p. 108) advocates for the maternal-feminine to be brought into language, stepping aside from dialectical opposites in order to avoid patriarchal categories. Her writings rest on poetics rather than politics. She wishes for a new model of ethics in relation to sexual difference, one in which one sexuated embodied subjectivity embraces the other in an act of love of 'otherness' (cited in Braidotti 1994, p. 133).

As articulated above, through my understanding of Malmgren's technique, any body in performance is part of a web of forces or understandings and each and every body that is encountered, including the materiality of the performer's own body, is to some varying extent an 'other' to the subjective position at any time. Malmgren's technique begins by highlighting the material 'otherness' of the actor's body to the actor herself. Through empathy or *Flow,* a body may be attracted to, or feel more congruent with others, including the otherness of one's own embodiment. However an embodied subject can only be partially aware at any time of what it is that she desires or by what she is motivated. This recognition of likeness can extend between the boundaries of sexually different bodies. Although there is a movement towards or away from something, or some body it is only partially conscious. Kristeva (1987, p. 6) reflects this understanding of the interplay between subjectivity, embodiment and desire when she writes,

> Your headache, your paralysis, your haemorrhage may be the somatic return of an unsymbolized repressed object. The repressed language of hatred or love, or of emotions too subtle for words, then reactivate energies no longer filtered by any psychic trace or representation, these attack and disrupt the functioning of the body's organs. Mute signs are deflected into symbols. Or perhaps you are obsessed by figments of your imagination, figures of your desire, stimulating enough to be exhausting, gloomy enough to be depressing.

Kristeva illuminates the material solidity of ways in which these pre-linguistic reflective symptoms are expressed. The trainee actors who lose their voices, who sicken or who are driven by obsessions about their own or others bodies, the students who are hardly able to concentrate in classes because of the imaginative landscapes that are driving them, are witnessed by both the Malmgren trainer as well as the others who are present in the studio. And yet these material signals are not fully conscious to the signaller or necessarily to those witnessing the signs. The possibility of congruence between consciousness and embodiment is alluring and yet never complete within the web of subjectivities present. As Fensham and Varney suggest (2005, pp. 35-36), a matrix of forces, social and biological, structure the performativity of gender and sexual difference where 'otherness' is about recognising or not recognising others' bodies as being like our own.

These images of drives and desires, the recognition of likeness or otherness, stand in direct contrast to the images of wants or objectives promulgated as the way in which a body moves in the conventional Stanislavskian actor training. In this technique the actor sets a character objective and plays the scene in order to achieve this. Young performers often perform on stage as if there is no problem and no risk in performing actions towards a fictional character's wants. This Cartesian styled body, where mind centred will is imagined as ruling a material body, is the dominant model in western actor training for ways of thinking about bodies. Leder (1998) calls this the dominant discourse of the 'Cartesian Corpse'.

Malmgren (2000) in speaking of having an objective emphasised:

> the excitement of having an objective. So there's conflict inside of me. So I risk something. So immediately I am in a *Mobile* state... [actors] must find the utmost distance to the motivation that creates the *Mobility*... All actors think that I have an objective, so I am safe. But ... in life you can never be certain.

In this experience of an excited body having an objective, the possibility of 'becoming' through action is made possible through an emergence of agency that extends the boundaries of the already known 'self'. The idea of Irigaray's 'overflow', a possibility of becoming more or different, provides the fuel to move beyond already determined or socially regulated behaviour and to meet what is different in others.

In the light of recent theorisations of sexual difference, the importance of the Malmgren technique may lie in its capacity to draw the trainee actor's consciousness towards the specific ways in which bodies behave and communicate through pre-linguistic reflective means. Actors in Malmgrens's technique are required to begin to differentiate these sequences of gestures and the ways in which 'otherness' is structured physically through their bodies. The *Inner Attitudes* and *Externalised Drives* are means of articulating partially unconscious desires, of considering the subtleties of the means by which any body transmits this information whilst not being fully aware of it.

8.4.1 Pedagogical considerations

As a reiterative behavioural practice, it is vital in the teaching of the Malmgren technique that formative movements presented by trainee actors are accepted by Malmgren trainers, rather than trainers establishing exclusionary limits of performed behaviour. The Malmgren trainer is a lynchpin in the processes of learning that occurs in any Malmgren studio. In the past, Malmgren trainers have been personally recommended to their positions by Yat Malmgren. Now, however another generation of Malmgren trainers are being sought after (V Mirodan 2007, pers. comm. 21 Nov.). Malmgren trainers are required to develop their observational abilities. However beyond this, as outlined in this chapter, bodies communicate at subtle levels whether they are attracted to or reject the behaviour patterns of others. An awareness of the affective transactions that are occurring in any Malmgren studio is a vitally needed quality in the teaching of the technique.

The Malmgren actor training technique relies on the identification of *working actions*. The content of scenarios and Solo presentations needs to remain in the control of the trainees for these choices to be experientially meaningful. *Flow* within the Malmgren studio is one of the principal differentiating factors in allowing transformative performances to emerge in trainee actors' work. This *Flow* needs to be initiated by the Malmgren trainer who must critically reflect on the *working actions* and *Inner Attitudes* being performed, whilst at the same time staying sensitive to the personal nature of the performed material. This balancing act may account for the distinct lack of written material about Malmgren's technique. Since *Flow* is a pre-linguistic reflective communication it is sensed but not verbalised. If shifting movements of subjectivity in the Malmgren technique allow new possibilities of agency to emerge, the technique needs to be taught where all interconnecting webs of audience and actors are moving within *Free Flow*.

Any Malmgren trainer needs to be aware of the ways in which subtle rejections of cultures or ideologies are expressed in a studio. The trainer is required to value the experience of each and every trainee actor and to allow her body to reflect this openness, despite any normative pressures to the contrary. As well an expression of the rejection of the Malmgren technique itself by trainees needs to be also openly received as perhaps being part of an expressive development. There is an ethical understanding required here of the Malmgren trainer, where the experience of the trainee is privileged over the performative form of expression that that trainee may exhibit.

The embodied subjects produced within this specific practice have opportunities to alter normative modes not only of viewing performing bodies but also of being performing bodies, through new movements within *Free Flow*. Perhaps what I am suggesting comes close to Irigaray's new language; the interconnections in the Malmgren studio between participants are heightened, erotic, full of excited possibilities and experiential. I am not suggesting that Malmgren's technique privileges interiority, rather that it provokes the meeting of desire and the will that enacts it.

8.5 Conclusions

This chapter has extended the research presented in Chapters 6 and 7 where an hermeneutic phenomenological investigation of actors in training in Yat Malmgren's actor training technique indicated that the process had the capacity to impact on the ways in which some actors conceived of themselves in relation to their bodies and their lived interactions in the world. This chapter theorises the possible bringing to consciousness of the meaning to the participants of the pre-linguistic reflective communications that occur through body-to-body transmissions.

Whilst the Malmgren technique never suggests that concrete meanings can be drawn from non-verbal communications, the Malmgren actor training technique can draw the attention of trainee actors to the subtle ways in which bodies move subconsciously. Bodily positions in space, gestures formed without awareness, unconscious sounds, all contribute to the ways in which bodies inhabit the ambiguous 'interplace' or *chiasm* of being both materiality and subjectivity. Whilst Malmgren directed the skill of recognising pre-linguistic reflective communication towards the creation of realistic characters for performance, this research has indicated that actors developing these skills may utilise them in order to reassess their embodied agency in their lived worlds. Through the development of the recognition of how flowingly or embracingly an actor meets her own body and the body of others and how these attitudes are expressed through pre-linguistic communication, new directed movements embodying a more conscious sense of agency may arise. I theorise in this chapter that the newly developing agency aimed for in the study of the Malmgren technique is shaped through placements of otherness and that through concepts and practices of *Flow* an evolution of 'becoming' can result where likeness between bodies can saturate performative spaces.

I acknowledge the many Foucauldian processes (cited in Braidotti 1994, p. 127) through which power and institutionalised normative forces shape bodies. However, this study suggests that corporeal processes, initiated through the Malmgren technique, may provoke a discernment of previously unconscious forces that shape actor's bodies in action, separating them or linking them with others. The possible developing awareness of pre-linguistic reflective communication is aimed at creating possibilities of new choices of action. These considerations may move actors into new styles and modes of performance and culture making, rather than reiterating the modes propagated in the training institution or mainstream theatrical milieux. Malmgren's actor training technique can bring 'otherness' to the foreground of attention of trainee actors and can be used to encourage new directions of applying this experiential knowledge about performative bodies.

CHAPTER 9

CONCLUSION: FOUR RIPPLES

> Imagine the icosahedron full of water, a *Mobile* atmosphere.
> We live in water in every articulation. Then I try to keep the
> *Mobility* open and risk and make myself vulnerable.
> Malmgren February 1998.

9.1 Introduction

This research has investigated the meaning of Yat Malmgren's method of actor training in the context of training actors in the twenty-first century, through the use of metaphor: expanding ripples of contextualisation. In posing the question: **In what way does Malmgren's actor training contribute to the understanding of the performative body?** the metaphor of ripples provided a multiperspective viewing of performing bodies undertaking the training.

The research process governing this eclectic viewing of the Malmgren actor training technique is predicated throughout the thesis on my own personal relationship with Malmgren and on the actor training and training as a Malmgren instructor that he undertook with me. These craft-based and orally transmitted training processes have shaped this thesis, directing the thesis towards a principally phenomenological, experientially based enquiry. The studio practice of an acting technique places the performer in a differing light than theatre studies or performance studies. The experience of actors in a particular training, in a studio practice setting, can be the principal means through which development in that training occurs. The Researcher's Journal is offered to readers in the light of this experiential placement, hopefully indicating the dialogic process between experience and embodied agency. Throughout the thesis this text has appeared as a subjective reflection of the author, fragmenting the academic writing, representing my own performative journey in undertaking this research. Phenomenology as a consistent and clearly articulated methodology does not undermine performance studies' theories of agency and embodiment recognising that both are shaped by socio-historic constructs. This thesis firstly offers two of these socio-historic discourses pertinent to Malmgren's actor training technique that have had limited academic attention; Chapter 2 sets the first ripple of contextualisation establishing the performative body undertaking Malmgren's actor training technique as conceptualised through Rudolf Laban's models of movement. Laban's models and language provide the substratum for all performative actions considered in Malmgren's actor training. Then in Chapters 3 and 5, the second ripple of contextualisation offers the contributions of Malmgren's technique as an actor training technique for the development of realistic characters for stage and screen, as Yat Malmgren's notes and teachings have internationally dispersed the technique. However from this point in the thesis, the research charts and offers new discourses about the Malmgren actor training technique, established through the author's phenomenological approach and with the aim of indicating the possible uses in actor training for the Malmgren training technique in a twenty-first century setting including uses in contemporary performance practice.

In Chapters 6 and 7, this research adds a third ripple of meaning for the performative body undertaking the training by revealing Malmgren's actor training technique as stimulating the possible development of processes of embodiment-to-consciousness for trainee performers. The fourth ripple of contextualising Malmgren's actor training technique expands in Chapter 8 to consider the technique's possible contribution to analysing pre-linguistic reflective communication. This research suggests that through Malmgren's actor training technique non-verbal means of establishing likeness and otherness can be brought to the attention of performers.

In this research, the ripples of understanding of Yat Malmgren's technique of actor training are located through the actor's body as an **experiencing** body, an intentional, desiring and directed body that has both temporal and spatial dimensions.

Malmgren's figure-of-eight process of *Externalised Drives*, crossing like two rivers, as a representation of the ongoing flow of intentionality and movement between a body and its response to its environment, allows for a dialogical interaction between the subjectivity and materiality of a performer's lived world. The image of Malmgren's 'crosses', linking the so called 'inner' lived world of the actor with her 'outer' or social and environmental lived world, preceded Elizabeth Grosz's (1994) similar schema of the body as a Mobius strip, with an outer and an inner in continual interaction with each other, by close to twenty years. Malmgren's 'crosses' identify the actor's body as a process of becoming, which is actional as well as relational. Similar to Merleau-Ponty's phenomenological notion of 'the flesh' (1968, p. 138), Malmgren's performative body is interlinked through a web of possibilities with organic others and inorganic materials, through a flow of action. The actor's body as considered in the Malmgren technique is a physical body, with specific desires and values, which operates within but yet is not reducible to a field of socially constructed meanings. Although the actor's body can be considered as a representation it can never be wholly reduced to one.

In this research I claim that the Malmgren technique can enable an experiential development of actors' awareness of embodiment and through these means offers a substantial training technique in any contemporary actor training course. The technique's heightened emphasis on physical expression can allow for the development of an awareness of an actor's agency in relation to an actor's material expression, generating new challenges of integrated performative positions.

9.2 Malmgren's technique: an actor training in sensation

Whilst a range of actor trainings offer the acquisition of performance skills and the application of these skills to a range of texts, scores and postdramatic performative events, Malmgren's actor training technique plunges trainee actors into an experiential and sophisticated investigation of the workings of the actor trainees' bodies.

Using a metaphoric language structure inherited from Rudolf Laban's Art of Movement, Malmgren's training begins by categorising performative action. As set out in Chapter 2, systematic structures of bodily movement, named through the use of Laban's *eight working actions, Motion Factors, Mental Factors* and *Motion Factor elements* are extended in Malmgren's technique to encompass dramatic action, including the vocal expression of language, in order to discern and differentiate performed action. Laban himself initiated the extension of his movement theories to dramatic action, in his latter teachings at The Laban Art of Movement Centre in Addlestone in Surrey in the early 1950s. Laban named this work Movement Psychology, combining the Jungian theories of William Carpenter with his own movement theories. This work, including Laban's *Glossary of Terms* in relation to this new development, was entrusted to Yat Malmgren (pers. comm. 29th

Nov. 2001; 29th. Jan 2001). Malmgren began teaching these theories to actors through movement training in his West Street Studio between the years of 1954 to 1963. He expanded his teachings and practices to a new system of actor training which he termed Character Analysis, developed through his years as the co-director of Drama Centre, London, with Christopher Fettes. Malmgren, together with Fettes, enabled Character Analysis to sit at the heart of Drama Centre actor training and theatrical productions, producing performances of radical re-interpretations of classical texts as well as new writings. Drama Centre, London became known for an intensity of performance propelling numerous actors to national and international fame.

Whilst the physically strenuous and emotionally demanding nature of actor training is well documented (Watson 2002) and the skilling of actors' bodies to produce specific sounds, shapes and actions has also been extensively documented (Zarrilli 1995, 1997), Malmgren's system of actor training whilst requiring these measures, differentiates itself from other actor trainings through the use of a concept of differing personality types, termed *Inner Attitudes*. Malmgren's *Inner Attitudes* distinguish performed action through the recognition of motivational differences affecting action in relation to any character's lived world. Using a concept of four *Mental Factors* of *Sensing, Thinking, Intuiting* and *Feeling*, Malmgren's *Inner Attitudes* are structured as differing modes of materially opening out upon an already imagined world. The being-in-the-world of each *Inner Attitude* is different. Body and mind in Malmgren's training are understood as a unity: any body/mind moves intentionally in an encounter through the *Mental Factors* with a lived world. Malmgren's *Externalised Drives* are structured as the means that body/minds, through habit and desire, relate with others, in encountering lived worlds. Both *Inner Attitudes* and *Externalised Drives* are structured through *Motion Factors* indicating that that it is through the moving body that these ways of perceiving and encountering any environment takes place.

As Chapters 3 and Chapter 5 claim, it is through the categorisation of performative action that Malmgren's actor training technique principally distinguishes itself. Whilst the concept of psychologically predisposed types is well recognised within the fields of psychology, education and management (Daniels 1979; Myers-Briggs 2007), it is less utilised in actor training. Skilling actors to recognise that in the same set of circumstances humans may respond in differing but yet systematised ways, suggests a means by which actors can sort, categorise and differentiate performed characters. Whilst interconnecting a character typology with particular movement patterns is evident in many forms of performance, from commedia dell'arte to ballet, pantomime, and farce, information about the behaviour patterns of personality types has not been extensively used in naturalistic actor training. It has however been extensively researched in dance/movement therapy, a field allied with Laban's movement theories (North 1972). The Malmgren technique suggests to actors in training that an actor cannot rely on habitual modes of performative action to formulate the necessary actions in character development for realistic performance.

Chapter 5 extends this argument and places the physical emphasis in Malmgren's actor training technique, including the viewing of the structural components of *Motion Factors*, *Motion Factor elements*, *Inner Attitudes*, *Externalised Drives* and *Action Attitudes*, as initiating a possible transformational process for trainee actors in sensation. Accordingly Chapter 5 sets out a six-step process whereby actors through Malmgren's actor training are prompted to develop their sensate communication with the audience and fellow actors in performance.

Transformative Actor-Training Processes in the Malmgren Technique (See Chapter 5, p. 139)
1. Expectations
2. First Steps – *Motion Factors* and their *Elements*
3. Considering *Inner Attitudes*
4. The Awareness of Being Viewed
5. The Beginnings of Transformation through Sensation
6. The Self-Reflexive Actor: *Externalised Drives* and *Action Attitudes*

Table 9.1 **Six-step transformative actor-training processes in the Malmgren technique**

This research proposes that a trainee actor's melding of viewed and experienced sensate impulses in the Malmgren technique can develop through the listed six steps (Table 9.1), although not necessarily in a uni-directional or temporally separated manner.

Three of the steps listed, Expectations, The Awareness of Being Viewed and the Beginnings of Transformation through Sensation, may describe stages of development encountered in other approaches to actor training. These steps may enable trainee actors to negotiate with their initial expectations as to the sensory demands of actor training; introduce trainee actors to an awareness that an audience's viewing has a distinctive validity; and extend the range of trainee actors' sensitivities to sensory impulses and communications.

The three steps identified in italics as dealing with First Steps–*Motion Factors and their Elements*, Considering *Inner Attitudes* and The Self–Reflexive Actor: *Externalised Drives and Action Attitudes*, are unique to the Malmgren training. It is these steps, each characterised by an actor's engagement with exercises focussed on the concepts with which they are identified that may enable actors to extend the specificities of their choice of actions; become cognisant of their unique vision of reality; and begin to take responsibility for their agency and interactions in their lived worlds. Malmgren's structured exercises open possibilities for new ways of taking action. Due to the breadth of the research undertaken, the specific developments in sensory communication for actors that Malmgren's structures of *Motion Factors* and the *Motion Factor elements, Inner Attitudes, Externalised Drives* and *Action Attitudes* offer to trainee actors have only been partially investigated in this thesis.

9.3 Malmgren's technique: directional bodies in space

The demands in Malmgren's actor training technique of communicating with an audience through non-habitual performative actions may provoke negotiations between the materially viewed body of the performer and the subjectively placed agency of the performer. In this research, hermeneutic phenomenology was the means by which to investigate the experiences of trainee actors undergoing the practices of the training to illuminate the embodied meaning of these practices for the trainees. Rather than assuming that these processes will always contribute to a growing ability to create realistic characterisations for performance, as the Malmgren technique initially intends, hermeneutic phenomenology, as a research methodology, has enabled a broader investigation into the outcomes and meanings of the use of the technique in actor training. This methodological approach was undertaken in specific recognition of the changing nature of theatrical practices in contemporary trainings. Malmgren's development of Character Analysis was for the performance of realistic characters set in Modernist play texts or scripts. I aimed to assess the meaning of the Malmgren's technique to actors in a twenty-first century setting, where postmodern performances are widespread, and poststructural theories of performance predominate. As well I have emphasised the retaining of Malmgren's name in the ongoing practice of his technique.

Chapters 6 and 7 outline the emergent interview themes of this hermeneutic investigation, revealing that the participants understand the practices of Malmgren's actor training technique as contributing to a wider frame of reference than for the creation of realistic characters for presentation on stage or screen. The six emergent themes arising from the hermeneutic phenomenological research reveal a possible meeting with and a possible development of the trainee's understanding of her own embodiment in her lived world. In this research I align these themes with the actor training steps set out in Chapter 5, indicating that the same structural elements of the Malmgren technique direct this wider possible development of an actor's understanding of embodiment. The phenomenological research illuminates that, through weblike processes of mimesis and flowlike processes of attraction and repulsion, trainee actors undergoing the Malmgren training and its practices are embodied through a flux of moving and fragmented subject positions. Through realigning bodily stances and gestures, in Malmgren's actor training practices, and through a growing awareness of the non-verbal ways in which bodies signal only partially conscious characteristics and desires, actors may use the Malmgren technique to transform their embodied agency in their lived worlds.

Using the metaphor of Merleau-Ponty's *chiasm*, the emergent themes in Chapters 6 and 7 reveal the participants through Malmgren's actor training technique as becoming aware that limited concepts of embodied identities and interactions with others restrict their range of expressive performative actions. Malmgren's *Inner Attitude* and *Externalised Drive* exercises can make the discontinuities between an imagined 'self' and a material 'self' apparent. They can highlight the ways in which actors' bodies resist or stay open to intentional desires. Possible re-assessments of agency for an actor are enabled through coming to grips with the materiality of intentional action. The exercises aim to develop an investigation of corporeally based performative processes. The circle of enquiry probing agency aims to extend to the practice of theatre itself, questioning whether and which performative practices can serve the agency of the actor.

For actors in training the self-direction of performance practices rests on the pedagogical discourses inherent in the training institution's curriculum. This study is limited to an exploration of experiencing bodies in Malmgren's actor training, but opens the possibility of further research as to how actor training in general can initiate new performative practices.

9.4 Malmgren's technique: flowing bodies

In placing the experiential and the sensory dimension of the actor's body as the primary site of learning in Malmgren's actor training technique, this research illustrates Malmgren's concept of *shadow moves,* revealing *Free* or *Bound Flow,* as the primary means by which the technique reflects on an actor's experiences of 'otherness'. Non-verbal, or as I have termed it in this research, pre-linguistic reflective communication, is the principal observational technique through which subtle changes in patterns of gestural actions are perceived in the Malmgren technique. Malmgren's *Inner Attitude* and *Externalised Drive* exercises may challenge an actor to differentiate between intentional action that openly merges with fantasies of fulfilment, and intentional action that blocks desires or blocks co-joining with others. *Flow* can be understood as a physical constriction or expansion, towards or away from a lived moment, reflected in small gestural movements. Malmgren's *Flow* is experienced in the first place as a unity or disconnection with the actor's intentional action. The materiality of the body is the first meeting place with 'otherness' for the trainee actor undergoing the technique, where this experience of 'otherness' may be a meeting with the materiality of the actor's body.

In this research I have linked Malmgren's concept of *Flow* with feminist concepts of affectivity. I have illustrated that through a developing awareness of the processes through which *Free* and *Bound Flow* function in an actor's body, actors can question the pre-formative ways in which they merge with their lived worlds. Concepts of otherness can be brought to consciousness. A more united agency of action can be developed for actors. The training initiates a sensed congruence between an actor's physical action and sense of 'self', as well as interlinking the actor's body to a more united vision of the audience. Again, through the breadth of the scope of this research, this arena of Malmgren's practices, the awareness of *Free* and *Bound Flow* for the performer, has by necessity been given only a preliminary review.

This research has begun the articulation of Yat Malmgren's technique of actor training which until now has received little academic attention. Where taught in actor trainings Malmgren's technique is often equated with Laban's movement techniques, a lack of differentiation, which this thesis intends to dispel. Malmgren's actor training technique is already in use in tertiary institutions and independent acting school courses in at least the United Kingdom, Australia, Sweden, New Zealand, Canada, and Israel. It extends the latter theories of Rudolf Laban's investigations into personality/movement types into the field of actor training. The Malmgren technique of actor training, with its heritage of language from Laban movement, offers new insights for trainee actors with respect to notions of embodiment. Malmgren's actor training technique can fundamentally alter actors' perspectives about processes of communication. The technique aims to draws trainee actors' awareness to processes of 'becoming', through heightened differentiation of sensory impulses and an integration of agency in intentional action.

9.5 The narrative description

I wish to conclude by using the voices of the research participants. As one means of capturing a possible holistic and affective voice of this research, I have synthesised a narrative of an encounter with Malmgren's actor training. As set out in Chapter 4, phenomenological research often culminates in a text, which seeks to carry an overarching meaning of the phenomenon under study. However in this context I acknowledge that no one overarching meaning is possible for this phenomenon. Instead, drawn from the phenomenological themes and gathered from among the participants, the created text offers readers a descriptive encounter with the phenomenon, a lived experience (Cohen, Kahn & Steeves 2000; Creswell 1998).

The following narrative is my construction and has been garnered from interviews with participants. It is a multi-vocal description of the phenomenon of studying Malmgren's technique of actor training, through which I aim to capture the felt meaning of the process. I have attempted, through placing the experiential at the heart of this research, to strengthen the new and feminine ways of conceiving both the performing body as well as Malmgren's technique as a site of 'becoming', where new and more united modes of being are made possible.

In offering this story, whilst using the words of the research participants, I situate the totality of this research as my viewpoint. It is one narrative existing within a context of many understandings of Malmgren's teachings. I make no attempt to conceal my own subjectivity; my aim has been to find a means to reveal the experiential, embodied realities that have propelled the research into being. The narrative is offered, particularly to those who have studied Malmgren's actor training with the sense that the technique is an experiential journey.

> I didn't have a clue how to get into drama school but I thought I'll audition for things. In fact one of the Drama Centre students who is in third year I met at a Guild Hall audition and the friend who was with him said of him, "Oh! He's got into Drama Centre. They love to break you down! It's a really hard school!" I'd never really heard of it before. I was thinking, "Is it true? Do they really? Do they really break you down? Do they really dissect your childhood?" So that's the way I heard about it. The school is based around a methodology. It has an ideology. It wasn't trying to create pretty faces. It was actually about acting. And it was dealing with the Laban method. I was really interested in the Laban work. I need to depend on structure because otherwise I can't articulate what I want.
>
> You start by watching yourself, what you're doing. The whole physical world is broken up into those *working actions*. The fact that you can categorise these things, thinking about psychology and what drives people and what people want and why they want it. Then just the way that Yat's formulated it makes sense. You are given this new body of work and it's something to explore within. So you'll just have to analyse a conversation or a way a person is behaving or an everyday incident. I had concerns whether I was analysing life too much and not living it! I stayed up nights just thinking about all sorts of things in relation to the Yat work and putting things into different perspectives and just thinking, constantly, to the point of not sleeping! At the beginning of it I found *working actions* and *Mental Factors* the most useful. *Working actions* especially in singing you can transfer that across to music a lot easier. For the analytical side of performance pieces I used *Inner Attitudes*.

It takes quite a lot to stay afloat because there are so many things to think about, so many things. And you set your goals so high, set yourself these ambitions that you really just want to do. You want to be so precise. You can, if you know when something is generalised or that it's habitual, you can be precise.

I can't let myself off the hook if I know that I didn't get it. 'Yat' is the only time I ever came to class terrified, the only time I ever came out terrified or empowered and ever felt I'd done something. It's the anticipation of doing something and exposing yourself. I know that I've tried to do what I thought were *free-flowing* scenarios and they were so clearly *bound-flowing* and everyone else in the room could see that, but I couldn't. I think I was concerned about my status within the group at first. That's kind of human isn't it? But it so doesn't matter now.

It just struck me that when you are trying to recreate a moment of your past that you are acknowledging fits in to one of these categories that we are looking at or that we are trying to identify throughout the work, that what can happen also is that you embody it with more of what you perceive to be that 'type' than was initially there. You're allowing that, that embodiment, to sit in a different way to what it would have sat in life because you're allowing it to, rather than simply in response to what is going on around you. You're now in response to being allowed to express these things in these ways. What's caused me to push something so far away from myself? You start to get a sense of what you've been missing out on.

There's a period when your body may be over reacting because you can't pin anything down in your mind and you can't put it into words but you keep going. Some people are more at ease with that – open throat, heart beating. But that's the aim for any activity, to be able to leave yourself behind, isn't it?

Look I have completely changed. When I think of the roles that I used to think I should go for and now. It's entirely different. It's an ongoing process to see things as they are. Definitely you understand more about your role in the world. You are always doing something and you are always affecting someone else, the place you are in and the rest of the planet. (Voices of Roger, Danny, Carmel, Douglas, Bella, James, Gillian, Suzi, Andy and Alex.)

9.6 Many splashes

Actor training deals with bodies. This research positions Malmgren's actor training technique as a unique training system, emphasising the experiential, meaning-making position of the actor's body. Whilst having clear connections to historical European styles of dance and actor trainings, Malmgren's actor training begins through an individual investigation of the ambiguity of being a performing body, both seen and unseen. Using a sophisticated and complex model inherited partly from Rudolf Laban, Malmgren's systematic series of actor training exercises places the actor's agency in question during actor training. This research reveals that the embodied learning process of Malmgren's actor training questions the way bodies are shaped and the role of the performer's agency in any performative action. The technique allows for the development of new processes of communication for the actor, encouraging risk taking in performative action, aligning actions with a developing sense of 'self'. This questioning of performative action extends to processes of actor training. Malmgren's actor training technique not only challenges performance courses where bodies are treated as signs, but it also challenges performance trainings which rely primarily on the acquisition of skills. Malmgren's actor training technique demands that actors be considered as more than signs or bodies to be shaped. Malmgren's technique, however, asserts that signing and shaping are fundamental aspects of 'becoming' wherever 'the flesh', the substance of being human, exists. Malmgren's actor training technique places the actor's body as a sensate, affective body in space with directional intentions, offering further possibilities always for the development of new forms, styles and means to cohere action with agency for the performer, and to cohere the performer with her viewing world.

REFERENCES

Al-Saji, A 2001, 'Merleau-Ponty and Bergson: bodies of expression and temporalities in The flesh', *Philosophy Today*, vol. 45, no. 5, pp. 110-124.

Artaud, A 1958, *The Theatre and its Double*, trans. M Richards, Grove Press, New York.

Auslander, P 1995, '"Just be yourself": logocentrism and difference in performance theory', in PB Zarrilli (ed.), *Acting (Re)considered: Theories and Practices*, Routledge, New York, pp. 59-68.

Barba, E 1995, *The Paper Canoe: A Guide to Theatre Anthropology*, trans. R Fowler, Routledge, New York and London.

Barker, C 1983, *Theatre Games*, Methuen, London.

--------- 2000, 'Joan Littlewood', in A Hodge (ed.), *Twentieth Century Actor Training*, Routledge, London and New York, pp. 113-128.

Barnes, P 1989, *Lulu: A Sex Tragedy*, adaption in English of *Erdgeist*, and, *Bruchse der Pandora* by F Wedekind, Methuen, London.

Barter, N 1995, 'Much better if she believed it', *The Guardian*, London. 26 September p. 16.

Benedetti, R 1986, *The Actor at Work*, 4th edn, Prentice-Hall, Englewood Cliffs NJ.

Bennan, JF 1967, *The Philosophy of Merleau-Ponty*, Harcourt, Brace and World, New York.

Benner, P 1994, 'The tradition and skill of interpretive phenomenology in studying health, illness,and caring practices', in P Benner (ed.), *Interpretive Phenomenology: Embodiment, Caring, and Ethics in Health and Illness*, Sage, London, pp. 99-127.

Berger, M and Levanthal, M 1993, 'The aesthetics of healing: reflections on the inner dance', in FJ Bejjani (ed.), *Current Research in Arts Medicine*, A cappela, Chicago, pp. 253-255.

Bergson, H 1913, *Matter and Memory*, trans. NM Paul and WS Palmer, George Allen, London.

--------- 1944, *Creative Evolution*, trans. A Mitchell, Modern Library, New York.

Blau, H 1982, *Take up the Bodies: Theater at the Vanishing Point*, University of Illinois Press, Urbana Ill.

Blau, H 1992, 'Ideology, performance, and the illusions of demystification', in JG Reinelt and JR Roach (eds.), *Critical Theory and Performance,* University of Michigan Press, Ann Arbor, pp. 430-445.

Bloch, S, Orthous, P and Santibanez, H 1996, 'Effector patterns of basic emotions', in PB Zarilli (ed.), *Acting (Re)considered: Theories and Practices,* Routledge, London and New York, pp. 197-218.

Bonner, CW 1999, 'The status and significance of the body in Lacan's imaginary and Symbolic orders' in D Welton (ed.) *The Body: Classic and Contemporary Readings,* Blackwell, Malden, Mass. pp. 232-251.

Braidotti, R 1994, *Nomadic Subjects: Embodiment and Sexual Difference in Contemporary Feminist Theory,* Columbia University Press, New York.

Brook, P 1972, *The Empty Space: A Book about the Theatre: Deadly, Holy, Rough, Immediate,* Penguin, London.

Brustein, R 2005, 'Mrs. Worthington's daughter's dilemma: actors are subject to both the pleasures of imitation and the rigours of an exalted calling', (Special Section: Approaches to Theatre Training 2005), *American Theatre,* vol. 22, pp. 46-51.

Buckbinder, D 1998, *Performance Anxieties: Reproducing Masculinity,* Allen and Unwin, Sydney.

Burgoyne, S, Poulin, K and Rearden, A 1999, 'The impact of acting on student actors: Boundary blurring, growth, and emotional distress', *Theatre Topics,* vol. 9, no. 2, pp. 157-179.

Burns RB 1994, *Introduction to Research Methods,* Longman Cheshire, Melbourne, Vic.

Butler, J 1988, 'Performative and gender constitution: an essay in phenomenology and feminist theory', *Theatre Journal,* vol. 40, pp. 519-531.

--------- 1989, 'Sexual ideology and phenomenological description: a feminist critique of Merleau-Ponty's "Phenomenology of perception"', in J Allen and IM Young (eds.), *The Thinking Muse: Feminism and Modern French Philosophy,* Indiana University Press, Bloomington, pp. 85-100.

--------- 1990, *Gender Trouble: Feminism and the Subversion of Identity,* Routledge, London and New York.

--------- 1993, *Bodies that Matter: On the Discursive Limits of 'Sex',* Routledge, London and New York.

--------- 1999, 'Foucault and the paradox of bodily inscriptions', in D Welton (ed), *The Body: Classic and Contemporary Readings,* Blackwell, Malden, Mass., pp. 307-313.

Butler, J 2004, *Undoing Gender*, Routledge, New York.

--------- 2005, '"There is a person here": an interview with Judith Butler', in MS Breen and WJ Blumenfeld (eds.), *Butler Matters: Judith Butler's Impact on Feminist and Queer Studies*, Ashgate, Burlington, VT, pp. 9-25.

Byron Dance Dynamics 2009, accessed 6/04/09
http://www.byrondancedynamics.com.au/page.asp?i=9

Callow, S 1995, *Being an Actor*, St Martin's Press, New York.

Campbell, J 1959, *The Masks of God: Primitive Mythology*, Viking Press, New York.

Carnicke, SM 1998, *Stanislavsky in Focus*, Routledge, London.

Carpenter, DR 2003, 'Phenomenology as method', in HJ Speziale and DR Carpenter (eds), *Qualitative Research in Nursing*, 3rd edn, Lipincott, Williams and Wilkins, Philadelphia, PA, pp. 51-73.

Case, SE 1988, *Feminism and Theatre*, Methuen, New York.

Casey, E 1998, 'The ghost of embodiment: on bodily habitudes and schemata', in D Welton (ed.), *Body and Flesh: A Philosophical Reader*, Blackwell, Malden, Mass., pp. 207-225.

Chaikin, J 1972, *The Presence of the Actor*, Atheneum, New York.

Chekhov, M 1985, *To the Actor: On the Techniques of Acting*, 2nd edn, Harper and Rowe, NewYork.

Chodorow, J 1991, *Dance Therapy and Depth Psychology*, Routledge, London.

Clurman, H 1972, *On Directing*, Macmillan, New York.

Coen, S 1994, 'Jewel Walker: body talk', (Special Section: Approaches to Theatre Training – Training Wheels), *American Theatre*, vol. 11, pp. 28-29.

Cohen, MZ and Omery, A 1994, 'Schools of phenomenology: implications for research', in JM Morse (ed.), *Critical Issues in Qualitative Research Methods*, Sage, Thousand Oaks, CA, pp. 136-156.

Cohen, MZ, Kahn, D and Steeves, R 2000, *Hermeneutical Phenomenological Research: A Practical Guide for Nurse Researchers*, Sage, London.

Cole, T and Chinoy, H (eds) 1995, *Actors on Acting: The Theories, Techniques, and Practices of the World's Great Actors, Told in their own Words*, Three Rivers Press, New York.

Connolly, M and A Lathrop 1997, 'Maurice Merleau-Ponty and Rudolf Laban – An interactive appropriation of parallels and resonances', *Human Studies*, vol. 20, pp. 27-45.

Crease, R 1994, 'Responsive order: the phenomenology of dramatic and scientific performance', in R Sawyer (ed.), *The Creativity of Performance*, Ablex, London, pp. 213-225.

Cresswell, JW 1998, *Qualitative Inquiry and Research Design: Choosing among Five Traditions*, Sage, London, New Delhi, and Thousand Oaks, CA.

Crotty, M 1996, *Phenomenology and Nursing Research*, Churchill Livingstone, Melbourne, Vic.

--------- 1998, *The Foundations of Social Research: Meaning and Perspective in the Research Process*, Sage, London, New Delhi, and Thousand Oaks, CA.

Csikszentmihalyi, M 1990, *Flow: The Psychology of Optimal Experience*, Harper and Row, New York.

--------- 1996, *Creativity: Flow and the Psychology of Discovery and Invention*, Harper Collins, New York.

--------- 1997, *Finding Flow: The Psychology of Engagement with Everyday Life*, Basic Books, New York.

Csordas, TJ 1999, 'Embodiment and cultural phenomenology', in G Weiss and HF Haber (eds), *Perspectives on Embodiment*, Routledge, New York and London, pp. 143-162.

Daniels, RN 1979, *Promoting Useful Managerial Learning: A Study of Relationships Between Personality Types, Learning Styles and Teaching Techniques*, British Library, West Yorkshire, UK.

Denzin, NK and Lincoln, YS 2005, 'Introduction: the discipline and practice of qualitative research', in NK Denzin and YS Lincoln (eds), 3rd edn, *The Sage Handbook of Qualitative Research*, Sage, London, New Delhi and Thousand Oaks, CA, pp. 1-32.

Department of Education, Employment and Workplace Relations, 2008, viewed 3 August 2008, http://www.dest.gov.au

Dezseran, LJ 1975, *The Student Actor's Handbook*, Mayfield, Palo Alto CA.

Diamond, E 1997, *Unmaking Mimesis: Essays on Feminism and Theater*, Routledge, London and New York.

Diekelmann, NL, Schuster, R and Lam, SL 1994, 'MARTIN, a computer software program: On listening to what the text says', in P Benner (ed.), *Interpretive Phenomenology: Embodiment, Caring, and Ethics in Health and Illness*, Sage, London, pp. 129-127.

Diprose, R 1994, *The Bodies of Women: Ethics, Embodiment and Sexual Difference*, Routledge, London.

Dolan, J 1988, *The Feminist Spectator as Critic*, University of Michegan Press, Ann Arbor.

Donnellan, D 2002, *The Actor and the Target*, Nick Hern, London.

Drama Centre London 2009, 'The methodological approach', viewed 22 March 2009, http://courses.csm.arts.ac.uk/drama/approach.asp?level=1

Drama Centre London Prospectus, 1963-2002, held at Drama Centre, London.

Du Bois, B 1983, 'Passionate scholarship: notes on values, knowing and method in Social science', in Bowles, G and Klein, RD (eds), *Theories of Women's Studies* Routledge, London, pp. 105-116.

Eagleton, T 1998, 'Body work', in S Regan (ed.), *The Eagleton Reader*, Blackwell, Oxford, pp157-162.

Eldredge, SA and Huston, H 1995, 'Actors training in the neutral mask', in PB Zarrilli (ed.) *Acting (Re)considered: Theories and Practices*, Routledge, New York, pp. 121-128.

--------- 1996, *Mask Improvisation for Actor Training and Performance: the Compelling Image*, Northwestern University Press, Evanston, Ill.

Ellen, R 1977, 'Anatomical classification and the semiotics of the body', in J Blacking (ed.), *The Anthropology of the Body*, Academic Press, New York, pp. 343-73.

Esslin, M 1987, *The Field of Drama: How the Signs of Drama Create Meaning on Stage and Screen*, Methuen, London.

Fairclough, N 2003, *Analysing Discourse: Textual Analysis for Social Discourse*, Routledge, New York.

Feldenkrais, M 1972, *Awareness Through Movement*, Harper and Row, New York.

Fensham, R 1996, review of 'Playing with time: women writers for performance', *Australasian Drama Studies*, vol. 29, Oct., pp. 235-238.

--------- and Varney, V 2005, *The Dolls' Revolution: Australian Theatre and Cultural Imagination*, Australian Scholarly, Melbourne.

Ferris, L 1990, *Acting Women: Images of Women in Theatre*, Macmillan, Hampshire.

Fettes, C 1989, 'The Drama Centre, London', in E Mekler (ed.), *Masters of the Stage: British Acting Teachers Talk about their Craft*, Grove Weidenfeld, New York, pp. 71-78.

\-\-\-\-\-\-\-\-\- 2002, 'Yat Malmgren' Obituary, *The Guardian*, London, 13 June 2002, Guardian Unlimited archive, viewed 22 March 2009, http://www.guardian.co.uk.

\-\-\-\-\-\-\-\-\- 2005, 'Reuven Adiv, inspirational drama teacher' Obituary, *The Guardian*, 31 January 2005, Guardian Unlimited archive, viewed 22 March 2009, http://www.guardian.co.uk.

Flynn, B 1973, 'The question of ontology: Sartre and Merleau-Ponty', in G Gillan (ed.), *The Horizons of the Flesh: Critical Perspectives on the Thought of\ Merleau-Ponty*, Feffer and Simons, London and Amsterdam, pp. 114-126.

Foster, J 1977, *The Influences of Rudolf Laban*, Lepus Books, London.

Foucault, M 1977, *Discipline and Punish: The Birth of the Prison*, trans. A Sheridan, Vintage, New York.

\-\-\-\-\-\-\-\-\- 1990, *History of Sexuality: vol. 1*, trans. R Hurley, Vintage, New York.

Gadamer, HG 1975, *Wahrheit und Methode*, 4th edn, Paul Seibeck, Tubingen.

\-\-\-\-\-\-\-\-\- 1984, 'The hermeneutics of suspicion', in G Shapiro and A Sica (eds.), *Hermeneutics: Questions and Prospects*, University of Massachussetts Press, Amhurst, pp. 58-60.

\-\-\-\-\-\-\-\-\- 1989, *Truth and Method*, 2nd rev edn, (1st English edn 1975), revised and trans J. Weinsheimer and D. Marshall, Crossroad, New York.

Garner, SB Jr. 1993, '"Still living flesh": Beckett, Merleau-Ponty, and the phenomenological body', *Theatre Journal*, vol. 45, no. 4, pp. 443-461.

\-\-\-\-\-\-\-\-\- 1994, 'Object, objectivity, and the phenomenal body', in *Bodied Spaces Phenomenology and Performance in Contemporary Drama*, Cornell University Press, Ithaca, New York, pp. 87-119.

Gaumer, D 1960, 'The art of movement in education', *Laban Art of Movement Guild Magazine*, vol. 24, pp. 32-42.

Geanellos, R 2000, 'Exploring Ricoeur's hermeneutic theory of interpretation as a method of analysing research texts', *Nursing Inquiry*, vol. 7, no. 2, pp. 112-119.

Geertz, C 1983, 'Blurred genres: The refiguration of social thought', in *Local Knowledge: Further Essays in Interpretive Anthropology,* Stanford University Press, Stanford, Palo Alto, CA, pp. 29-35.

Georgi, A (ed.) 1985, *Phenomenology and Psychological Research*, Duquesne University Press, Pittsburgh, PA.

Gorky, M 1972, *Enemies*, trans. J Brooks and K Hunter-Blair, Methuen, London.

Gronbeck-Tadesko, JL 1992, *Acting through Exercises: A Synthesis of Classical and Contemporary Approaches*, Mayfield, Mountain View, CA.

Grosz, E 1987, 'Notes towards a corporeal feminism', Special issue, 'Feminism and The body', J Allen and E Grosz (eds), *Australian Feminist Studies*, vol. 5, Summer, pp. 1-5.

-------- 1990a, 'Contemporary theories of power and subjectivity', in S Gunew (ed.), *Feminist Knowledge: Critique and Construct,* Routledge, London and New York, pp. 59-120.

-------- 1990b, *Jacques Lacan: A Feminist Introduction*, Allen and Unwin, Sydney.

-------- 1994, *Volatile Bodies: Toward a Corporeal Feminism,* Indiana University Press, Bloomington.

Grotowski, J 1975, *Towards a Poor Theatre,* E Barba (ed.), Methuen, London.

Guba, EG and Lincoln, YS 1981, *Effective Evaluation*, Jossey-Bass, San Francisco, CA.

-------- and Lincoln, YS 2005, 'Paradigmatic controversies, contradictions and emerging confluences', in NK Denzin and YS Lincoln (eds.), *The Sage Handbook of Qualitative Research*, 3rd edn, Sage, London, Delhi and Thousand Oaks, CA, pp. 183-190.

Hadreas, PJ 1986, *In Place of the Flawed Diamond: An Investigation of Merleau-Ponty's Philosophy,* Peter Lang, New York.

Hagen, U 1973, *Respect for Acting,* Macmillan, New York.

Hall, CS and Nordby, VJ 1973, *A Primer of Jungian Psychology*, Mentor, New York and Scarborough, Ontario.

Halprin, A 1995, *Moving Toward Life: Five Decades of Transformational Dance,* R Kaplan (ed.), University of New England Press, Hanover, NH.

Hanna, JL 1983, *The Performer-Audience Connection*, University of Texas Press, Austin, Texas.

Hart, L 1993, 'Introduction', in L Hart and P Phelan (eds.), *Acting Out: Feminist Performances,* University Michigan Press, Ann Arbor, pp. 1-12.

Hayes, J 1996, 'Movement Psychology: the Yat technique, a method training for the nineties', paper presented at Together as One, 5th. Australasian Theatre Conference, Toi Whakaari New Zealand Theatre School, Wellington, New Zealand, 7-10 July 1996.

--------- 1999, 'Performing bodies: Space for women on stage', paper presented at Sensational: Images and Bodies Conference, College of Fine Arts, University of NSW, Sydney, NSW, 12 November, 1999.

Heidegger, M 1996, *Being and Time*: *A Translation of Sein und Zeit,* ed. and trans. J Stambaugh, State University of New York Press, Albany, NY. (original work published in 1927).

Herrington, J 2000, 'Directing with the Viewpoints', *Theatre Topics*, vol.10, no. 2, pp. 155-168.

Higgs J 1998, 'Structuring qualitative research theses', in J Higgs (ed.), *Writing Qualitative Research,* Hampden Press, Sydney, NSW, pp. 137-150.

Hirsch, F 1984, *A Method to their Madness: The History of the Actors Studio,* Norton and Co., New York.

Holdsworth, N 2006, *Joan Littlewood,* Routlege, London and New York

Holstein, J and Gubrium, J 1995, *The Active Interview,* Sage, Thousand Oaks, CA.

Husserl, E 1952, *Ideas; General Introduction to a Pure Phenomenology,* trans. F Kersten, Martinus Nijhoff, Boston, Mass. (original work published in 1913).

--------- 1970, *The Idea of Phenomenology,* Martinus Nijhoff, The Hague.

Huxley, M and Witts, N (eds.) 1996, *The Twentieth Century Performance Reader,* Routledge, London.

Innes, C 1981, *Holy Theatre: Ritual and the Avant-Garde,* Cambridge University Press, Cambridge and New York.

International Council of Kinetography Laban/Labanotation, 2007, viewed 27 September 2007, http://www.ickl.org/

Irigaray, L 1985, *This Sex which is not One,* trans. C Porter and C Burke, Cornell University Press, Ithaca.

--------- 1992, *Elemental Passions,* trans. J Collie and J Still, Athlone Press, London.

--------- 1993, *An Ethics of Sexual Difference,* trans. C Burke and GC Gill, Cornell University Press, Ithaca, New York.

Jardine, L 1983, *Still Harping on Daughters: Women and Drama in the Age of Shakespeare*, Harvester, Sussex.

Johnson, M 1987, *The Body in the Mind: The Bodily Basis of Meaning, Imagination and Reason*, University of Chicago Press, Chicago.

Jonas, H 1994, 'Philosophy at the end of the century: a survey of its past and future', *Social Research*, vol. 61, pp. 813-833.

Kendall, D 1984, 'Actor training in Australia' in Performing Arts in Australia Special Issue, *Meanjin*, vol. 43, no. 1, pp. 155-160.

Kiernander, A 2000, 'The unclassic body in the theatre of John Bell' in P Tait (ed.), *Body Shows: Australian Viewings of Live Performance*, Rodopi, Amsterdam, pp. 124-135.

Krasner, D 2000, 'Strasberg, Adler and Meisner: Method acting', in A Hodge (ed.), *Twentieth Century Actor Training*, Routledge, London and New York, pp. 129-150.

Kristeva, J 1980, *Desire in Language; A Semiotic Approach to Literature and Art*, LS Roudiez (ed.), trans T Gora and AA Jardine, Columbia University Press, New York.

-------- 1987, *In the Beginning was Love: Psychoanalysis and Faith*, trans. A Goldhammer, Columbia University Press, New York.

Kumar, R 1996, *Research Methodology: A Step-by-Step Guide for Beginners*, Longman, Melbourne, Vic.

Laban, R 1948, *Modern Educational Dance*, Macdonald and Evans, London.

-------- 1950, *The Mastery of Movement on the Stage*, Macdonald and Evans, London.

-------- 1954, 'Movement Psychology: Glossary of terms and six tables', unpubl. held by Drama Centre, London.

-------- 1966, *Choreutics*, Macdonald and Evans, London.

-------- 1960, *The Mastery of Movement*, 2nd edn, L Ullmann (revised and enlarged), Macdonald and Evans, London.

-------- 1971, *The Mastery of Movement*, 3rd edn, L Ullmann (ed.), Macdonald and Evans, London.

-------- 1975, *Laban's Principles of Dance and Movement Notation*, 2nd edn, R Lange (ed.), Macdonald and Evans, London.

-------- and Lawrence, FC 1947, *Effort*, Macdonald and Evans, London.

Laban, R and Lawrence, FC 1974, *Effort: Economy of Human Movement*, 2nd edn, Macdonald and Evans, London.

Laban Centre London, 2007, viewed 27 September 2007, http://www.laban.org/

labanotation 2007, *Encyclopaedia Britannica*, accessed 6 September 2007, http://www.britannica.com/eb/article-9046696

Lacan, J 1999, 'Towards a genetic theory of the ego', in D Welton (ed.), *The Body: Classic and Contemporary Readings*, Blackwell, Malden, Mass.

Lacey, S 1995, *British Realist Theatre*, Routledge, London.

Lamb, A and Watson, E 1979, *Body Code: The Meaning in Movement*, Routledge, London.

Lampe, E 1998, 'SITI-A site of stillness and surprise: Ann Bogart's Viewpoints training meets Tadashi Suzuki's method of actor training', in I Watson (ed.), *Performer Training: Developments Across Cultures*, Harwood Academic, Amsterdam, pp. 171-189.

Langer, SK 1953, *Feeling and Form: A Theory of Art Developed from Philosophy in a New Key*, Charles Scribner's Sons, New York.

Lather, P 1991a, *Feminist Research in Education: Within/ Against*, Deakin University Press, Geelong, Vic.

Lather, P 1991b, *Getting Smart: Feminist Research and Pedagogy with/in the Postmodern*, Routledge, New York and London.

--------- 1992, 'Critical forms in educational research: feminist and post-structural perspectives', *Theory Into Practice*, vol. 31, no. 2, pp. 87-99.

Laverty, SM 2003, 'Hermeneutic phenomenology and phenomenology: A comparison Of Historical and methodological considerations', *International Journal of Qualitative Methods*, vol. 2, no. 3, article 3, viewed 25 January 2008, http://www.ualberta.ca/~iiqm/backissues/2_3final/pdf/laverty.pdf

Lawler, J 1998, 'Adapting a phenomenological philosophy to research and writing', in J Higgs (ed.), *Writing Qualitative Research* Hampden, Sydney, NSW, pp. 47-56.

Leahy, K 1996, 'Power and presence in the actor-training institution audition', *Australasian Drama Studies*, vol. 28, pp. 133-9.

Leder, D 1990, *The Absent Body*, University of Chicago Press, Chicago.

Leder, D 1998, 'A tale of two bodies: the Cartesian corpse and the lived body', in D Welton (ed.), *Body and Flesh: A Philosophical Reader*, Blackwell, Malden, Mass., pp. 117-129.

\--------- 2005,'Moving beyond "mind" and "body"', *Philosophy, Psychiatry and Psychology*, vol. 12, no. 2, pp. 109-113.

Legrand, D 2007, 'Pre-reflective self-consciousness: On being bodily in the world', *Janus Head*, vol. 9, no. 2, pp. 493-519.

Lindholm, M, Uden, G and Rastam, R 1999, 'Management from four different perspectives', *Journal of Nursing Management*, vol. 7, pp. 101-111.

Love, L 1995, 'Resisiting the "organic"', in PB Zarrilli (ed.), *Acting (Re)considered: Theories and Practices*, Routledge, London, pp. 275-288.

Lulu: A Sex Tragedy 2000, by P Barnes, director J Kevin, produced by Faculty of Creative Arts, University of Wollongong, Illawarra Performing Arts Centre, Wollongong, NSW, 10-20 May.

Macauley, A 2003, 'Don't tell me show me: directors talk about acting', *Equity*, Spring, pp. 14-19.

McCaughey, J 1988, 'Bodies of opinion: acting out images of real life', *New Theatre Australia*, vol. 6, pp. 8-10.

McCracken, G 1988, *The Long Interview*, Sage, London.

Macke, FJ 2005, 'Seeing oneself in the mirror: critical reflections on the visual experience of the reflected self', *Journal of Phenomenological Psychology*, vol. 36, no. 1, pp. 21-44, viewed 21 August 2007, *Expanded Academic ASAP*, Gale, University of Wollongong database.

McNiff, S 1981, *The Arts and Psychotherapy*, Thomas Books, Springfield, Illinois.

Madison, GB 1981, *The Phenomenology of Merleau-Ponty*, Ohio University Press, Athens.

\--------- 1992, 'Did Merleau-Ponty have a theory of perception?', in TW Busch and S Gallagher (eds.), *Merleau-Ponty, Hermeneutics and Postmodernism*, State University of New York Press, Albany, NY, pp. 83-108.

Maggs-Rapport, F 2001, '"Best research practice': In pursuit of methodological rigor', *Journal of Advanced Nursing*, vol. 35, no. 3, pp. 373-383.

Malmgren, Y 1979-2002, Character Analysis, unpubl. Lecture notes held by Drama Centre London.

\--------- Jan. 1988, Feb. 1998, Nov. 2000, personal records of Malmgren studio classes, Drama Centre, London.

Malmgren, Y 2000, taped interviews 28 and 29 Nov. 2000.

Martin, R 1990, *Performance as Political Act: The Embodied Self*, Bergin and Garvey, New York.

Marton, F 1992, 'Phenomenography and 'the art of teaching all things to all men'', *Qualitative Studies in Education,* vol. 5, pp. 253-267.

Merleau-Ponty, M 1962, *The Phenomenology of Perception*, trans. C Smith, Routledge and Kegan Paul, London.

Merleau-Ponty, M 1964, 'Philosophy and the sciences of man', in JM Eadie (ed.), *The Primacy of Perception and Other Essays Part 1*, trans. JM Eadie, Northwestern University Press, Evanston, Ill., pp. 12-27.

--------- 1965, *The Structure of Behaviour,* trans. A Fisher, Methuen, London.

--------- 1968, *The Visible and the Invisible,* Claude Lefort (ed.), trans. A Lingis, Northwestern University Press, Evanston.

Merlin, B 2001, *Beyond Stanislavsky: The Psycho-Physical approach to Actor Training*, Nick Hern London.

Mill, J 2002, 'In conversation with Tony Knight', *Equity,* Winter, pp. 16-17.

Miller, JA (ed.) 1988, *The Seminars of Jacques Lacan. Bk. 1: Freud's Papers on Technique 1953-1954*, trans. J Forrester, Cambridge University Press, Cambridge.

Mirodan, V 1997, 'The way of transformation: The Laban-Malmgren system of Dramatic character analysis', Department of Drama, Theatre and Media Arts, Royal Holloway College, PhD thesis, University of London.

Moore, S 1979, *Training the Actor: The Stanislavski System in Class*, Penguin, New York.

--------- 1991, *Stanislavski Revealed: The Actor's Guide to Spontaneity on Stage,* Applause Theatre Books, New York.

Moran, D 2000, *Introduction to Phenomenology,* Routledge, London.

Morse, JM (ed.) 1994, *Critical Issues in Qualitative Research Methods,* Sage, Thousand Oaks, CA.

Myers-Briggs Personality Types, 2007, viewed 26 September 2007, http://www.personalitypathways.com/MBTI_articles.html

Newlove, J 1993, *Laban for Actors and Dancers,* Nick Hern Books, London.

Newlove, J and Dalby, J 2004, *Laban for All,* Nick Hern Books: London.

Noland, C 2007, 'Motor intentionality: Gestural meaning in Bill Viola and Merleau-Ponty, *Postmodern Culture,* vol. 17, no. 3. pp. 1-29. Viewed 2 May 2009, http://muse.uq.edu.au.ezproxy.uow.edu.au/journals/postmodern_culture/v017/17.3noland.html

North, M 1990, *Personality Assessment through Movement,* Northcote House, London.

Nussbaum, M 1999, 'The professor of parody: the hip defeatism of Judith Butler', *The New Republic,* vol. 220, 22 February, pp. 37-45.

O' Brien, L 1999, *Phenomenology,* notes and reference list, Research Methods for Humanities and Social Sciences, Postgraduate Seminar Series, University of Western Sydney, Kingswood NSW, delivered 24th April.

O'Connell, S 1999, 'Claiming one's identity' in G Weiss and HF Haber (eds), *Perspectives on Embodiment: The Intersections of Nature and Culture,* Routledge, London, pp. 61-78.

O'Connor, B 2001, 'Mapping training/mapping performance: current trends in Australian actor training', in I Watson (ed.), *Performer Training: Developments Across Cultures,* Harwood Academic, Amsterdam, pp. 47-60.

O'Toole, J 2002, 'Scenes at the top down under: drama in higher education in Australia', *Research in Drama Education,* vol. 7, no. 1, pp. 114-121.

Olkowski, D 2000 'The end of phenomenology: Bergson's interval in Irigaray', *Hypatia,* vol. 15, no. 3, pp. 73-91.

Ong, WJ 1982, *Orality and Literacy: The Technologizing of the Word,* Methuen, London and New York.

Osborne, J 1957, *Look Back In Anger,* Faber and Faber, London.

Parr, B 2005, 'The misfit male body in Adelaide theatre, 1959', *Australasian Drama Studies,* vol. 46, pp. 20-37.

Patton, M 2002, *Qualitative Research and Evaluation Methods,* Sage, Thousand Oaks, CA.

Pearlman K 1998, 'Learning to read the physical mind' in P Tait (ed.), *Body Shows: Australian Viewings of Live Performance,* Rodopi, Amsterdam, pp. 217-228.

Pease, A 1987, *Body Language: How to Read Others' Thoughts by their Gestures,* Camel, Avalon Beach, NSW.

Phelan, P 1993, *Unmarked: The Politics of Performance,* Routledge, London.

Phelan, P and Lane, J 1998, *The Ends of Performance*, New York University Press, New York.

Plager, KA 1994, 'Hermeneutic phenomenology: a methodology for family health and Health promotion study in nursing' in P Benner (ed.), *Interpretive Phenomenology: Embodiment, Caring and and Ethics in Health and Illness*, Sage, London, pp. 65-83.

Pradier, J-M 1990, 'Towards a biological theory of the body in performance', *New Theatre Quarterly*, vol. 21 no. 6, pp. 86-98.

Preston-Dunlop, V 1998, *Rudolf Laban: An Extraordinary Life*, Dance Books, London.

Ray, MA 1994, 'The richness of phenomenology: philosophic, theoretic, and methodologic concerns', in JM Morse (ed), *Critical Issues in Qualitative Research Methods*, Sage, Thousand Oaks, CA, pp. 117-133.

Rayner, A 1994, *To Act, to Do, to Perform: Drama and the Phenomenology of Action*, University of Michigan Press, Michigan.

Redfern, HB 1973, *Concepts in Modern Educational Dance*, Henry Kimpton, London.

Reinelt, J 1995, 'Theatre on the brink of 2000: shifting paradigms'. *Theatre Research International*, vol. 20, no. 2, pp. 123-132.

Reynolds, J 2002, 'Maurice Merleau-Ponty (1908-1961)', *Internet Encyclopedia of Philosophy*, viewed 21 January 2007, http://www.iep.utm.edu/m/merleau.htm#SH3b

Richards, T 1995, *At Work with Grotowski on Physical Actions*, Routledge, New York.

Ricoeur P 1981, *Hermeneutics and the Human Sciences: Essays on Language, Action\ and Interpretation,* J Thompson, (ed.) and trans, Cambridge University Press, Cambridge.

Riley, SR 2004, 'Embodied perceptual practices: towards an embrained and embodied model of mind for use in actor training and rehearsal', *Theatre Topics*, vol. 14, no. 2, pp. 445-471.

Risum, J 2001, 'A study in motley: the Odin actors', in I Watson (ed.), *Performer Training: Developments Across Cultures*, Harwood Academic, Amsterdam, pp. 93-115.

Rolf, IP 1977, *Rolfing: The Integration of Human Structures,* Dennis-Landman, Santa Monica, CA.

Roose-Evans, J 1984, *Experimental Theatre from Stanislavsky to Peter Brook*, Routledge and Kegan Paul, London and Melbourne, Vic.

Rosen, S 1997, 'Horizontverschmelzung' in LE Hahn (ed.), *The Philosophy of Hans-Georg Gadamer,* Open Court Publishing, Chicago, Illinois, pp. 207-218.

Roth, G 1989, *Maps to Ecstasy: Teachings of an Urban Shaman*, Nataraj, Novato, CA.

Rothwell, R 1998, 'Philosophical paradigms and qualitative research', in J Higgs (ed.), *Writing Qualitative Research*, Hampden, Sydney, NSW, pp. 21-28.

Rubin, D (ed.) 1994, *The World Encyclopaedia of Contemporary Theatre: Vol 1 Europe*, Routledge, London and New York.

Russell, J 1958, *Modern Dance in Education*, Macdonald and Evans, London.

Saint-Denis, M 1982, *Training for the Theatre: Premises and Promises*, S Saint-Denis (ed.), Theatre Arts Books, New York.

Schechner, R 1968, 'The politics of ecstasy', in *Public Domain: Essays on the Theater*, Avon, New York.

-------- 1985, *Between Theater and Anthropology*, University of Pennsylvania Press, Philadelphia.

-------- 1988, *Performance Theory*, Routledge, New York.

-------- 2003, *Essays on Performance Theory, 1970-1976*, Routledge, London and New York.

Sellers-Young, B 1998, 'Somatic processes: convergence of theory and practice' *Theatre Topics,* vol. 8, no. 2, pp. 173-187.

Seton, M, 2004, 'Forming (in)vulnerable bodies: intercorporeal experiences in actor training in Australia', Department of Performance Studies, PhD thesis, University of Sydney.

Sisholm, C 2000, 'Crossing lovers: Luce Irigaray's *Elemental Passions*, *Hypatia,* vol. 15, no. 3, pp. 92-112.

Smith, ACH 1972, *Orghast at Persepolis*, Eyre Methuen, London.

Stanislavski, K 1963, *Creating a Role*, trans. ER Hapgood, Geoffrey Bles, London.

-------- 1973, *Stanislavsky on the Art of the Stage,* 3rd edn, trans. And intr. essay by D Magarshack, Faber and Faber, London.

-------- 1988, *Building a Character*, trans ER Hapgood, Methuen, London. [first copyright, 1948, Theatre Arts Incorporated, USSR]

Stanislavski, K 1989, *An Actor Prepares*, trans ER Hapgood, Routledge, New York. [first copyright 1936, Theatre Arts Incorporated, USSR.]

Stanton-Jones, K 1992, *An Introduction to Dance Movement Therapy in Psychiatry*, London, Routledge.

States, BO 1985, *Great Reckonings in Little Rooms: On the Phenomenology of Theater*, University of California Press, Berkeley and Los Angeles, California.

Stoller S 2000, 'Reflections on feminist Merleau-Ponty skepticism', *Hypatia*, vol. 15, no. 1, pp. 175-185.

Sullivan, S 1997, 'Domination and dialogue in Merleau-Ponty's Phenomenology of Perception', *Hypatia*, vol. 12, no. 1, pp. 1-19.

Suzuki, T 1986, *The Way of Acting: The Theatre Writings of Tadashi Suzuki*, trans. JT Rimer, Theatre Communications Group, New York.

--------- 1996, 'Culture is the body', in PB Zarrilli (ed.) *Acting (Re)considered: Theories and Practices*, Routledge, London, pp. 155- 160.

--------- 2000, 'Fragments of glass: A conversation between Hijikata Tatsumi and Suzuki Tadashi' moderated S Akihiko, *TDR*, vol. 44, no. 1, pp. 62-70.

Tait, P 1998, 'Performing sexed bodies in physical theatre' in V Kelly (ed.), *Our Australian Theatre in the 1990s*, Rodopi, Atlanta, CA., pp. 213-228.

--------- 2000, 'Fleshed, muscular phenomenologies: across sexed and queer circus bodies', in P Tait (ed.), *Body Shows: Australian Viewings of Live Performance,* Rodopi, Amsterdam and Atlanta, GA, pp. 60-78.

--------- 2008, 'Bodies perform inner emotions: Stanislavski's legacy', *Australasian Drama Studies*, vol. 53, October, pp. 84 -102.

Taylor, C 1985, *Human Agency and Language: Philosophical Papers (Vol. 1),* Cambridge University Press, Cambridge, UK.

Taylor, S and Bogdan, R 1984, *Introduction to Qualitative Research Methods*, Wiley, New York.

Theatre School 1993, 'Part 1 Getting in, Part 2 Being there, Part 3 Getting your act together, Part 4 Uncertainties', television program, British Broadcasting Corporation, BBC2, London, 5, 12, 19, 26 October 1993.

Thompson, J 2002, 'How we met: Pierce Brosnan and Christopher Fettes', *The Independent*, London, January 27, 2002, viewed 25 March 2009 http://findarticles.com/p/articles/mi_qn4158/is_20020127/ai_n9674926

Tolan, K 2004, 'Returning to the well: the Actors Center is an oasis for actors hungry to learn and survive', (Special Section: Approaches to Theatre Training 2004), *American Theatre*, vol. 21, pp. 46-49.

van Maanen, J 1988, *Tales of the Field: On Writing Ethnography*, University of Chicago Press, Chicago.

van Manen, M 1990, *Researching Lived Experience: Human Science for an Action Sensitive Pedagogy*, University of New York Press, New York.

Verve Studios 2009, accessed 6/04/09
http://www.vervestudios.com.au/team.html

Viola B 1998, *The Passions*, J.P. Getty Museum, Los Angeles.

von Eckartsberg, R 1998, 'Introducing existential-phenomenological psychology', in R Valle (ed.), *Phenomenological Inquiry in Psychology: Existential and Transpersonal Dimensions*, Plenum, New York and London, pp. 3-20.

Warburton, D 1993, 'Speaking as a director and an actor', in *Proceedings of the 1993 4th. National Conference of Network Voice Teachers of Australia and New Zealand*, University of Western Sydney Nepean, Sydney.

Watson, I (ed.) 2001, *Performer Training: Developments across Cultures*, Routledge, London.

--------- 2002, 'Actor training in the USA', in I Watson (ed.), *Performer Training: Developments Across Cultures*, Harwood Academic, Amsterdam, pp. 61-82.

Webb, P and Pollard, C 2006, 'Demystifying a hermeneutic approach to research', *Australasian Journal of Information Systems*, vol. 12, no. 2, pp. 31-47.

Weiss, G 1992, 'Context and perspective', in TW Busch and S Gallagher (eds.), *Merleau-Ponty, Hermeneutics and Postmodernism*, State University of New York Press, Albany, New York, pp. 13-24.

Whitehead, L 2004, 'Enhancing the quality of hermeneutical research: decision trail', *Journal of Advanced Nursing*, vol. 45, no. 5, pp. 512-518.

Willis, P 2004, 'From "The things themselves" to a "Feeling of understanding": finding different voices in phenomenological research', *Indo-Pacific Journal of Phenomenology* vol. 4, no.1, pp. 1-13, viewed 27 January 2008,
http://www.ipjp.org/back.html#v4el

Willson, FMG 1997, *In Just Order Move: The Progress of the Laban Centre for Movement and Dance 1946-1996*, Athlone Press, London.

Wilson, N 2005, 'Butler's corporeal politics: matters of politicised abjection', in MS Breen and WJ Blumenfeld (eds.), *Butler Matters: Judith Butler's Impact on Feminist and Queer Studies*, Ashgate, Burlington, VT., USA, pp. 161-173.

Wilshire, B 1991, *Role-playing and Identity: The Limits of Theatre as Metaphor*, Indiana University Press, Indianapolis, I.

Winearis, J 1968, *Modern Dance: The Jooss-Leeder Method*, foreword R Laban, Black, London.

Wolford, L 2001, 'Ambivalent positionings: Grotowski's art as vehicle and the paradox of categorization', in I Watson (ed.), *Performer Training: Developments Across Cultures*, Harwood Academic, Amsterdam, pp. 117-132.

Woollard, J 2002, 'More than skills and showreels', (Education feature: training the actor), *RealTime,* vol. 50, p. 43.

'Yat Malmgren', *The Times*, London, 15 June 2002, p.35.

Young, IM 1989, 'Throwing like a girl: a phenomenology of feminine body comportment, motility, and spatiality', in J Allen and IM Young (eds.), *The Thinking Muse: Feminism and Modern French Philosophy,* Indiana University Press, Bloomington, pp. 51-70.

Yule, A 1994, *Sean Connery: Neither Shaken nor Stirred,* Warner, London.

Zarrilli, PB 1992, 'For whom is the king a king? Issues of intercultural production, perception and reception in a *Kathakali King Lear'*, in JG Reinelt and JR Roach (eds), *Critical Theory and Performance*, University of Michegan Press, Ann Arbor, pp. 16-40.

--------- 1995a, 'Between theory and practice', in *Acting (Re)considered: Theories and Practices, (*ed.) PB Zarrilli, Routledge, London, pp. 1-4.

--------- 1995b, '. ...on the edge of a breath looking', in P. Zarrilli (ed.), *Acting (Re)considered: Theories and Practices*, Routledge, London, pp. 177-196.

--------- 1997, 'Acting "at the nerve ends": Beckett, Blau, and the necessary', *Theatre Topics*, vol. 7 no. 2, pp. 103-116.

--------- 2001, 'Negotiating performance epistemologies: Knowledge about, for, and in', *Studies in Theatre and Performance*, vol. 21, no. 1, pp. 31-46.

--------- 2002, 'The metaphysical studio', *TDR*, vol. 46, no. 2, pp. 157-170.

--------- 2004, 'Toward a phenomenological model of the actor's embodied modes of experience', *Theatre Journal,* vol. 56, no. 4, pp. 653-666.

VDM publishing house ltd.

Scientific Publishing House
offers
free of charge publication

of current academic research papers, Bachelor´s Theses, Master's Theses, Dissertations or Scientific Monographs

If you have written a thesis which satisfies high content as well as formal demands, and you are interested in a remunerated publication of your work, please send an e-mail with some initial information about yourself and your work to *info@vdm-publishing-house.com*.

Our editorial office will get in touch with you shortly.

VDM Publishing House Ltd.
Meldrum Court 17.
Beau Bassin
Mauritius
www.vdm-publishing-house.com

VDM Verlag Dr. Müller

LAP LAMBERT Academic Publishing

SVH Südwestdeutscher Verlag für Hochschulschriften

Printed in Great Britain
by Amazon